The
Taming
of the
Canadian
West

THE CANADIAN WEST

McCLELLAND AND STEWART LIMITED/ILLUSTRATED BOOKS DIVISION

M c C L E L L A N D   A N D   S T E W A R T   L I M I T E D / T H E   C A N A D I A N   P U B L I S H E R S

McClelland and Stewart Limited
ILLUSTRATED BOOKS DIVISION
150 Simcoe Street, Toronto 1, Ont.

PUBLISHER	*Jack McClelland*
EDITORIAL DIRECTOR	*Pierre Berton*
CREATIVE DIRECTOR	*Frank Newfeld*
EDITOR	*Leslie F. Hannon*
ART DIRECTOR	*Hugh Michaelson*
ART ASSISTANT	*Don Fernley*
PICTURE EDITOR	*Jane Murdoch*
ASSISTANT EDITOR	*Walt McDayter*
EXECUTIVE ASSISTANT	*Ennis Halliday*

This volume designed by Frank Newfeld

First Ship of the Far West

On September 20, 1788, John Meares launched the *North West America* at Nootka Sound — the first ship built on the Pacific Coast, 10 years after the first white man, Captain James Cook, set foot there. In 1789 Spaniards seized Nootka Sound and four ships belonging to Meares, and war between Spain and Britain over this Vancouver Island inlet seemed inevitable. But a year later, Spain reluctantly relinquished her claims to the northwest coast.

TRAPPERS IN THE WILDERNESS

MURDER OF A SETTLER'S FAMILY

A BRIGADE OF RED RIVER CARTS

SUPPLY TRAIN IN THE FOOTHILLS

A SETTLER'S SHANTY

AN ENGLISH IMMIGRANT'S HOME

WHISKY ON THE PLAINS

SULKY PLOUGHING, ASSINIBOIA

AN INDIAN RAID

MASSACRE AT FROG LAKE

CUMBERLAND MISSION, THE PAS

A TRAVELLING PRIEST

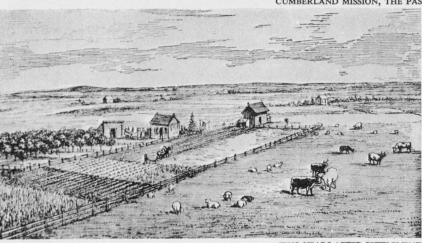

TWO YEARS AFTER SETTLEMENT

The decisive battle of the 1885 Northwest Rebellion was won when the impatient Canadian volunteers disobeyed their cautious commander and routed the *Métis* of Louis Riel.

The Settlers Steam West

A smoke, a drink, a game of cards: en route to a new life, settlers idle away the hours in a C.P.R. colonial car.

A long way west, 2,262 miles from Montreal, a train arrives with new citizens for the new town of Calgary, 1887.

Contents

The best of Indian drawing and painting on the plains was
done on the walls of the *tipis*, often recording great victories in
the hunt or in battle, or depicting sacred birds and animals.

A Note by the Author

This book has been for me a personal voyage of exploration into the poorly charted seas of Western Canadiana. I found remarkable things there: high adventure and low comedy, heroes and rascals, tragedians and buffoons, and everywhere achievement, beauty, folly, bravery, magnificent defiance of the Canadian wilderness. My expedition lasted five years, and I hope that those of my countrymen who have accepted the myth that Canadian history is dull will now share some of the elation I felt when making my discoveries.

Wherever possible, I have used the actual words from the journals and diaries of the explorers and pioneers. They were on the scene and nobody is better equipped than they to describe their exploits. But, primarily, I have considered my function to be that of the story-teller. I have adopted the credo of the late Bernard DeVoto. In clothing the bare bones of the past with flesh, he hoped "to bring history out of the seminar and restore it to the living room, where it was once acknowledged to belong."

In my fashion, that is what I have attempted to do in this work.

1867 1967

The author acknowledges the assistance of the Centennial Commission.

To Hugh MacLennan,
a novelist who believes
that Canadian history
can be as human as a novel,
and to Dr. William Kaye Lamb,
a Canadian historian who
believes that no novel
can be as full of human
stories as history.

I

The Noble Barbarian

BY the time the first white men came, there were in the four million square miles now called Canada some fifty tribes, about a quarter of a million Indians. The raven-haired Indians of the Canadian West, with whom this book is concerned, can be divided into three main groups. The prairie tribes were buffalo-hunting warriors on horseback. They ruled an empire of waist-high yellow grass. The tribes of the Northwest Territories included nomads of the tundra. In their fight to survive, to catch the caribou, they used wolflike dogs and their women were little better than beasts of burden. The tribes of the Pacific Coast were either aristocrats, commoners, or slaves. Living in the shadow of the "Shining Mountains" – as they called the Rockies – along the protected fiords, they ate the salmon and whale. For transport, they had huge ocean-going cedar canoes. The lucky well-born few had "potlatch" parties and totem pole rites and harems of slave wives for their Oriental potentate taste.

The white men who conquered them did not understand their complex culture. Today, we understand only a little more. Consequently, these early Americans are still shrouded in myth and half-truth. "Indian," the very name imposed by the white man, was a misnomer. When Christopher Columbus set sail from Spain in 1492, he was so certain he would reach Cathay – as China was then called – that he bore letters of introduction from Queen Isabella of Spain to the Chinese Grand Khan. Columbus carried an interpreter who could speak Chinese, Hebrew and Arabic, but not the language of India. Consequently, when Columbus landed in the New World, and his interpreter could not understand the language of the natives, the explorer assumed he was on one of the islands off the southeast tip of Asia, then known as the "Indies." So he called the aborigines "Indians."

It is just as wrong to consider them "beardless redskins." When John Cabot discovered Newfoundland in 1497, he found the now-extinct Beothuk Indians there. Their faces and hands were smeared with red clay to ward off the mosquitoes, and so he named them "redskins." In actual fact, the skin colouring of the Canadian Indian ranges from dusky chocolate through coffee brown and pale yellow to near white. And, despite the popular impression that Indians never have to shave, the early explorers of the West all noted how the Indians painfully plucked their beards, using clam shells as hair tweezers.

The greatest misconceptions of all arose about their morality and way of life. Two extremist schools of thought have painted the Indians in hues of black or white.

One group, observing that the Indians had never discovered the wheel or the keystone arch, sneered at them as a race of uncivilized primitives, heathen barbarians and butchers of the white man. Typical of this school, which expected the Indian to be fashioned in the white man's image of godliness and etiquette, was James Isham. He was an English governor of the Hudson's Bay Company fur-trading post at York Factory. Writing in the style of the 1730s, Isham poked fun at the Indians' habit of biting off each other's fingers and noses when in a rage: "No poizen is so Venemous as their teeth." Scorning their lack of chastity, their polygamous way with wives, he called them, "A crafty sort of people, Lewd from their cradle."

The opposite school romanticized the Indian. To these sentimentalists the Indian embodied the noble savage of Jean-Jacques Rousseau and James Fenimore Cooper. He lived a life of immaculate simplicity and stoic dignity. True, the Canadian Indian didn't know iron or gunpowder, but he had maple syrup and corn, tobacco and turkey, the birchbark canoe and the snowshoe, the toboggan and lacrosse. True, the Indian didn't have a written language, but he had oratory and drama, dancing and songs, painting and blanket-weaving, herbal medicine and cosmetics. This idealized portrait of the Canadian "child of nature" induced the English poet, Alexander Pope, to lament:

Lo! the poor Indian, whose untutor'd mind,
Sees God in clouds or hears Him in the wind.

Both extremists were telling the truth: a coloured version. In reality the Canadian Indian was neither "good" nor "bad." He simply did not adhere to the moral precepts of the white man. He had his own values, his own vision of truth, according to the time and place of his society. And the mores of his civilization could be as diverse, as intricate, as contradictory as any contrived by the palefaces.

The Canadian Indians could be cannibals. One western explorer, Daniel Williams Harmon, tells of an Indian woman who ate fourteen relatives in a single winter. Another fur trader, Alexander Henry the Elder, describes a conquering tribe who ripped open the bellies of their victims with tomahawks, scooped up the blood in their cupped hands, "and quaffed amid ferocious shouts of victory." And yet no squeamish follower of the English fox-hunt could be as contrite about killing animals. A Pacific Coast tribe, the Nootkas, after hunting a grizzly bear, would respectfully bring the dead beast into their underground house. They would sit it up in a ceremonial hat like an honoured guest, toss handfuls of eagle down in the air to show their good will, puff the smoke of peace into its jaws and beg, "Please forgive us, O bear, since we had to kill you to eat food."

The Canadian Indians could be as sensuous in their all-night banquet orgies as the Romans. And they could be as hygienic as the Finns. Indeed, they used "sweat bath lodges" akin to the saunas of Finland, and after steaming in these huts of bended willows with red-hot stones, the cleansed bathers would plunge naked into the snow.

They could be as cruel and as ostentatious as the ancient Egyptians. After the death of some chiefs, protocol demanded that dozens of their slaves be roasted alive in the funeral pyre, that their white dogs be sacrificed, that totem poles be erected to perpetuate the departed one's glory. And yet the Indians could be truly democratic. Of the individual equality in a Montagnais tribe, a Jesuit missionary said: "All the authority of their chief is in his tongue's end: for he is powerful only in so far as he is eloquent: and, even if he kills himself talking and haranguing, he will not be obeyed unless he pleases the savages."

They could be as grotesquely vain as the African Ubangis. Tattooing and pierced-nose pendants were common. One west-coast tribe, the Salish, bound the skulls of their babies to flatten their heads; another, the Kwakiutl, intentionally deformed their children in the cradle to produce pointed heads; and a third, the Babines or "Big Lips," as a special mark of beauty, plugged three-inch long labrets of wood into the jutting,

A warrior of Nootka Sound.

saucer-like lower lips of their daughters. They could be as refined in their poetry as the Japanese. Their eleven separate languages, split into 50 dialects, produced such imagery as "Moon of Exploding Trees" for the month of January and "Moon of the Flying Up of Young Ducks" for August. Their exquisite fables, which personified the raven as comically greedy and the wolf as trickily treacherous, make Aesop seem a rather humourless spinner of folk tales.

The Canadian Indians could be as clannish as the Scots. Family fraternities and secret societies had their own heraldic armour and eagle-claw plaid-like kilts, and a single murder could keep an inter-clan blood feud raging for decades. And they could be as neurotic as some modern North American suburbanites. Wife-swapping, incest and homosexuality were not uncommon, though generally regarded as taboo, and were usually punished by that potent code of unwritten law – ostracism from the tribe.

They could be as fanatically superstitious as any fakir from India. Their *shamans* (sorcerers) walked over red-hot embers, and their masked witch doctors preached reincarnation and communion with ghosts. And yet they could be as orthodox in their religion as any Bible Belt fundamentalist. They widely believed in the Good spirit, *Kitche-Manitou*, who maintained for the virtuous a happy hunting-ground beyond the gleaming "Mountains of the Setting Sun." And they believed in a Bad Spirit, *Mutche-Manitou*, who kept the wicked wandering alone in a purgatory beneath a swamp. Being practical people, more concerned with the present than the hereafter, their prayers were primarily designed to propitiate the devil.

Finally, like people everywhere, the Canadian Indians were often cold, often hungry, often lonely, often frightened of the gales and blizzards that howled with elemental fury across their large and empty land. They were, as Stephen Vincent Benét expressed it:

Neither yelling demon nor Noble Savage.
They were a people not yet fused.
Made one into a whole nation, but beginning . . .

The most glamorous of the western Indians were the tribes of the Great Plains. They tended toward six-foot physiques with hawk-nosed features and long black hair. Like knights, they wielded shields, made of moose-hide and engraved with emblems of past deeds of valour. They loved brightly-plumaged war bonnets and brace-lets of antelope teeth, and they painted their bodies with yellow and scarlet stripes.

It was terrifying, and yet thrilling, to see a band on the warpath. Stripped to their breech-clouts, clutching their lances or swinging their stone-headed clubs, the warriors charged at full gallop, bodies crouched low to their horses' withers, eagle feathers flying, their fear-some war cries echoing across the plains.

"Strapping, fine-looking Indians," they were des-cribed by the Wesleyan missionary, Reverend John McDougall, in the 1860s. "Surely the bravest and most expert hunters of all the aboriginal peoples in this wide Dominion. I often asked myself, 'Who taught these wandering people the art of carrying themselves with such grace and dignity?' "

Alexander Mackenzie, explorer for the Canadian Nor'westers in the 1780s, felt that "their women are the most comely of all the nations which I have seen on this continent. The regularity of their features would be acknowledged by the more civilized people of Europe." James Isham had to concede, grudgingly, that the prairie squaws "are Very Bewitchen when Young." They could, moreover, be great coquettes. Daniel Wil-liams Harmon, the pious Nor'wester (who took one of them as a wife, and had 14 children by her) described the flirts of the prairie tribes in his journal *Sixteen Years in the Indian Country*: "The young girls often make ornamental garters, neatly worked with porcupine quills, and present them to their favourites. The stand-ing of a young male among the young females may often be determined by the number of garters which he wears."

The men of the prairie tribes sought supremacy in three pursuits: waging war, stealing horses, and hunting buffalo. Most adventuresome were tribesmen of the Blackfoot confederacy. "Tigers of the plains," they were to some white men, but they were "kind people" to Anthony Henday, the first European to see the Rocky Mountains of Canada. This Hudson's Bay Company adventurer was dumbfounded when in 1754 he first spotted the Blackfoot braves on their pawing steeds of war – their "big dogs," which had been introduced to the Indians by the Spanish conquistadores via Mexico.

The Blackfeet at once named the speedy horse *Chistli* – Seven Dogs. The introduction of the horse into his culture turned the Blackfoot into a mystic. On horse-back he felt closer to his god; he felt god-like himself. He had time to smell the first pale pink roses of summer, and to notice the curly grass bending under the hoofs of his pony, and to hear the coyotes wailing in the aspen coulées, and to feel the immensity of his domain stretch-ing endlessly under the wide and starry sky. In the still-ness and the solitude he dreamed of the horses he longed to capture and the women they would buy, of the enemy he would conquer, of the way he would die.

The Blackfoot braves were the Ishmaels of the Prairies. Their long war lances were raised against every neighbour. Their confederacy was an alliance of three tribes who roved from the foothills of the Rockies, across southern Alberta, and deep into what is now Montana. There were the Blackfeet proper (named after the stain left on their white buckskin moccasins by burned-over prairie). There were the Piegans (whose name meant "Poorly Dressed Skins"). And there were the Bloods ("Many Chiefs").

"The aristocracy of the plains," Rev. John McDougall said of the Blackfoot warriors. "Proud arrogance and intense self-sufficiency seemed to speak out in their every word and action." The parson found there was only one plains tribe the Blackfeet would not attack, and that was because they lived so far away. These were the Saulteaux (pronouced "Sootoo"), named after the rapids of Sault Ste. Marie, and sometimes known as Chippewa or Ojibwa. This branch of the Algonkian-speaking tribes seldom ventured from what is now Manitoba and Ontario, which restricted their warfare to the Sioux of North Dakota and Minnesota.

Intermittently, the Blackfoot alliance would raid the tribes to the west and south, the Sarcees ("Not Good"), and the Gros Ventres ("Big Belly" or "Gut People," a name derived from the sign language in which they begged for food to fill their aldermanic stomachs). But the Blackfoot's bloodiest battles were with the eastern Saskatchewan plainsmen, the Crees ("Pleasant Speak-ing People"), and the tribe to the north, the Assini-boines, or Stonies ("People Who Cook With Hot

Stones"). Indeed, to the Crees and the Assiniboines, the Blackfoot were known by one dread name – *Archithinues*, meaning "The Enemy."

To become a warrior was the goal of every prairie Indian boy. At birth he would be baptized by an old tribal warrior with a name derived from some former feat in battle. A name possessed magical virtues and with appropriate rites, could be changed, sold, or pawned, until a boy assumed his permanent name on reaching manhood.

Some of the names, suggested by a vision or an exploit, sound bizarre to white ears. A youth who rode so hard and long on the warpath that he did not have time to change his saddle was named "Stinking Saddle Blanket." The fastest runner among the Bloods was called "Bad Dried Meat." Youths, who graduated from one juvenile secret society to another as they grew adept as racing jockeys, were not without humour in awarding nicknames. One Blackfoot, noted for his stinginess, suffered the name, "Johnny Belches When He Eats." On reaching manhood, he formally requested the tribal council to rid him of this embarrassing sobriquet. But at the feast required for this ceremony, the tight-fisted fellow served his guests small, stringy portions of moose. To his disgust his fellows conferred upon him a new name, "Johnny Does Not Belch When He Eats."

Every youth aspired to be a member of one of the tribe's 12 military societies – elite police cavalry corps with such titles as "The Crazy Dogs." Before reaching this goal the would-be warrior had to endure a gruelling ritual. At 13 he had to go off by himself and lie for four nights in the snow or rain. Gashing his breast with a flint knife to excite pity, he would fast and pray to the gods of the sun and thunder to send him a "guardian spirit." He might be rewarded in his dream by the vision of a hawk. Afterward, he would catch a hawk, and insert its body in a pouch of skin, and this "medicine bundle" would be his guardian angel in time of war.

Initiates had to endure the agony of the Sun Dance. This ritualistic self-torture was performed each July. Young warriors to prove their bravery would pierce sharp, wooden skewers under the skin of their chests or backs. The skewers were attached to rawhide thongs, strung to the top of a sacred pole and to the end of buffalo skulls. The young men would dance and writhe at the end of a Maypole rope until their skin ripped, freeing them from the cowardice of the flesh.

An Indian raid had its code of rules like any sport. The sovereign object was less to kill than to expose yourself to danger. Consequently, when a war party travelled as far as 400 miles to enemy territory, no special precautions were taken for concealment, though

some famous Crees, like Chief Poundmaker, wore magical shirts which they believed would make them invisible. As the advance scouts of the war party approached, columns of smoke signals, made by damping a fire with a blanket, passed the warning from camp to camp: "The enemy comes!"

The war party would circle the camp, and, just as in the movies, gallop around and around ever closer, shooting willow arrows. A prairie warrior, guiding his steed with knees only, had his hands free for weapons. He could cling to his horse's neck out of sight and shoot beneath its belly, or nimbly swing onto or off his pinto at full gallop.

But, unlike the movies, scalping an enemy was not as daring an exploit as "counting coup" – touching him with an ash bow or a spear. It was a more valorous deed to thwack your foe and make him dismount, like a knight with a lance, than to shoot him from a safe distance. To get near enough to strike a personal blow meant running a genuine risk and you kept careful score of these *coups,* the French traders' word for "blows."

Nor did you necessarily kill a foe when you scalped him. To "scalp" was to slice off a round patch of skin from behind the crown of a man's head, usually with a scalp lock of hair attached. It was not necessarily fatal. Many victims were "scalped," and then allowed to go free, bloody but still alive, 99 per cent intact.

When the war party with their blood-dripping trophies returned home, the warriors would paint their exploits on buffalo hides, the wallpaper of their cone-shaped *tipis,* or tepees. The women would hang the scalps on the lodge poles and dance around them rattling their *shishiquoi,* or tambourines, and brag in song about their victorious menfolk. But there were sometimes young men who deserted the war party for the arms of a maiden back in camp. "These men are treated with contempt," wrote Daniel Williams Harmon, and he added a wry note on the fickleness of the female, who after attracting them back, "frequently composed songs of derision in regard to their behaviour."

Horse-stealing was a stealthier sport, as tricky and honourable an art as stealing bases in baseball. The Assiniboines, who were masters in it, disguised themselves as antelopes. They could approach a camp at dawn and untether the horses without alarming a single Indian guard. Then leaping on the horses while still in their antelope skins and horns, they would gallop off with what was called a blood-curdling "hunting halloa."

An Assiniboine's viewpoint in swapping his horse for something he needs is described by Harmon: "Immediately before delivering him to the purchaser, he

To the plains Indians, the buffalo was a roaming department store. The horns provided spoons and the backbone, dice.

steps up to the favourite animal, and whispers in his ear. He tells him not to be cast down or angry with his master for disposing of him to another. 'For,' he adds, 'you shall not remain long where you are. Before many nights have passed, I will come and steal you away.' "

In buffalo-hunting, the most expert prairie tribesmen would disguise themselves in buffalo skins. These "wild cattle" roamed the plains in the tens of thousands. The cow grew a coarse tawny mantle across its humped shoulder, displayed a black billy-goat beard and a shaggy Hottentot hairdo, and it nursed its young from four nipples of a milk pouch suspended beneath its series of stomachs. The early French *voyageurs* called them *les boeufs,* meaning "oxen," and out of this came the English *buffle, buffelo,* and finally *buffalo.*

Indian hunters used two techniques to slay their shaggy prey: the "surround" and the "pound." The first method was the sportiest, sometimes akin to a Spanish bullfight. A band of hunters might set the prairie grass afire in a wide circle surrounding the small herd of buffalo to hamper their escape. Then the yelling

Indians would close in from all sides. With extraordinary speed they would shoot their arrows through the lungs of the bellowing monsters. One powerful hunter was noted for allegedly being able to drive an arrow through one buffalo and pierce the heart of the next.

The Indians trained their fleetest horses to race close beside their prey, for it was considered unsporting to waste more than one shaft on a buffalo. But sometimes a partially wounded bull would plunge forward and gore the horse to death. Then the dismounted Indian had to flee for his life. The buffalo is a rather stupid, near-sighted grass-eater, almost totally dependent on its sense of smell to locate an attacker, but a wounded bull is a vicious 1,800-pound powerhouse, able to gut an Indian with a sharp twist of its short horns. George Catlin, the Pennsylvania artist, who lived among the prairie Indians in the 1830s, drew a vivid sketch of a hunter trying to escape by leaping astride the backs of two charging buffaloes:

"Many warriors, who were thus dismounted, saved

themselves by the superior muscles of their legs. Some, closely pursued by the bulls, wheeled suddenly and, snatching the part of a buffalo robe from their waists, threw it over the horns and eyes of the infuriated beast. Then, darting by its side, they drove the arrow or lance into its heart."

Impounding a big herd of buffalo was a community sport, not unlike a tiger "beat" in India. Keeping to windward of a herd, Indians disguised in buffalo skins would act as decoys and stampede the beasts toward a two-mile-long, V-shaped corral. The wings of the V consisted of women and children, who flapped blankets and pounded gourds to keep the crazed buffalo running forward. The end of the V was a shut-in enclosure of strong logs, where the trapped bison would be slaughtered with spears; or sometimes it was the edge of a cliff, and the buffalo would plunge blindly to their death.

While the men of the tribe would go off to gorge themselves on buffalo tongues, their squaws would proceed with the butchering. As the camel was to the Arab, the buffalo was to the Indian: a walking delicatessen and hardware store. The buffalo stomach became a pot, and meat was boiled by the laborious process of dropping fire-heated stones into this hanging paunch of water. The buffalo hides, scraped and tanned in the sun, became *tipi* walls, warm clothes, and winding sheets for the dead. From the back fat came ornamental hair grease: from the sinews, snowshoes and bow strings. The horns yielded cups, awls, and spoons. The backbone produced knives for their kitchens, toboggans for their children, and dice for their husbands' gambling. Buffalo claws hung from the *tipi* as a door bell. Buffalo dung — "bois de vaches," the French called it, ("cow wood") — was chipped into a campfire as coal. The buffalo tail and beard found use as fly swatters.

The bulk of the buffalo meat was cut into strips, like rashers of bacon, and hung on wooden racks to dry. Then it was pounded into powder, put into rawhide bags, and, like modern canned meat, sealed over with hot melted fat. Months later in the winter, this *pemmican* would be eaten with dried chokecherries, saskatoon berries, and a few crushed leaves of peppermint. Travellers called it "rubaboo" and thought it piquant. Some disagreed. The Earl of Southesk, in his *Narrative of Travel, Sport and Adventure During a Journey through Saskatchewan and the Rocky Mountains*, said:

"Take scrapings from the driest outside corner of a very stale piece of cold roast beef. Add to it lumps of tallowy rancid fat. Then garnish with long human hairs and short hairs of oxen, dogs, or both. You will then have a fair imitation of *pemmican* — though I should rather suppose it to be less nasty."

The prairie squaws were the happiest of all Canadian Indian women. They did not drown their baby girls at birth like some of the mothers of the Northwest Territories, who could not bear to deliver a girl into virtual slavery. The prairie mothers carried their papooses everywhere in a painted buckskin cradle slung to their backs. Moss between the child's legs, changed occasionally, served as a diaper, and the mother would nurse her child by throwing her breast backward either over her shoulder or under her arm. The young girls were given toy dolls and, in winter, whipping tops to spin on the ice.

An adolescent girl, after commencing her menstrual cycle (which required her to live apart in a brush hut), was ready for courtship. A medley of beaux would crawl into the family tent on different nights, and softly try to woo her. If the groom was a chief's son, his parents would lead a string of gift horses to the *tipi* of the bride's parents, and the couple would live in a honeymoon lodge of their own. But if the groom was poor, he would move in with his in-laws. Like the Hebrews in the Bible, the Indian Jacob would buy his bride, Rachel, over a period of years by giving her parents all the produce of his hunting. Only on the birth of his first child would he have the right to move out of the parental tent and become master of his own lodge.

It is true that the prairie husband was lord supreme of his own lodge. But he would often condescend to help his womenfolk load the horse-drawn *travois* — a platform of two long tent poles tied in an A-shaped triangle with a buffalo skin stretched across. It is also true that in a domestic spat the husband had the right to "bung her in the eye," as one startled paleface observer put it, and "yank her two braids of hair, and snap off her nose with one bite, so that the shrew would lose her beauty to other men." At the same time her husband might be passionately jealous of her — even though she were one of his several wives.

A prairie tribesman usually took as wives girls who were sisters. He held the rather dubious belief that sisters tended to quarrel less than strangers. The first wife a man wed was supposed to be the head wife, with the right to boss the others. But this arrangement by no means quietened the tongue-wagging. To diminish wrangling, a rich Blackfoot chief might provide each wife with a special lodge, and sleep for a single night with each lady of his harem in order of rank. One poor Blood, married to two squaws, found that to avoid perpetual bickering he had to bed down in one blanket precisely between them.

Except for occasional clashes over women, the prairie tribesmen lived in peace with their clansmen.

Their deadpan sense of fun often puzzled the palefaces. Paul Kane, the Toronto artist who roved and painted the pioneer West, tells of fishing a brave from freezing water.

"Are you not cold?" Kane asked him.

"My *clothes* are cold," the Indian said, "but *I* am not."

Despite the white man's stereotype of a tight-lipped, impassive Indian, the tribesmen were often cheerful and talkative. Their rhetoric was rich with simile and metaphor, and they frequently staged contests to see who could compose the lustiest songs. "When fifteen or twenty of them get into a lodge," wrote Daniel Williams Harmon, "they make an intolerable noise. Men, women and children keep their tongues constantly in motion. And, in controversy, he who has the strongest and clearest voice is, of course, heard the most easily, and consequently, succeeds best in his argument. They take a great delight, also, in singing, or humming, or whistling. In short, whether at home or abroad, they can hardly be contented with their mouths shut."

The most loquacious were the prairie elders who were held in respect, unlike the old in the Northwest Territories, who, when unable to hunt or prepare food, were left to perish.

On the Prairies, elderly people were given a generous share of each buffalo hunt. "On the first news of the buffalo hunters' approach," observed Alexander Henry, "it is customary for the old men and old women, who have no sons nor any particular friend to assist them, to crawl a mile or more out of the villages, and sit by the wayside. There almost every hunter in passing drops them a piece of meat."

The toothless old crones helped their granddaughters sew moccasins, and they held an honoured place rattling the gourds at the Ghost Dance or Chicken Dance. They acted as midwives – a role an old woman could perform only after eating the flesh of bitch puppies and drinking the broth in which the pups were boiled. The old men won renown as *shamans*, sucking out a disease with a long tube and magical incantations; as camp criers, wandering through the village shouting reports of council decisions – a sort of talking news service in several befeathered editions.

The ancient warriors on both the plains and west coast were revered as story-tellers. The Old One would gather the children around the campfire in the evening, and between slow puffs on his redstone pipe, he would tell them legends of "Thunderbird," the eagle who created thunder and lightning after the big flood; and of "Napiwa," the old man of the dawn who nurtured life in the warm seasons, and his perpetual struggle with "Stony Coat," the god of ice and winter; and of "Windigo," the long-nosed witch cannibal, who kidnapped bad children. And the Old One would invariably conclude each tale with a moral: "Don't laugh at cripples, blind people, or those who are poor, or you may become like them yourself."

The prairie tribesmen had their hard times too. In the winter, when the buffalo herds had migrated south, even the wolves had to scramble for a lean jackrabbit. Then it seemed no use for the *shaman* to peer through the smoke hole of his lodge at the still starlit face of the night, and implore the *Kitche-Manitou* for a blizzard of "moose snow."

The most poignant tragedy was when the baby son of a prairie brave died. Even the father was unashamed to show his tears, for he knew the infant would not be strong enough to fend for himself in the sunset land beyond the sand hills. The child's body was laid in a birch branch-covered grave, the buckskin blanket around him never sewn, lest he should be unable to shake it off with ease when he arrived in the land of the souls. For 12 moons the father lamented, and the mother was inconsolable, pulling out all her hair, cutting her face, arms and legs, burning all her clothes except the few rags she wore, trying to make herself as wretched as she believed her child was.

If a prairie chief died, his wives, their tormented faces daubed black, would sometimes try to throw themselves into the fire. The chief would be robed in his gayest battle regalia, and his body would rest on a high wooden scaffold on a hill, his moccasined feet always turned toward the west. His favourite horse of the buffalo chase would be killed and laid beside him. A wooden dish of venison would be set nearby to feed him during his journey to the land of the spirits, along with his pipe and tobacco and his sturdiest bow and arrow. Then the tribal orator would stand up and deliver a funeral eulogy, extolling the chief's virtues before the assembled wailing tribe.

In 1890, Crowfoot, chief of the Blackfoot confederacy, perhaps the greatest of all prairie Indians, lay dying in his *tipi*, and the melancholy drumming of the warriors ceased as he delivered his last message to his people. In it we glimpse the unfulfilled poetry and philosophy of a race:

"A little while and Crowfoot will be gone from among you – whither, he cannot tell. From nowhere we come, into nowhere we go. What is life? It is as the flash of a firefly in the night. It is as the breath of a buffalo in the winter time. It is as the little shadow that runs across the grass and loses itself in the sunset. My children, I have spoken."

The Proud People

They came in many migrations – beginning some 25,000 years ago – across the Bering Strait from somewhere in Asia, a people high of cheekbone and brown of skin. They populated two continents, from the Mackenzie delta south to Tierra del Fuego. Those who settled on the western plain and north Pacific Coast are shown in photograph and contemporary painting on the pages that follow.

Among the tribes there were as many rivalries, jealousies and resulting wars as between the nations of Europe. Their art, tools, clothes, food and language varied, depending on where they made their homes – the open spaces of the prairie, the forests to the north, the protective battlements of the mountains, or near the warm waters of the Pacific. This painting by A. J. Miller shows Blackfoot warriors, stately riders of the plains.

The Prairie Nobles

Through the eyes of the early artists who
ventured onto the plains, the Indians were not
just "redskin savages": they saw in them
a dignity of bearing and a nobility of face,
and their pictorial impressions remain,
portraits from yesterday of a proud people.

*Nomads of the plains, the Assiniboines ranged
between the Saskatchewan and Assiniboine Rivers.
The painting is by Swiss artist Karl Bodmer.*

A Blackfoot and a Piegan chief. The illustration is by Karl Bodmer, 1832-34.

Mexkemahuastan, chief of the Gros Ventres. His Saskatchewan plains tribe was pushed southwards by the Cree and Assiniboines.

Ojibwa market woman: a touch of panache with bustle and white man's hat. Artist, John Reade.

Ojibwa chief Manitowwahbay painted in oil by Paul Kane, 1845. The Ojibwa domain extended to the plains.

Sioux Indians, by George Catlin, 1830s. He went west as an artist-historian.

The fierce-fighting Cree rode the plains and the northern woods. This was a woodland camp near present-day Edmonton.

The Cree: Warriors of Plains and Woods

Left, *Cun-Ne-Wa-Bum, a comely half-breed Cree maiden of Fort Edmonton. The artist was Paul Kane: he went west in 1846 to spend two and a half years studying Indian life.*

Right, *a Cree warrior outside his crude skin tent on the prairie, proudly hugging his repeating rifle. Near his feet can be seen another white man's tool: a steel axe.*

A Dream of Peace

*This romantic family scene was captured in
watercolour by Peter Rindisbacher, who in 1821 came
to the West from Switzerland as a boy of 15
to settle with his family at Selkirk's Red River
Colony. Although Indians were inveterate
gamblers, the tepee with some tribes, particularly the
Piegans, was something they would never risk in a game.*

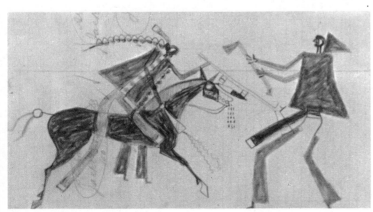

A Dance of War

To the frenzied rhythm of drums, brandishing
tomahawk and spear, these Indians performed their
dance of war. They crouched, they leaped and
whooped, then savagely struck the post they surrounded.
The War dance was a primitive form of play,
a mimetic drama of an attack against an enemy camp.
The large watercolour is by Seth Eastman.

The Ordeal of the Sun Dance

Each tribe had its own secret ceremonies, dances and religious rites, but the Sun Dance, shown in these rare photographs, was common to almost all the plains Indians. Staged at midsummer, it lasted about three or four days, and involved little "dancing" apart from a slight shuffle. Sometimes the tribe would simply sit around in a circle and stare at a central figure, as the photograph of a Blackfoot ceremony (top) reveals. The celebrants occasionally went without food or water for the entire period, hoping for a trance or a vision. In some tribes, the Sun Dance was the time to test the courage of young warriors. A brave would pierce the flesh of his back or chest with thongs, and attach these with a rope to a ceremonial pole. He would then writhe and twist, tearing his flesh free. Note the Indians in the bottom picture, hiding from the camera.

The Dance of the Snowshoes

To the Indians of the wooded regions,
the snowshoe could mean the difference
between life and death in the
lean season of winter, for without
it they would not be able to
hunt in the deep, soft snows of the
forests, and hunger might soon
haunt their camps. The Ojibwa had
a special rite, the Snowshoe
Dance, shown in the painting (right),
by George Catlin, dated 1830 – 1833.

On the Pacific Coast, a tribesman's status was measured by the gifts he could afford at a feast called a "Potlatch."

Salish woman weaving a blanket. Woolly dogs supplied the yarn, and colour-fast vegetable dyes provided the decoration.

Beyond the 'Shining Mountains'

Left, *the inside of a house at Nootka Sound, British Columbia, from an engraving by John Webber. Some Nootka wooden houses could hold 800 people during ceremonials.*

Right, *two West Coast chiefs resplendent in their regal robes. Intricately designed, made of the wool of three mountain goats, some shoulder capes took a year to weave.*

The Salmon Eaters

*Indian lodges near Fort Colvile, on the Columbia River,
as painted by Paul Kane. The matted roofs were used to stack
salmon for drying, unlike the elaborate smoke-houses
built by the Tsimshian Indians to the north. Catching the
plentiful salmon was sometimes simpler than storing
it: some tribes such as the Salish constructed caches on
stilts to protect their food supply from prowling animals.*

*Portrait of a murderer. This oil painting by Paul Kane
shows To-Ma-Kus, a Cayuse Indian who on November 29, 1847, killed
Marcus Whitman, Oregon country pioneer and missionary.*

II

The Pathfinders

IT was a warm June Sunday afternoon in 1793, high in the Canadian Rockies. Alexander Mackenzie, a handsome, 30-year-old Nor'wester fur trader with curly brown hair and a dimpled pugnacious chin, sat in his birchbark canoe. He and his six French *voyageur* paddlers, two Indian guides, another Scot fur trader named Alexander Mackay, and a dog, were seeking that elusive will-o'-the-wisp – a river route across Canada to the Pacific.

Mackenzie was not normally a poetic nature lover. He was a dour Stornoway Scot who had adventured to Montreal as a boy of 16. But as he made the first crossing of the Rockies by a white man he was moved to write in his diary of the "exuberant verdure" of this "magnificent theatre of nature, the most beautiful scenery I had ever beheld." He was entranced by the "velvet rind" of the arching willow and blossoming alder branches. He was enchanted by white mountain goats and what looked like purple humming birds; by the lush wild strawberries, the perfume of roses and camas lilies. And though he and his men had to wade to their thighs through "boiling and hissing" mountain streams carrying each other on their shoulders, he could not help admiring the limestone-bedded river with its water "the colour of asses' milk."

Suddenly, around the bend of what he named the "Bad River," Mackenzie sighted two savages. On their naked chests bristled necklaces of white grizzly bear claws. They brandished arrows and six-foot bows of polished cedar. Their fists were clenched in the classic gesture of hostility.

Mackenzie disarmed them with an equally classic gesture. He stepped forward and shook each of them by the hand. "This was the first time they had ever seen a human being of a complexion different than their own," he wrote. "They examined everything about us with minute and suspicious attention. However, they laid aside their weapons. One of them, but with a very tremulous action, drew his knife from his sleeve, and presented it to me as a mark of his submission to my will and pleasure."

Mackenzie was impressed by the new breed of Indians he saw here and in the riverside villages en route to the "Stinking Lake," as the natives called the salt waters of the Pacific. One tribe of fish-eaters was of such a "cheerful and pleasing aspect" that he named the camp, on the bank of the Bella Coola River, the "Friendly Village."

The men wore sea otter and ermine robes tied loosely over their shoulders, and they would lay aside these regal cloaks quite casually to stride about totally naked. The chief's son, a beardless giant of six-feet-four, was treated with deferential respect by the other tribesmen. He offered Mackenzie a feast of roast salmon and roe, and the explorer was much taken by his "affable manners" and "prepossessing appearance."

His father wore a royal beard, so Mackenzie presented this *tyee*, or "chief," with a pair of steel scissors. His Majesty immediately used it to clip his whiskers. The chief was so grateful that he insisted on giving Mackenzie one of his females as a bed companion that night. "Notwithstanding his repeated entreaties," Mackenzie confides in his diary, "I resisted this offering of his hospitality."

The women wore fringed sea otter aprons. Their short hair was capped with gaily woven spruce bonnets, looking like an upturned flower basket, and several women had macaroni-like sea shells jutting from their perforated nostrils.

Mackenzie found the women lusty, but inclined to be fat. He assumed their dumpy legs resulted from their "posture of always sitting at their domestic engagements." These chores included splitting and cleaning stacks of 500 salmon with mussel-shell scrapers.

Mackenzie was astonished at the wealth of the coastal capitalists, at their pomp and splendour. Their 50-foot dug-out canoes, the prows carved with garish faces, could carry 50 people. Like merchant princes, they traded up and down the coast, dealing in shipments of slaves and mountain goat wool and *oolakan* (candle fish) oil. They reckoned wealth in money: strings of white dentalia sea shells and strips of copper.

In 1793, Alexander Mackenzie became the first white man to cross the Rockies, following the churning mountain streams to the salt waters of the Pacific. Today, the longest river system in Canada bears his name.

Their lodges were not movable tents but permanent cedar-plank "temples." These big rectangular mansions, carved with an elk-horn adz, teetered on steps above the gravelly banks. Inside, rows of benches lined the walls as in an amphitheatre. Outside, totem poles loomed 20 feet high, their grotesque sculpture heralding the wealth and glory of each nobleman. "They were painted with hieroglyphics and figures of different animals," reported Mackenzie, "and with a degree of correctness not to be expected from an uncultivated people."

Unlike any other Canadian Indians that Mackenzie had ever seen, these natives had a strong sense of property rights. Each salmon-fishing weir on a river bank belonged to one family of noblemen through inheritance. It was their exclusive domain. Poachers dared not trespass. This aristocratic class-consciousness possibly recalled to the lowly-born Scot the rank and estate of the English country gentlemen, and he wrote: "Of the many tribes of savage people whom I have seen, these appear to be the most susceptible of civilization."

To end his expedition among the Pacific Coast Indians, he took vermilion mixed with bear grease and painted these words on the southeast face of a rock jutting into the Pacific:

ALEXANDER MACKENZIE FROM CANADA,
BY LAND, THE TWENTY-SECOND OF JULY, 1793.

Four years before, Mackenzie had blazed a trail north, exploring the river that bears his name to the Arctic Ocean. Here he observed the poorest and least civilized of western Indians, the tribes from the treeless tundra, the nomads who snared the caribou in the no-man's-land of the Northwest Territories.

It was in June, July and August, 1789, that the young Highland Scot made this expedition. Yet even in these 102 summer days he was appalled by the ice and sleet and cold on what, in dismay, he named, "River of Disappointment."

Still trying to find a passageway west to the Pacific, the Nor'wester fur trader set out from Fort Chipewyan on Lake Athabasca in what is now northeast Alberta. This time his birchbark canoe was manned by four *voyageurs*. His guide – an obstreperous Indian nicknamed "English Chief," accompanied by his two squaws – had to be regaled finally with rum and pleaded with to continue the bleak trek into the "land of the never-setting sun."

Spilling down the rapids of Slave River and onto the solid slab of ice crusting Great Slave Lake, Mackenzie suffered qualms. When it was hot, he was tormented by swarms of gnats that bit implacably until the blood came, and he had to pull the canoe through swamps up to his armpits. When it was cold, he was beset by hailstones, "boisterous hurricanes whose gusts blew our tents away," and frost "so severe that our axes became almost as brittle as glass."

Snaking down the Mackenzie River, he found few things to please him. Overhead against a steel-blue sky, curlews wheeled and screamed as though in protest against their fate. To be sure, in the lower forests of stunted pine and scraggly larch and dwarf spruce he saw dun-coloured summer foxes and some herds of caribou. And among the misty bogs here were ptarmigan and fat lemmings. But further north, on the bald rock, mossy lichen and primordial frost the land seemed naked and lonely.

"This country is one continual morass, where the ground never thaws above five inches from the surface," Mackenzie noted in his journal one July midnight, with the sun blazing overhead. "I could never force a blade into it beyond a depth of six or eight inches."

The people were not much more prepossessing than the wilderness they thinly inhabited. Before he planted a wooden post bearing his name on the Arctic fringes of Whale Island, Mackenzie met several of these "edge-of-the-woods" tribes. They were largely Chipewyans and Dogribs, who tracked the caribou in the migratory seasons – spearing them on the Barrens in the summer, snaring them in the timber during winter.

"They are a meagre, ugly, ill-made people," Mackenzie observed when a tribe of men and women staged a "promiscuous dance of antic postures" for him. "Their complexion is swarthy. Their stature has nothing remarkable in it. Their features are coarse: and their hair lank, but always of a dingy black. Nor have they universally the piercing eye, which generally animates the Indian countenance."

He felt that their music, which consisted of the men howling like wolves, was absurdly "inharmonious." Their dancing, in which the women's arms hung down limply, was ungainly. "They might be supposed to be ashamed of both recreations," he moralized. He particularly disliked their nagging and complaining. "This they express by a constant repetition of the word *eduiy* – 'it is hard' – in a whining and plaintive tone of voice."

The men, who wrestled each other to grab off a woman for the night, were at least built robustly. They wore jackets of muskrat or marten skins with a tail flopping behind in case they wanted to sit on the ice. Their cheeks were tattooed with four straight blue lines made by drawing coloured threads painfully under their skin. Their sole attractive ornament was yellow and red embroidery on their leather headbands and leggings.

These were laced with porcupine quills "of very neat workmanship."

The women dressed like the men, except for roomier hoods about the shoulders, allowing them to sling suckling babies on their backs next to their skin. Mackenzie was shocked that the women "have no covering on their private parts, except a tassel of leather, which dangles from a small cord."

He was distressed to see the men treating their wives as slaves. The women pulled heavier packs than those of their scruffy toboggan dogs. The men, carrying only their few weapons, refused to help the women but even so, were remarkably jealous of their many wives. A husband might put an unfaithful wife to death, beating her with a moose-horn club, or killing her with a stone from his slingshot. "Notwithstanding the vigilance and severity," Mackenzie wrote, "it seldom happens that a woman is without her favourite, who, in the absence of the husband, exacts the same submission, and practises the same tyranny. And so premature is the tender passion, that it invigorates a girl as young as twelve."

Their physical possessions were primitive. Their one-man canoes, carved out of swamp spruce, were like the Eskimo *kayak*. A hunter might paddle his canoe right up onto the shoulders of a caribou that was swimming with its herd across a stream. Then, picking up his bone spear, the hunter would stab to right and left until his mount reached the far side and toppled over dead.

Their *tipis*, Mackenzie reported, were little more than a brush lean-to. "A few poles supported by a fork, with some branches or a piece of bark as a covering, constitutes the whole of their native architecture." By striking a flint and a piece of yellow pyrite together over dried grasses and kindling wood, an open fire would be lit between two such rude huts and the heat would be cast into both lodges. "Notwithstanding the cold, and having neither skins or garments of any kind to cover them," Mackenzie said, "they laid themselves to sleep around the fire, like so many whelps."

Mackenzie regarded the northern Indians with condescension. But he had spent only three months with them – in 1789. Another explorer, Samuel Hearne, a Hudson's Bay Company trader, lived with them for four years—from 1769 to 1772, alternately loving and hating them.

Mackenzie wrote them off as "uncivilized" in the ghost-written epic, *Voyages to the Frozen and Pacific Oceans*, that won him a knighthood. Hearne wrote only a diary, *Journey To The Northern Ocean*, but it was a masterpiece. For Hearne laced his objectivity with wit and gave the northern Indians rare understanding.

Samuel Hearne was just 24 when he set off across the frozen wastes on his first expedition in November of 1769. From the stone gateway of Fort Prince of Wales on Hudson Bay, at the mouth of the Churchill River, seven cannons fired a farewell. He was a Londoner, a one-time cabin boy in a Royal Navy warship who had sailed around the world under Admiral Hood, and then as mate of a whaling sloop for the Hudson's Bay Company.

One does not get a true picture of the man from the one painting of him that survives. It shows him laced and ruffled in a blond wig, elegant in cravat, vest and waistcoat, his widely separated blue eyes staring mildly out of a rather pasty face. Another great explorer, David Thompson, who served a one-year apprenticeship under Hearne at the Bay, describes him as "a handsome man of six feet in height, of a ruddy complexion and remarkably well-made, enjoying good health."

Young Hearne was a nonconformist, and an admirer of Voltaire. He also had a genuine love for birds and animals and he wrote of them with artistry and the clarity of a naturalist. He collected a menagerie – bald eagles, lemmings, silver foxes, beavers, mink, ermine, squirrels, snow buntings, horned owls – and studied them carefully.

Before setting out on his expedition, Hearne had toughened himself. In the winter of 1767 he had walked both ways carrying mail, across the desolate 150 miles separating York Factory and Fort Churchill. He had camped out in winter with the Indians, snaring ptarmigan and racing after moose, until he was "celebrated," he said, "for being particularly fleet of foot in snowshoes."

Now the fur-trading company was sending him on foot with a band of Chipewyan Indians to track down an El Dorado of copper, rumoured to exist at the mouth of a river flowing into the far-off Arctic Ocean. All Hearne had to go by was a rude map of the north country drawn on a caribou skin with charcoal by an Indian who claimed to have found enormous lumps of copper ore.

On that first trip, Hearne walked only 200 miles. His Indian guide, "a sly artful villain" named Chawchinahaw, persuaded the others to desert one night with Hearne's ammunition and ice chisels. "I was under the necessity of hauling the sledge back," Hearne explained, "which however was not very heavy, as it scarcely exceeded sixty pounds."

Hearne's second expedition was likewise fruitless. His new Indian guide, a fumbler named Connee-queese, led him on a wild goose chase to the Barrens. Moreover, he allowed a marauding band of Chipewyan "ravagers" to commandeer their supplies. Hearne asked the brigands to give him back, at least, his razor and soap. They also handed back, "a knife to cut my victuals, an awl to mend my shoes, and a needle to mend my other clothing – though not without them making me understand I ought to look upon it as a great favour." A stray gust of wind smashed his direction-finding quadrant, and his sleigh dog froze to death. Yet after nearly nine months Hearne managed to get back to the fort, half-starved but resolved to try again. "I endeavoured, like a sailor after a storm," he said, "to forget past misfortunes."

The Indian who guided his third walking expedition of almost 19 months epitomized, for Hearne, all the virtues and defects of the northern tribesmen. He was the famed Matonabbee. Shortnecked, copper-coloured, with a Roman nose and six-foot stature, this Chipewyan radiated a dauntless will and an amiable philosophy.

"I have met with few Christians who possessed more good moral qualities, or fewer bad ones," Hearne wrote. "His features were regular and agreeable; and yet so strongly expressive, that they formed a complete index of his mind. In conversation, he was easy, lively, but exceedingly modest. To the vivacity of a Frenchman, and the sincerity of an Englishman, he added the gravity and nobleness of a Turk."

Matonabbee told Hearne that the reason for the failure of his last two expeditions was elementary. He had neglected to take along wives to lug his packs.

"Women were made for labour," Matonabbee told Hearne with a laugh. "One of them can carry or haul as much as two men. They also pitch our tents, make and mend our clothes of the hunt, keep us warm at night. More than this, women can be maintained at a trifling expense. For, as they always cook, the very licking of their fingers in scarce times is sufficient for their sustenance."

Matonabbee maintained seven strapping wives. They were built, Hearne dryly observed, like "good grenadiers." But they were also the cause of a main defect: Matonabee's inordinate jealousy. Hearne could not understand why anybody would want to philander with these plodding drudges. "Their senses seem almost as dull and frigid as the zone they inhabit," he recorded in his diary. "Still, I suppose it only requires indulgence and precept to make some of them as lofty and insolent as any women in the world." Hearne conceded that the northern women were accomplished actresses. "I can affirm with truth I have seen some of them, with one side of the face bathed in tears, while the other has exhibited a significant smile."

Hearne commented on an example of female flirtation as his expedition tramped across 14 miles of ice

covering Partridge Lake in bitter February cold. The thighs and buttocks of one of Matonabbee's wives became encrusted with freezing snow. "The pain the poor woman suffered was greatly aggravated by the laughter and jeering of her companions. They said she was rightly served for belting her clothes so high. I must admit I thought she took too much pains to show a clean heel and a good leg. Her garters were always in sight."

Hearne was surprised to see how closely the parents kept watch over their unbetrothed daughters. "From the age of eight," he observed, "the girls are prohibited from joining in the most innocent amusements with male children. They are guarded with an unremitting vigilance that cannot be exceeded by the most rigid discipline of an English boarding school." At 12, the girls had to seclude themselves in a hut near camp for the onset of their menstrual cycle. They returned from this *thunnardy*, or "monthly living alone," wearing a beaded veil. This showed that they were eligible for marriage – usually with a man 20 years older.

Thunnardy, Hearne noted with amusement, was used by married women as "an excuse for a temporary separation. I have known some sulky dames to leave their husbands and tents for five days at a time, and repeat the farce twice or thrice a month. The poor men have never suspected the deceit – or, if they have, delicacy has not permitted them to inquire into the matter. I have known Matonabbee's handsome wife to live apart from him for several weeks, under this pretence, and then she eloped. Matonabbee seemed quite inconsolable. His wife had chosen to return to the sprightly young fellow of no note who had been her former husband, (from whom Matonabbee had seized her by force in a wrestling match) rather than have the seventh share of the affection of the greatest man in the country. I am sorry to mention it, but Matonabbee had no sooner heard of this man's arrival near our camp at Clowey Lake than he took out his box-handled knife and went into the man's tent. Without any preface, he took him by the collar and began to execute his horrid design. The poor man fell on his face and called for help. But before it came, he had received three wounds in his back. Matonabbee returned to his tent afterwards. He sat down composedly, called for water to wash his bloody hands, lit his pipe, and asked me, 'Did you not think I had not done right?' "

Walking as much as 20 miles a day across spongy muskeg, Hearne found it a land of "all feasting or all famine." Once his band of 16 nomads travelled for two days on nothing but melted snow water and a pipeful of tobacco. On another fast of seven days, Hearne, like

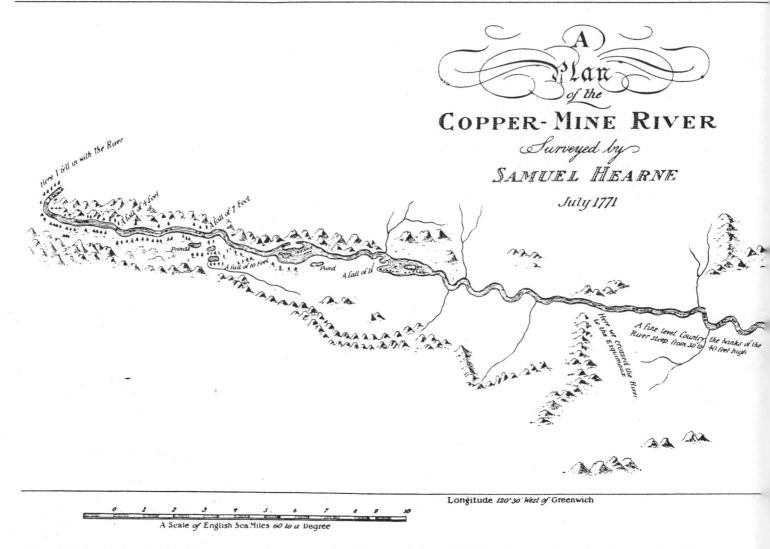

Samuel Hearne's map, with his own notations, recording his expedition of 1771 to the mouth of the Coppermine River.

Charlie Chaplin in *The Gold Rush*, was forced to eat a boiled pair of boots.

Unlike Mackenzie, Hearne recorded cannibalism and its aftermath: "For having eaten human flesh, the pariah is shunned and detested . . . obliged to wander up and down, forlorn and forsaken even by his own relations, like Cain after he killed his brother Abel. I have seen several of these poor wretches. And though they were much esteemed persons before hunger drove them to this act, afterwards they were so despised, that a smile never graced their faces. Deep melancholy was seated on their brows. And their eyes seemed to say: 'Why do you despise me for my misfortune? The period is probably not far distant when you too may be driven to the like necessity.' "

After these stretches of starvation, Hearne could

understand the gluttony the men showed in the periods when the white Arctic hare, partridge, whitefish and caribou were abundant. No sooner would a moose be killed than the hunter would rip open the stomach, thrust in his arm, snatch out the kidneys, and gobble these delicacies warm before the animal was quite dead. An unborn fawn, ripped out of the belly of its mother, was considered fit for a gourmet. Hearne saw Maton-abbee devour raw even the acidy flesh of the muskox "eating as much as six men" with only mild indigestion.

"Notwithstanding that they are voracious on occasion," Hearne said, "yet the northern Indians bear hunger with a degree of fortitude which, as has been said, 'is much easier to admire than to imitate.' I have often seen them, at the end of a three-day fast, as merry and jocose on the subject as if their abstinence from

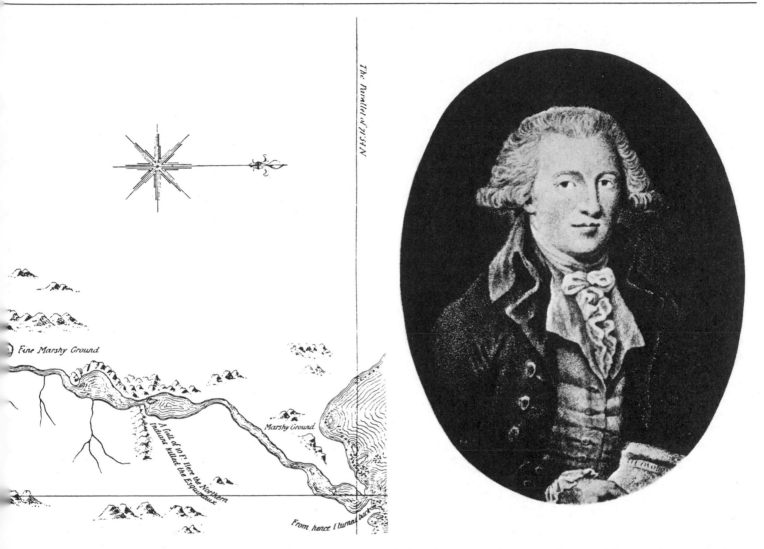

The Parallel of 71.54 N.

Fine Marshy Ground

A fall of 10 Ft. Here the Northern Indians killed the Esquimaux

Marshy Ground

From hence I turned back

It was a journey to disappointment: Hearne never found the El Dorado of copper that lured him to the Arctic Coast.

food had been self-imposed. They would, for instance, ask each other, in the plainest and merriest mood, 'Do you have any inclination for an intrigue with a woman?' "

There were northern Indian rituals that Hearne found enchanting. When two bands of people met on the lone tundra, an orator from each would recite the calamities and deaths endured since each party had last seen each other. This was followed by a "crying match," in which each party vied in wailing and howling their sympathy: it was climaxed by the cheerful passing around of a pipe and the smiling exchange of the good news. Hearne was diverted by their nude dances, too. Lines of naked Indians curtsied to each other formally, as though in a minuet, lifting their feet high like cranes to the pounding beat of a caribou-skin drum as they

sang a sprightly chorus of *"Hee, hee, hee! Ho, ho, ho!"*

Hearne enjoyed their game of quoits, called *holl*, and their interminable gambling with the Indian version of the game, "Button, button, who's got the button?" As his party neared the Arctic Ocean, Hearne's Indians supplicated the *nantena*, fairies who were supposed to control the wind and the sea and the air. And the aurora borealis, with its brilliant curtain of yellows, crimsons and greens, was to them the *edthin*, or "cloud caribou." On a still night Hearne heard these Northern Lights "make a rustling and cracking noise, like the waving of a large flag in a fresh gale of wind," which the Indians romanticized as the spirits of their dead friends dancing and making merry in the sky with the caribou.

When his band reached the banks of the Copper-mine River on July 13, 1771, Hearne was far from charmed by his companions. A village of Eskimos was camped beside a waterfall and Matonabbee was determined to massacre the helpless natives in their sleep. Hearne vainly tried to dissuade Matonabbee from this "brutish slaughter" but his heretofore easy-going friend seemed to be fired with a fierce hatred for the Eskimos. With a discipline and murderous zeal that Hearne had not seen before, Matonabbee led his savage crew in painting images of the sun and moon and the Arctic bear on their caribou-hide shields. They smeared red-and-black stripes on their faces, and tied their hair back to keep the wind from blowing it into their eyes. "And though the mosquitos were so numerous as to surpass all credibility," Hearne wrote, "yet some of the Indians actually pulled off their jackets, and prepared to enter the lists quite naked except for their breech-clouts and moccasins."

Creeping quietly to where the Eskimo families were sleeping in their tents, the Indians rushed down the bank, brandishing spears. Those men, women and children not immediately stabbed to death ran naked into the snow until the Coppermine River cut off their escape. Twenty northern Indians pierced one elderly Eskimo man "until his body was like a sieve." They poked the eyes from an old Eskimo woman and then butchered her. After chopping up the women, the Indians stood over them. A few Eskimos managed to scramble into knee-deep water. And the Indians formed a circle on the hill, raised their spears high and clashed their shields together, and to deride their victims, jeered, *"Tima! Tima!"* – Eskimo for "Good friend! Good friend!"

Hearne was aghast when a young Eskimo girl of about 18, transfixed by an Indian spear, threw herself writhing and clutching at his feet. "She twisted herself around my legs so that it was with difficulty I could disengage myself from her dying grasp. Two Indian men were pursuing this unfortunate victim. I begged very hard for her life. The murderers made no reply, until they had struck both their spears through her body. They then looked me sternly in the face, and ridiculed me by asking, 'Do you want an Eskimo wife?' They paid not the smallest regard to the shrieks and the agony of the poor wretch, who was still twining round their spears, like an eel."

Hearne pleaded with them, "Please, dispatch this poor girl out of her misery. Otherwise, out of pity, I will have to put an end to her." One of the Indians obligingly pulled his spear from her body and thrust it through her breast near the heart. Such was the love for life, Hearne noted, that the Eskimo girl made feeble efforts with her arm to ward off this blow of mercy and then, at last, she died. "Even at this hour," Hearne wrote in his diary years later, "I cannot reflect on the transactions of that horrid day without shedding tears."

Dismayed and disenchanted, Hearne left this scene of carnage, known forever after as "Bloody Falls." He was still downhearted as he and his band of "wanton" Indians proceeded down the Coppermine River to its mouth at the Arctic Ocean. There, at one o'clock in the morning of July 18, 1771, with the sun flickering through fog and drizzling rain, "I erected a mark, and took possession of the coast, on behalf of the Hudson's Bay Company."

His triumph was a bitter one. The fabled El Dorado of copper, supposed to be rich enough to fill an entire ship, proved "no more than an entire jumble of rock and gravel." A four-hour search yielded only a single four-pound chunk of metal.

The dejected Hearne left on his long hike home, brooding about the northern Indians and their "inhospitable land" on the cap of the continent. "It must be allowed that they are the greatest philosophers," he mused, "for they never give themselves the trouble to acquire what they can do well enough without. Being destitute of all religious control, these people have, to use Matonabbee's own words, 'nothing to do but consult their own inclinations and passions; to pass through this world as contentedly as possible, with no painful fear of punishment in the next.'

"Even when that greatest calamity of the northern Indian befalls them, old age, and they are no longer capable of walking, and they are left alone to perish, they submit patiently to their lot without a murmur. Like other uncivilized people, they bear bodily pain with great fortitude."

Not all men thought the habitat of the northern Indians unlovely. Years later, when more white men came to the Barren Grounds, and a missionary preached the beauties of the Christian heaven, an ancient Dogrib Indian named Saltatha replied earnestly:

"My father, you have spoken very well. You have told me that Paradise is very beautiful; tell me now one thing more. Is it more beautiful than the land of the muskox in summer, when sometimes the mist blows over the little lakes in the early morning, and sometimes the water is blue, and the loons cry very often? Can I see the caribou roam where I look, and can I feel the wind, and be like the wind? That is beautiful: and if Paradise is still more beautiful, my heart will be glad, and I shall be content to rest there till I am very old."

The Hunters

On the wide Canadian plains, the hunt went on in every season. The teeming herds of buffalo gave the Indian his food, his clothes, and his ancient weapons. There was a savage beauty in the hunt, triumph and sometimes tragedy, and travelling artists who came to the early West were thrilled and inspired by the spectacle.

The Lumbering Prey

Feast or famine for the people of the plains depended on the appearance of the great herds near the tribal hunting grounds.

For the prairie Indian, bison provided fresh meat in summer, dried "pemmican" in winter, hides for clothes and shelter. In the U.S., the senseless slaughter of the herds by white hide-hunters sparked several fierce Indian wars, and it was partly because settlers were forcing the buffalo off the Canadian plains that Indian and Métis buffalo hunters answered Louis Riel's call to arms in 1885. Early painters, professional and amateur, began to record the hunt before this, and so glamorized did the Canadian West become in European eyes that many artists tried to join the vogue without ever going there. Having nothing but hearsay to tell them whether a buffalo had one hump or two, it's not surprising that their art was more humorous than accurate.

△ *Horses came to the plains in the early 1700s, and a buffalo pony was a brave's proudest possession. This hunter isn't doing well, for using more than one arrow was "unsporting."*

▽ *A hunter could become the hunted, but even the mighty bison bulls, 2,000 pounds of muscle, were no match for the white man's deadly rifle. For the great herds, it spelled extinction.*

The Fatal Plunge

The "surround" and "pound" methods of hunting buffalo on the Canadian plains are known to have been used by Stone Age Europeans in hunting mammoths. In the first plan, the prey is surrounded by the hunters, or encircled by a grass fire, and individuals in the trapped herd can be picked off. In the pound method, the herd is stampeded into a corral, and then killed. Sometimes, as shown here, buffalo were stampeded over cliffs.

With Spear and Snowshoe

When the deep snows came, the hungry hunters
set out on the trail of the moose and other game.

*The spear was more effective than the arrow when
tackling the moose in winter. The Athapaskans to the
north, however, found the snare even more reliable.
In summer, a lucky hunter might chance to see a
moose swimming, and could spear it easily from a canoe.*

△ *The drama of a winter moose hunt is shown in this amusing early 19th century painting by John Reade. To lure the male moose, Algonkian tribes made "moose calls" out of birchbark.*

▽ *This native had a powder-and-ball rifle for duck hunting. Plains Indians – the buffalo eaters – would often rather go hungry than eat ducks, rabbits or other small game.*

Stalking the Herd

At the risk of being charged and gored, a pair of hunters under camouflage close in on a huge herd grazing in the "sea of grass."

The wolf was the traditional enemy – so why didn't the herd trample them? A prairie conundrum caught on canvas by George Catlin, who first went to the West in 1832. The hunters more commonly used buffalo robes for camouflage. If a bull charged, the hunter would dodge and throw the robe over the animal's head, then plunge a lance into its heart. In lush times, even the Indian was wasteful: he would kill a buffalo and remove only the tongue, leaving the remainder of the huge carcass to rot on the plains.

III

Blood and Furs

ALEXANDER HENRY paused uneasily in his writing of a letter to be taken by birchbark canoe to Montreal. Outside he could hear 400 Chippewa Indians whooping and hollering as they played a boisterous game of lacrosse outside the cedarwood stockade of Fort Michilimackinac. It seemed an exceedingly large number of players. Why had the redskins asked yesterday to buy his entire stock of tomahawks? Did Chief Pontiac still resent the Paris peace treaty that had given French Canada that year to the British without as much as a pow-wow with the Indians?

From where Henry was writing his letter that day in June 1763, he could see two English brass cannons on the bastions. Within the stockade were 30 neat wood houses of conquered, but supposedly friendly, French-Canadian traders. But Henry reassured himself with the fact that Michilimackinac (Indian for "Big Turtle") had a garrison of 92 English soldiers under Major George Etherington. On the south bank of the strait linking Lake Huron and Lake Michigan, the fort was now the meeting place of all free-lance Indian traders. From there, they portaged beaver furs to Montreal.

Henry was known as "the handsome Englishman," despite the fact that he was born in New Jersey. He was stocky and tough, with candid blue eyes, pink cheeks, and fair hair that fell to the collar of his buckskin shirt. Though he was afterwards called Alexander Henry the Elder (to distinguish him from his nephew, Alexander Henry the Younger, a later Nor'wester), Henry was only 24. He was a witty man who knew the poetry of Milton. And he had those two fevers that afflicted every Canadian Nor'wester frontiersman – a wanderlust and a profitlust.

As he continued to write his letter, Henry remembered what had happened a year earlier on his way to Michilimackinac. He had canoed from Montreal with trading trinkets and rum. The Chippewa had been so hostile to the British that Henry had tried to disguise himself as one of his French-Canadian *voyageurs*. He had put on a fringed buckskin shirt, a buffalo coat, and a red worsted cap. He had smeared dirt on his face and wielded a paddle. A Chippewa chief saw through the disguise. Henry was surrounded by 60 braves brandishing tomahawks and scalping knives, their naked chests painted for war. The chief spoke ominous words to Henry; he used what Henry recognized as his formal "war council voice."

"Englishman! You know the French King is our father. We promised to be his children. During his sleep you took advantage of him and possessed yourselves of Canada. Englishman, although you have conquered the French, you have not yet conquered us." Amid approving grunts of "Eh" from his warriors, the Chippewa chief continued: "Englishman! Our father, the King of France, employed our young men to make war upon your nation. In this warfare many of them have been killed. And it is our custom to retaliate . . . until such time as the spirits of the slain are satisfied." Only by ladling out "English milk" – as the Indians called his casks of liquor – had Henry escaped.

One Chippewa, however, had taken Henry aside and laid gifts of beaver skins and dried venison meat at his feet. It was Wa-wa-tam, a 45-year-old chief of great dignity. He had dreamed of adopting an Englishman as his blood son and brother. "I recognize you as the person whom the Great Spirit pointed out to me in my dream," Wa-wa-tam said shyly. "I hope you will not refuse my presents, so now I may regard you as one of my family."

Wa-wa-tam had reappeared at Fort Michilimackinac with his wife the previous day. Both begged Henry to leave with them immediately for Sault Ste. Marie. They hinted of some sinister Indian scheme; Wa-wa-tam spoke of the "disturbing noise of evil birds."

Henry wrote later: "The Indian manner of speech is so extravagantly figurative that I turned a deaf ear. I left Wa-wa-tam and his wife to depart alone, with dejected countenances, and not before they had each let fall some tears."

Now, in the bright June morning, as Henry blotted his letter with sand, he suddenly heard the "noise of evil

To the victor went the scalp; it mattered little whether the victim was still breathing.
Artist, Peter Rindisbacher.

birds": an ear-piercing Indian war cry. In the comparative safety of his office, he stood at the window, horrified at the spectacle.

The Indians had batted the lacrosse ball, by seeming accident, over the palisade. Under the pretext of recovering it, 400 athlete-warriors had streamed inside the fort and then pulled tomahawks from under their sports robes.

"Through the window," Henry wrote, "I beheld, in shapes the foulest and most terrible, the ferocious triumphs of barbarian conquerors. I saw the Indians, within the fort, furiously cutting down and scalping every Englishman they found. I saw several of my countrymen fall, and more than one struggling between the knees of an Indian, who, holding him in this manner, scalped him while yet living.

"The dying were writhing and shrieking under the unsatiated knife and tomahawk. And from the bodies ripped open, their butchers were drinking the blood, scooped up in the hollow of joined hands, and quaffed amid shouts of rage and victory. I was shaken, not only with horror, but with fear. The sufferings which I witnessed, I seemed on the point of experiencing."

During the slaughter, Henry noticed that the allies of the Indians, the French-Canadian traders, were looking on from their houses within the stockade. They did not lift a hand to protect the English, nor were they touched by the rampaging Chippewa. Climbing over a low backyard fence, Henry raced next door to the house of a plump Frenchman called Charles Langlade. He begged with Langlade to hide him. The Frenchman looked for a moment in Henry's face, turned to look at the scene of carnage before him, then gave a Gallic shrug: "I can do nothing for you."

"This was a moment for despair," Henry recalled. "But the next moment, a Pawnee Indian woman, a slave of Monsieur Langlade's, beckoned me to follow her. She brought me to a door which led to the garret, where I must go and conceal myself. I joyfully obeyed her directions. And she, having followed me up to the garret door, locked it after me, and with great presence of mind took away the key." Through the knothole in the dark windowless garret Henry peered out at the butchery in the fort. Soon he heard the savage cry, "All is finished!" At the same instant he saw a bunch of Indians trooping up to Langlade's front door. With his ear against the plank floor boards of his garret, Henry could hear the Chippewa questioning Langlade: "Do you have any Englishmen hidden in your house?"

"I cannot say," Langlade repied. "I do not know of any."

The Indians persisted: "How about your garret?"

With dismay Henry heard Langlade say, "Come on upstairs and examine it for yourself."

In mounting panic Henry looked for a hiding place. Piled in a corner were vessels used for making maple sugar. He had barely crept behind them when Langlade unlocked the door and led in four blood-smeared Indians armed with tomahawks.

"I could scarcely breathe," Henry wrote. "I thought that the throbbing of my heart occasioned a noise loud enough to betray me. The Indians walked in every direction about the garret. One of them approached me so closely that had he put out his hand he would have touched me. After telling Monsieur Langlade how many they had killed, and how many scalps they had taken, they returned downstairs. And I, with sensations not to be expressed, heard the door, which was the barrier between me and my fate, locked for the second time."

Henry threw himself down on a feather bed on the floor, and in his exhaustion slept until dusk of the next evening. Then the attic door opened again and he was awakened by Langlade's wife. She was surprised to see him but consented to give him a drink of water, leaving Henry on a "rack of apprehension."

Next day, at sunrise, he heard the Indians banging on the front door. "The Englishman, Henry, is not among the dead," someone was shouting at Langlade. "He must be concealed here." Madame Langlade, in rapid French, told her husband, "Let us deliver the Englishman to his pursuers. Otherwise, the Indians may take revenge on our children. Better that *he* should die than they."

"I have just been told that the Englishman is in my house," Langlade told the Chippewa. "He came here without my knowledge. Come and I will put him in your hands."

"I now resigned myself to the fate with which I was menaced," Henry wrote. "I arose from the bed, and presented myself full in view to the Indians who were entering the room. They were all in a state of intoxication, and naked, except about the middle. One of them, named Wenniway, I had previously known. He was upward of six feet in height, and had his entire face and body covered with charcoal and grease. Only a white spot, of two inches in diameter, encircled either eye. This man walked up to me. He seized me with one hand by the collar of the coat, while in the other he held a large carving knife as if to plunge it in my breast. His eyes, meanwhile, were fixed steadfastly on mine. At length, after some seconds of the most anxious suspense, he dropped his arm, saying, 'I won't kill you!'"

Chief Wenniway stripped Henry to his shirt and locked him in an Indian lodge with 20 other prisoners – including Major Etherington and a Jewish trader, Ezekiel Solomon – each tied with a rope around his neck and fastened to a stake. While the Chippewa decided whether to behead them or hold them for ransom, they fed their starving captives a single loaf of bread, sliced with the bloody knives they had used in the massacre. "The blood, they moistened with spittle," Henry said, "and rubbing it on the bread, they offered this for food to their prisoners, telling us, 'Eat the blood of your countrymen.'"

While waiting for chance to determine his destiny, Henry was overjoyed to see his adopted Chippewa "blood brother," Wa-wa-tam, enter the lodge. In passing, Wa-wa-tam managed to whisper to him, "Take courage." At the tribal council that followed Wa-wa-tam and his wife laid many presents at the feet of the chiefs. After a smoking of pipes he addressed them earnestly. "Friends and relations," Wa-wa-tam began. He pointed to Henry. "See there my friend and brother among the slaves – himself a slave! You all well know I adopted him as my brother. And because I am your relation, he is therefore your relation, too. So how, being your relation, can he be your slave?"

Wa-wa-tam let that thought sink in. Then he continued: "On the day the war began, you were fearful lest, on his account, I should reveal your secret. You requested that I leave the fort and cross the lake. I did so. But now I bring these goods to buy off every claim any man among you may have on my brother." This appeal visibly touched them.

Chief Wenniway arose and replied, "My relation and brother. I am very glad for your friend, the Englishman. We accept your presents. And you may take him home with you."

Wa-wa-tam led Henry to his family tent, a few yards away from the lodge containing the English prisoners.

Wa-wa-tam's wife, three children and daughter-in-law greeted him with elation, and gave their paleface "relative" his first full meal in days. Henry's appetite flagged when Wa-wa-tam returned a little later with remnants from the tribal victory feast. In a wooden dish Wa-wa-tam was carrying what looked like a human hand. Nonchalantly he admitted that seven of the fattest English prisoners had been selected for the feast. Their heads had been severed and their sliced flesh boiled in tea kettles.

"I did not relish the repast," Wa-wa-tam explained. "But it has always been our custom, when overcoming our enemies, to make a war feast from among the slain. This inspires the warrior with courage in attack, and breeds him to meet death with fearlessness."

Henry learned he was not yet out of the soup himself. The Chippewa were debating whether Henry would inform the English about their massacre. Almost immediately a band who were fighting with Chief Pontiac in his uprising against nearby Fort Detroit came to Wa-wa-tam's tribe to muster recruits. When Wa-wa-tam would not help them, they proposed to kill Henry "in order to give their friends a mess of English broth, to raise their courage."

Wa-wa-tam hid Henry, then disguised him as an Indian. The family painted Henry's skin with stripes of red and black. They strung *wampum* beads around his neck, silver armbands around his wrists. They dressed him in a vermilion-greased buckskin shirt, red leggings, and scarlet coat, shaved him bald except for a scalp lock, and crowned him with feathers. "The ladies of the family appeared to think my person improved," Henry said. "They now condescend to call me handsome, even among Indians."

For the next nine months Henry trapped for beaver with his Indian family in the Great Lakes wilderness, becoming "as expert in the Indian pursuits as the Indians themselves." With a lancet he bled rheumatic Indians and won a reputation as a great medical "juggler."

"I sometimes bled a dozen women in the morning, as they sat in a row, along a fallen tree," Henry wrote. "In every Chippewa village, this service was required of me, and no persuasion of mine could ever induce a woman to dispense with it."

Eventually Henry was offered canoe passage to Sault Ste. Marie and he took emotional leave of his adoptive family. Wa-wa-tam embraced him and said: "My son, this may be the last time that ever you and I shall smoke out of the same pipe." When the canoe was pushed off, Wa-wa-tam began to pray, beseeching the *Kitche-Manitou* to take care of his brother till they should next meet. But Henry never saw Wa-wa-tam

again. His "blood brother" turned blind and died soon after.

Henry eventually joined the avenging forces of General John Bradstreet, who promised to recover Fort Michilimackinac for him. Ironically, the General put Henry in charge of his "Indian Battalion," 96 friendly Chippewa warriors. He was present when the siege of Fort Detroit was lifted and Chief Pontiac fled for his life. Henry was one of the victors who signed a peace treaty with the Chippewa chiefs of Fort Michilimackinac. And he survived, like Ezekiel Solomon, who was ransomed at Montreal, to launch the great trading war for the northwestern fur empire.

With Pontiac's conspiracy broken, British free-lance explorer-traders were able to plunge into the Indian country west of the Great Lakes. It was a rich territory, so far tapped only by the trickle of French-Canadian fur traders who had followed the 17th century trails of Pierre Esprit Radisson and his brother-in-law, Médart Chouart, Sieur des Groseilliers. "Mr. Radishes and Mr. Gooseberries," the English called them. But these were the founding fathers of the Hudson's Bay Company, swashbucklers who penetrated as far north as James Bay, and as far west as "the shore of that sweet sea," Lake Superior.

Radisson, the chronicler of their exploits, was a likeable vagabond with a knowledge of human frailties. When he first set out from Ville Marie de Montreal with his load of cheap trading trinkets, he knew he would have no trouble recruiting *coureurs-de-bois*. "For where there is lucre," he wrote, "there are people enough to be had."

Arriving among the "cruel barbars" of the West, he threw gunpowder into the fire to show what would happen if the redskins tried to molest him. "The wildman durst not speake," he said, "because we weare demi-gods."

When the Indians were reluctant to guide his party into enemy territory Radisson beat their strongest warrior with a beaver skin and taunted: "For my part, I will venture, choosing to die like a man than live like a beggar." The shamed tribesmen lifted the white man on their shoulders, "like a couple of cocks in a banquette," Radisson wrote. "We weare Cesars, being nobody to contradict us."

Radisson's story of the immense harvest of furs to be reaped in the New World induced King Charles II of England in 1670 to grant his cousin, Prince Rupert, a trading monopoly over one and a half million square miles drained by Hudson Bay. The royal charter gave Prince Rupert, and his Committee of 17 London merchants who invested in his mercantile enterprise, "sole

Trade and Commerce" rights — on condition that they undertook expeditions of discovery into "the north west part of America." With this agreement they were named "The Governor and Company of Adventurers of England trading into Hudson's Bay." Not a single partner in the original "Honourable Company" ever visited the shores of Hudson's Bay, and few of their humble servants shipped out from England were "Gentlemen Adventurers."

These early English Canadians considered the French traders out of Montreal to be "Slie, Subtle and artful to perfection." The dandies wore plumed hats and lace ruffles, swaggered when they carried their *fleur-de-lis* banners to Indian *tipis*, and were liberal in pouring French brandy. As long as the French did not trade near the English forts on Hudson Bay, the Honourable Company looked the other way. Consequently, the French Canadians, led by Pierre Gaultier de Varennes, Sieur de la Verendrye, had built a string of log forts in the southern Canadian West. Their trading route by canoe portage wound from Fort Michilimackinac, through the interlacing chain of lakes and rivers between Lake Superior and Lake Winnipeg, as far west as the forks of the Saskatchewan River.

The English traders had the luck to be on the right side when Wolfe defeated Montcalm in 1759, and the Peace of Paris ceded New France to the British in 1763. The French-Canadian forts west of the Great Lakes had crumbled from decay and the humble servants of the H.B.C. prepared to continue their lackadaisical trade around the rim of their private sea.

Suddenly, a renewed craze for beaver fur hats swept Europe and a group of opportunists formed the North West Fur Trading Company. The newcomers portaged west across the lakes and rivers, and adopting French-Canadian trading techniques, galvanized the lethargic H.B.C. servants in their stone forts. For the next 60 years the new company presented cut-throat competition. To the Honourable Company, the newcomers were the "Pedlars from Quebec." To free-lance Yankee traders, who admired their spunk and their style, they were "the lords of the lakes and the forests." The traders themselves preferred the name "Nor'westers."

Some of the "Pedlars" were French-Canadian *voyageurs*, at loose ends since Wolfe conquered Quebec. A few were Yankee frontiersmen, like the Jewish Ezekiel Solomon, thrown up in the freebooting ferment that produced John Jacob Astor's American Fur Company. Most were Scottish Highlanders, clans of McTavishes, McDonalds, McGillivrays and McKenzies. Several had migrated to New England, then pushed north to Canada as United Empire Loyalists in the wake of the American War of Independence in 1776. Most were daredevils, proud, ruthless, sometimes murderous, driven by private demons of restlessness and greed.

In their rivalry for beaver furs, both groups pampered and corrupted the Indians. Flintlock firearms, gunpowder and steel traps were handed out to the natives on "easy-credit terms." Some Indians were lured with tall stove-pipe hats once worn by Dickensian dandies, or by ruffled waistcoats, the former pride of a Restoration fop, or by ostrich plumes, that once drooped in halcyon glory over the bonnet of a London dowager. The traders robbed the Indians blind and the factors at the Hudson's Bay Company forts were particularly adept at short-changing them. The standards for measuring gunpowder, for example, were "improved" so that an Indian would sometimes get two ounces instead of a pound. One Indian complained to Governor James Isham of York Factory, "Tell your servants to fill the measure and not to put their fingers within the brim." Fourteen beaver skins were supposed to be worth one muzzle-loading musket, but it was claimed that Bay traders demanded a stack of beaver pelts to the height of the gun.

Firewater was the most potent medium of exchange. The Bay servants attempted to imitate the French with "English brandy," which was really raw gin tinctured with molasses: the Nor'westers preferred rum, which they called "licker." Both sides diluted their spirits heavily with water. One pint of *hootchenoo* (an Indian term soon shortened to "hootch") brought one fine dark beaver skin. It also produced some of the rowdiest "deboches" recorded on the plains. After pushing all his pelts through the barred wicket of a trading post, a rum-inflamed brave would trade his horse, his tents, even his wives and daughters, for an extra gulp of firewater. And if supplies ran out, a debauched Indian would shoot burning arrows over the stockade: for hell had no fury like that of a hungover Indian denied a hair of the dog that bit him.

In his journal, *Travel & Adventures in Canada and the Indian Territories*, Alexander Henry left an imperishable record of the Indians whose insatiable appetites the Nor'westers had to placate, of the rapids they had to run and the gumbo bogs they had to portage as their free-lance argosies invaded the unmapped country northwest of Superior. After eleven years in the fur trade around Sault Ste. Marie, Henry and his partner, Jean Baptiste Cadot, set out in June of 1775 on a voyage to the Saskatchewan River. With them was Matthew Cocking, a trader at the Bay's new Cumberland House on the Saskatchewan River. His first glimpse of Henry's French-Canadian *voyageurs* was disappointing. They were virtually dwarfs; few were more than five feet tall. But it was a revelation to see them portage through ankle-deep muck, each bare sweating back bent beneath two 90-pound packs, each pack supported by leather tumplines strapped around the forehead. "The Canadians," he wrote to his head office, "are chosen Men, inured to hardship & fatigue under which most of Your Present Servants would sink."

Alexander Henry appreciated the qualities of the *voyageurs*. He had hired fifty-two to man his "brigade" of 16 canoes, which were heaped to the gunwales with baubles and rum worth 3,000 pounds in Montreal. "The best men in the world," he described them. "They rarely murmur at their lot, and their obedience is yielded cheerfully." They had a proud tradition of their own, these *mangeurs du lard* with their scarlet bandanas wrapped around their head, and their bright sashes swinging at their waists. "Pork-eaters," they were called; they loved fat pork. They owned little more than their short clay pipes and their long green paddles but they could subsist on Indian corn and wild swamp rice, flailing the kernels into their moving canoe with their paddles. Their endurance was formidable. Two racing brigades were known to paddle for 40 hours without pausing, dipping their blades forty strokes to the minute, swaying in rhythm to endless choruses of the "Rolling Of My Ball":

> *En roulant ma boule roulant,*
> *En roulant ma boule . . .*

Usually, though, the steersman commanded his *voyageurs* to pause at well-defined points for a pipeful of twist tobacco. Each stopping point was measured as a "pipe." There were, besides, 90 portages, "carrying places," before their 500-pound-canoes, each with four tons of cargo, completed the route from Montreal up the Ottawa River to Lake Nipissing and across Georgian Bay to Grand Portage on the western shore of Lake Superior.

Grand Portage was the last outpost, the jumping-off point for the interior *pays d'en haut*. It was swarming with free-lance traders when Henry's brigade arrived on June 28. Here, Henry noted in his journal, "I found the traders in a state of extreme reciprocal hostility, each pursuing his interests in such a manner as might most injure his neighbour."

Henry and his partner, Cadot, quickly set their *voyageurs* at the task of crossing the "great carrying place." Nine miles separated Grand Portage from Pigeon River, a Rubicon of sheer cliff and tumbling waterfall. The canoemen – who received a Spanish dol-lar for each extra 90-pound pack carried – backpacked as much as 270 pounds each. It took "seven days of severe and dangerous exertion," Henry wrote. The French Canadians celebrated its end with a regale of rum. At the encampment called Height of Land, Henry had acquired smaller, 250-pound canoes and for $400 each, had hired a veteran headman and sternman to guide the expedition up Rainy Lake and Lake of the Woods. Now the oldest of these guides broke off a wet cedar bough. Solemnly commanding each *voyageur* to kneel, he initiated each as knight of the waterways, *un homme du nord*. And over a tot of rum each new North-man had to swear never to kiss the Indian girlfriend of a fellow canoeman without his permission.

This vow was challenged after the expedition had paddled the wildly foaming Winnipeg River (Cree for "muddy waters"). Four canoemen drowned in a gale, and the woman of a Cree stirred the other French Canadians with amour. "They omit nothing to make themselves lovely," Henry wrote of the Cree girls with their earrings, their tinkling brass bracelets, and their red cosmetics painted on their cheeks. "Not content with the power belonging to these attractions, the beauties condescend to beguile with gentle looks the hearts of passing strangers." Henry noted that the Cree husbands, often encumbered with three wives each, actually encouraged their women to have affairs with his *voyageurs*. "One of the chiefs assured me," he wrote, "that the children born by their women to Europeans were bolder warriors and better hunters than themselves. The Cree husbands make no difficulty in lending one of their wives and the women, so selected, consider themselves as honoured."

From "these amicable people" Henry acquired *pemmican* and rice giving in exchange rum and gun-powder. While the men grew tipsy their women soberly bartered. But by the time Henry left two days later they were all drunk, although, he was pleased to see, "very peaceably drunk."

It was a different story at a Cree village further north. On the beach of the Pasquia River they were met by Chief Chatique, "the Pelican," an Indian robber baron. He was a corpulent six-footer surrounded by 30 warriors bristling with bows and arrows and spears. Chatique invited the paleface traders into his tent to smoke a pipe, and then blandly demanded a river toll fee of guns, gunpowder and rum. The traders paid him off and hastily left.

It began to appear obvious that these free-lance traders needed to pool their forces in order to combat Indians bent on bargaining by force. An amalgamation, they thought, would also hamstring competition from the Hudson's Bay Company. Henry hatched this plan for an alliance when he met four Pedlars, whose brigades were paddling north on Lake Winnipeg toward the "Sascatchiwaine River" (Cree for "swift-flowing waters"). These four "wintering partners" – and their grubstake supply merchants back in Montreal – formed the nucleus of what was to become officially in 1779 – the North West Company.

Least-known of the four was Charles Paterson, a hard-bitten Scot fired with the "ancient North West spirit." He had no hesitation in bribing away the Bay's most skilful guide for 30 English pounds. Paterson helped build Fort des Prairies, just below the Grand Forks of the Saskatchewan River and, with the beaver he took there, his backer, James McGill, was able to found a university back in Montreal. Paterson made a dramatic exit by drowning in 1788. One stormy day he forced his *voyageurs* out on "water white as a sheet." His body was found next morning half-buried on the sandy shore of an island. He was clutching the hand of his Indian slave girl, whom he had tried to rescue from drowning. Even in death Paterson was guarded by his giant white dog, which had to be driven off with sticks.

Henry's other partners were Thomas and Joseph Frobisher, two muscular brothers from Yorkshire, traders of shrewd and ruthless acumen. They were equipped with goods by an older brother in Montreal, Benjamin Frobisher. Tom ultimately built a fort at Ile-à-la-Crosse Lake, on the Churchill River, about 190 miles northwest of the Bay's post of Cumberland House. Here he intercepted Indians en route to Cumberland and Fort Churchill. Joe Frobisher shoved northeast on the Churchill River to Frog Portage. He, too, waylaid Indians whose furs were committed to the H.B.C. with such success that Frog Portage was renamed "Portage du Traite."

As Joe Frobisher grew rich, he almost starved. In his first winter at Portage du Traite, a Bay man reported, "One or two of his men died for real want. One of them was shot by the Indians for eating human flesh – the corpse of one of their deceased friends. Mr. Frobisher himself was so distressed that he ate all the parchments and many of his furs. Even a few garden seeds, which he proposed to have sown the following Spring, he ate to satisfy his hunger."

Peter Pond, the fourth founder of the Nor'westers, was the most intriguing. "A trader of some celebrity in the North West," Henry wrote on first meeting this Connecticut Yankee on Lake Winnipeg. "Odd in his manners," another Pedlar described him. "He thought himself a philosopher." He was odd, indeed, this dreamy, violent and semi-illiterate son of of a shoe-

maker. A soldier-of-fortune with the British, at 16 Pond thought nothing of killing an Indian trader in a duel over a trifle. "We met the next morning eairely," Pond described one affair, "and discharged pistels in which the pore fellowe was unfortenat."

Yet Pond was an enterprising visionary, the first white man to cross the Methy Portage and discover the Athabasca River and Lake Athabasca. He built a cabin on the Athabasca River, 40 miles south of Lake Athabasca, where Chipewyan Indians brought thousands of the silkiest prime beaver, for which he traded the clothes off his back. It was Pond who opened what became the Nor'westers' richest territory. The Indians told him of a wonderful river that flowed out of Great Slave Lake to the Pacific Ocean. So Pond sat down at his homemade table, in weather so cold that his ink froze, and drew with his quill pens the first map of what is now Canada's Northwest Territory. He dreamed of presenting this masterpiece to the Empress of Russia. Eventually, he was forced to retire from the Nor'westers on a charge that he was implicated in the murder of two fur-trading rivals. Pond died back east in poverty, cursing his original grubstaker, the Montreal capitalist to whom he sold his share in the North West Company for a picayune 800 pounds.

This was Simon McTavish, merchant prince and backstage wire-puller. At 13 McTavish had emigrated from the Highlands, but he grew to be a handsome man-about-town in Montreal, loving "good wine, good oysters and pretty girls . . . always like a fish out of water when not in love." He was an organizer, and intriguer, and an autocrat. By elbowing his way to the top of the North West Company, he became the richest man in Montreal. His partners called him "The Marquis," "The Old Lion of Montreal" or "The Premier." He acquired an elegant seigniory in the Quebec countryside, with liveried servants and four-horse carriages, and at the foot of Mount Royal built Montreal's tallest sandstone mansion. He amassed it all in the fur wars without ever seeing the battlefield.

In the far-off Saskatchewan wilderness in the winter of 1775, Alexander Henry and his wintering partners were working hard. Henry himself had built a fort at Beaver Lake, and while on a 25-day snowshoe expedition in below-zero weather "to gratify my curiosity" about the foothills of the Rockies, had almost starved. Only a meeting with Indians en route to a Bay fort had saved him.

As he left for Montreal, his canoes piled high with furs, Henry dreamed of what the Chipewyan Indians had told him. Two rivers, they said, came out of Lake Athabasca; one at least flowed into the Northwest Passage, which wound over the "Shining Mountains" to the Pacific Ocean. Henry himself had caught glimpses of mountains northwest of the Saskatchewan River: "Masses of rock, large as houses, lay as if they had first been thrown into the air, then suffered to fall fractured into their present posture of chasms." And in Montreal, where he became one of the company's wealthiest supply merchants, he nursed his vision of the Nor'westers crossing the Rockies. He talked about it as he was presented to Queen Marie Antoinette at the court of France. He enlarged on it speaking in London to the president of England's Royal Society of scientists and explorers, Sir Joseph Banks.

Henry was still expounding his dream in 1785, when he founded Montreal's exclusive dining club of the fur barons. The Beaver Club at first limited its membership to 18 other Nor'westers who had spent at least one winter in the *pays d'en haut*. Each member was obliged to wear on a blue ribbon a brilliant gold medal bearing the inscription "Fortitude In Distress," and the date of the adventurer's first trip to Indian country. But then the rules were relaxed, and Henry, the Frobishers, Peter Pond and the other veteran front-liners allowed honourable membership to such *grands seigneurs* of the fur trade as Simon McTavish and James McGill.

The carousing of these "hyperborean Nabobs" was accompanied by a ritual as formalized as an Indian dance. A fine of six bottles of Madeira wine was imposed on the reveller who dared deviate from the order of the toast list. Glasses were smashed after each toast to "The Mother of all Saints," "The King," "The Fur Trade in all its Branches," "*Voyageurs*, Wives and Children," and "Absent Members." A calumet – the Indian peace pipe – was lit and passed from mouth to mouth with Indian whoops and Highland hoots. Amid mahogany, silverware and candleglow, the diners sat down to a banquet imported from the Saskatchewan. Nostalgically they stuffed themselves on *pemmican*, buffalo tongues, roasted beaver tails, and sturgeon with wild rice. They

drank until early morning, and then climaxed their festivities with an uproarious *Grand Voyage*. Members and gentlemen guests sat on the carpet in two swaying rows. Wielding fire tongs, canes and swords as paddles, they merrily dipped and pulled in a make-believe canoe to the rhythm of the *voyageurs'* "Rolling Of My Ball" chanson.

One of Henry's guests at the Beaver Club was John Jacob Astor. This German butcher's son had arrived in New York with a pack of seven cheap flutes which he peddled to the Indians. From this start he had risen to head the American Fur Company, and at this time was leasing a Montreal warehouse to store pelts bought for resale in New York. Henry fired Astor's imagination with his dream of a Northwest Passage, a Pacific outlet from which fur merchants could trade more directly with China, where Canton mandarins paid for furs with silk, tea and spices.

Indeed Henry poured out his dream to anyone who would listen. On March 5, 1786, he sat down in his big warehouse on St. Paul Street in Montreal to write to his fur-trading friend in New York, William Edgar. He was now the King's Auctioneer of Montreal, affluent and dignified. At 47 he was an old man by the standards of western explorers. Almost a quarter of a century had passed, he reflected, since he picked up his quill at Fort Michilimackinac to write the letter that saved him from Chief Pontiac's Indian massacre.

"Dear Edgar," Henry began. "I find you intend to become an adventurer in the China trade. A better scheme I am sure you could not undertake." And with all his old verve and vitality Henry wrote of his "favourite plan" that anticipated the exploration of the Fraser, Mackenzie and Thompson . . . "a river communication with those parts of the Northwest I was at, by which a road would be opened across the Continent. Were I without a family, I would set off immediately. For there is no one I could recommend so well as myself, nor no voyage could please me so well."

IV

Through Hell's Gate

SIMON FRASER was a prickly paradox. He was not unlike the great river that now bears his name: turbulent, yet magnificent in the arrogance of strength. Of all the Nor'wester explorers, he was the most unattractive but his feats and hairbreadth escapes were the most heroic. When he first crossed the "Shining Mountains" in 1805 he was only 29 but already a full Nor'wester Company partner. He was short-tempered, snub-nosed, turtle-mouthed, squat. His tousled sideburns stuck out. His icy blue eyes snapped from under a sloping forehead.

He had been born a farmboy in Bennington, Vermont, but his immigrant parents were Scottish through and through. His father had died in an American prison fighting against the Revolution. His mother, Isabella, of the Highland clan Daldregan, fled with her eight children to Canada. In Montreal, after only two years of schooling, 16-year-old Simon was articled as a Nor'wester clerk and rose fast. Bumptious, unpolished, but bull-headed in his tenacity, he was sent west. Here he was no less contrary.

Indians who cringed were held in contempt. "Damned blockhead!" was Fraser's epithet for his Indian guide, Ranchuse. Yet Ranchuse directed Fraser's birch-bark canoes across the mountains of British Columbia to the upper reaches of the Peace and Parsnip Rivers, enabling Fraser to hack from the bush the first four trading posts west of the Rockies.

These "wild and romantic" ramparts of northern British Columbia, draped with jade-green pine and fir and hemlock, at first struck an imaginative spark. The Cariboo country reminded him of his mother's tales of the Scottish Highlands and he christened the region New Caledonia. Yet he came to hate its loneliness; and the rain gusting down from the mountains made him ache with what he called "come-riddle come-raddle."

In 1806 Fraser and his young clerk, John Stuart, stepped from their birchbark canoes on the shore of a lake that Fraser named after Stuart. Carrier Indians gathered to gape at these palefaces from beyond the horizon. The white men discharged a musketry volley and the Indians fell to the ground in fear. The savages watched astonished as the palefaces put knobbed sticks in their mouths and puffed fire and smoke. "These magic sky people must come from the land of the ghosts," the Indians whispered, "for they are blowing spirits up in the air."

Fraser's notion of humour was to hand out cakes of soap to the squaws; thinking the gifts were chunks of bear fat, the Indian wives tried to eat them and to their feared dismay, began to foam and froth at the mouth.

Even stranger were the rites by which the palefaces celebrated the completion of Fort St. James, on Stuart Lake. A Carrier Indian named Staquisit never tired of telling the eerie tale around the campfire: "A white witch doctor picked up what appeared to be a crane. He put the bird's legs over his shoulder. Then he blew, and made his fingers dance on the bird's bill. And, lo, what spooky sounds were made – a noise like the demons of the *Mutche-Manitou*, that whistled all the way up the lake and whistled all the way back again." It must have sounded unearthly, indeed, the first time the wilds of British Columbia echoed with the dirge of a Scottish bagpiper. The parodoxical Fraser handed out rum for trade but meted out stern punishment, if the "lazy, thievish, roguish vagabonds" let their orgies affect their trapping.

"Of course," Fraser noted, "the Indians require to be kept at a proper distance." He did not, however, take his own advice and, apparently, he left behind a dark-skinned progeny at each of his four forts. "Yes, my friend, I have once more entered upon the matrimonial state," he wrote to a Montreal man in 1807. "P.S. Anything that the Children are in want of, and that can be had, please give it to them & Charge the same to my acct." Yet the glum Roman Catholic Scot forbade amours for his *voyageurs*. One of his canoemen, La Malice, had bought an Indian girl for 300 pieces of silver and wanted to bring her on one of Fraser's expeditions to keep himself warm, he said, during the cold nights in the mountains.

"Take your choice," Fraser declared peremptorily.

*The indomitable Simon Fraser:
his perilous journey down an unnamed river to the
Pacific Coast staked the Nor'westers' claim
to the furs west of the mountains.*

"Accompany me without her. Or go back alone to Montreal." However, he relented and allowed him to take his girlfriend but then, typically, Fraser carped at the number of *pemmican* berry cakes that La Malice consumed after a liaison with his girl.

Fraser was obsessively jealous of Alexander Mackenzie, first to find the Northwest Passage envisioned by Alexander Henry the Elder. With nine men and a dog, Mackenzie had pushed up the Peace and Parsnip Rivers, around the Fraser's headwaters, down the Bella Coola River to the Pacific. He was now Sir Alexander Mackenzie, a dominant partner in Simon Fraser's own fur-trading company. Fraser peppered his diary with slurs of "The Knight" for not noticing certain land-

marks. He criticized his omission of the Fraser River's northerly tributary, the Nechako, at whose mouth Fraser erected Fort George. He accused "Sir A.M.K." of "indulging himself in sleep" at the helm of his canoe; of being "very inaccurate with a compass." And then recalling his Christian precepts, he writes in May, 1806: "But then, he was the first that passed, and it was pardonable for him, and I have not the least desire to detract from his merits. His perseverance was commendable, and he succeeded where, perhaps, many others would have failed."

Fraser was sure that *he* would never have failed. All one needed to achieve posterity was a gifted ghostwriter to give literary grace to one's diary. Indeed, in 1807 Fraser tried to persuade his clerk, John Stuart, to edit his journal, which he admitted was "exceeding ill wrote, worse worded and not well spelt." Though Fraser did not know it, Sir Alexander Mackenzie's published journal had already touched off a transcontinental race to the Pacific Ocean. Thomas Jefferson, President of the United States, had sent a secret message to Congress, asking $2,500 for an expedition to be sent to the mouth of the Columbia River. The project was labeled as "literary," meaning scientific; but that was a smokescreen. Its real object was to take possession of the fur trade in the Far West for the fledgling American Republic before Canadians moved into that rich coastal territory. Even as Fraser had crossed the Rockies in 1805, United States pirogues and a keelboat had advanced to the headwaters of the Missouri. Now the packhorses of the Yankees were approaching the gateway of the Rockies to the south.

The American expedition – 45 men and a shaggy Newfoundland dog – was far better equipped than Fraser's. In charge was Jefferson's private secretary, Captain Meriwether Lewis, a moody, 29-year-old scholar who later committed suicide. His lieutenant was William Clark, a gregarious frontiersman of 33, known to the Indians as "Redheaded Chief." On November 7, 1805, Clark drank from the "handsome, bold-running, cold, clear water of the great Columbia River" and exclaimed in his diary: "Ocian in view! O! the joy!"

His enthusiasm was dampened by a miserably rainy winter in log shacks, dubbed Fort Clatsop, on the south bank of the Columbia, where that green brawling river spills from the present states of Oregon and Washington into the sea. Chinook Indians revealed that ocean pedlars had already been there and taught them such British and Yankee phrases as "damned rascal," "heave the lead," and "sun of a pitch." The Yankee newcomers hung Jefferson medals around the neck of one-eyed Chief Comcomly and told the Indians they were now subjects of the great American "White father." Under no circumstances were they to recognize any British Nor'wester traders.

As his expedition started homeward the following March, Lewis had prophetic qualms. This lower loop of the Columbia River, he predicted, was destined to be a scene of strife as the boundary line between the United States and British Canada.

He was right. In Montreal the gentlemen partners of the North West Fur Company were stunned to hear that the Americans were claiming the mouth of the Columbia. In a panic they pressed Fraser to move faster.

They were making an understandable blunder in geography. They thought that Fraser, who was in reality in northern British Columbia, was camped on the upper reaches of the Columbia. The partners ordered him to explore his uncharted river down to its mouth immediately. If he was successful, the stakes were large: Canadian ownership of a fur kingdom stretching from Fort George in B.C.'s interior to the Yankees' Fort Clatsop on the Pacific.

Fraser was chafing to start but he had no supplies. In December of 1806, he informed his Montreal partners that "it would be a little short of madness to attempt going down the Columbia in a starving state without an ounce of provisions." The supplies did not reach him until the autumn of 1807. It was now too late in the season to run the Fraser. It was not until May 28 of 1808 that Fraser left Fort George on his great adventure.

It was characteristic of him that he gave his four fragile canoes such imposing titles as *Perseverance* and *Determination*, as though to steel his own resolve. The birchbark boats, loaded with trading trinkets, were paddled by 19 French-Canadian *voyageurs*, gaudy in scarlet leggings, purple capots and sashes, with yellow or pink feathers tucked in their red wool caps. As interpreters Fraser picked two Carrier Indians, giving them each "a blanket and breeches – that they may appear decent and Englishfied amongst the strangers." As lieutenants he took the literary Scot, John Stuart, and Jules Maurice Quesnel, the 22-year-old son of a Montreal poet and musician, after whom Fraser named the first big tributary stream they passed.

As they paddled between the steep riverbanks, green with juniper and sky-blue with lupins, the faces of Indian spies appeared for "a peep at us *en passant*." Then the scouts, via moccasin telegraph, flashed ahead the news of palefaces approaching the villages in godlike habiliments. At every village stopover Fraser shrewdly put on a good show. Freshly shaven and wearing his beaver-trimmed silk topper, he would have himself carried regally from his canoe on his *voyageurs*' shoulders. He would then startle the natives with a volley on his "thunderstick." Then he shook hands with as many as 1,200 villagers who would crowd around to stare. If children were sick, Fraser would solemnly dip his finger into a vial of opium tincture and with his magical finger touch their foreheads.

After three hours of oratory from the tribal council, Fraser would pin a shiny brooch on the head of the highest chieftain. In gratitude, the chief would agree to send porters and guides with the expedition to the next village. In exchange for a couple of calico nightgowns and a tea kettle, Fraser's *voyageurs* were entertained with all-night dances, girls, and feasts of strawberries, oysters, baked salmon, and roast dog with wild onion sauce. Fraser remained obdurately condescending. To him the songs the Indians composed and crooned in his honour made "a terrible racket." The women's hair, pomaded festively with fish oil, made them "dirty and smelly." And their gifts of striped red-and-blue rugs, woven from dog's hair, were attractive only in that "they resemble, at a distance, Highland plaid." After one Lillooet Indian village danced and serenaded him all night, he expressed his view in his diary: "However kind savages may appear, I know it is not in their nature to be sincere in their professions to strangers. The respect and attention, which we generally experience, proceed, perhaps, from an idea that we are superior human beings . . . At any rate, it is certain the less familiar we are with one another, the better for us."

At a village of Atnah Indians, their handsome and friendly "Great Chief" tried to dissuade Fraser from continuing. "The river below, he warned, was a succession of falls and cascades . . . impossible to pass. Whirlpools will swallow up your canoes." And the entrance to the sea was guarded by fierce Cowichan Indians, "bad men who go about in the dark." Fraser's expedition, he said, should go overland by packhorse. "But going to the sea by an indirect way was not the object of this undertaking," Fraser answered in his diary. "I, therefore, would not deviate."

Soon Fraser was admitting that this challenge to the river's 500 miles of whirlpools, rocks and rapids was "a desperate undertaking!" He had reached that part where the river rages between narrowing canyon walls. His expedition was caught in a life-and-death struggle with a chain of foaming cataracts so powerful that salmon were thrown from the water against the cliffs. At the Iron Rapids, Fraser felt dizzy at the sight of the river "which does not exceed 30 yards in breadth, passes between two precipices, and is turbulent, noisy, and awful to behold! . . . Our canoes are within an ace of being dashed to pieces against the rocks . . . One of the canoes was sucked into a whirlpool, whose force twisted off the stern. But this happening near the bank and the end of the rapid, the men were saved." On another day a *voyageur* named D'Alaire was left sitting with feet astride half a canoe as he rode three nightmarish miles down the boiling maelstrom.

At the Couvert Rapids, near Deadman's Creek, "the great difficulty," Fraser wrote, "consisted in keeping the canoes clear of the precipice on one side, and of the gulfs formed by the tumultuous waves on the other. Thus, skimming along like lightning, the crews cool and determined, followed each other in awful silence. And when we arrived at the end, we stood gazing on our narrow escape from perdition."

Near Jackass Mountain, the expedition was forced to climb cliff banks slippery with slime. "We had to plunge our daggers into the high and steep bank," Fraser said. "We cut steps, then fastened a line to the front of the canoe. Some of the men ascended in order to haul it up; while the others supported the canoe upon their arms . . . Our lives hung, as it were, upon a thread. For failure of the line, or a false step of the men, might have hurled the whole of us into eternity."

As the gorge's walls grew higher and closer together they had to cache their canoes. Lugging 90-pound packs on their backs, they inched along cliff ledges so narrow that it was "difficult even for one person sideways." Thorns tore and blistered their feet. Rocks gave way beneath them. "From this cause," Fraser wrote, "one of our men was much hurt . . . With a large pack on his back, he got so engaged among the rocks, that he could neither move forward nor backward; nor yet unload himself without imminent danger. Seeing the poor fellow in this predicament, I crawled to his assistance. Not without great risk, I saved him. His load, however, dropped off his back, and tumbled over the precipice into the river."

At Black Canyon, Fraser finally acknowledged the valour of the Indians. "Nimble as goats, they leaped from rock to rock to the summit and pulled up the palefaces with a long pole. In places where we were obliged to hand our guns from one to another, and where the greatest precaution was required to pass even singly, the Indians went through boldly with loads."

Their courage was badly needed at Hell's Gate Canyon where the frothing river thunders far below dark overhanging cliffs. "I cannot find words to describe our situation," Fraser wrote. "We had to pass where no human being should venture. Yet in these places there is a regular footpath impressed, or rather indented, by frequent travelling upon the very rocks. And besides this, steps are formed like a ladder, or the shrouds of a ship, by poles hanging to one another, and crossed at certain distances with twigs and tree boughs . . . Add to this that the ladders were often so slack, that the smallest breeze put them in motion — swinging them against the rocks." The Indians crawled up this web like spiders, and helped the white men, too. At the end of the canyon, Fraser sat down to rest his nerves and record that "the Indians deserve our thanks . . . they went up and down these wild places with the same agility as sailors on board a ship."

Ragged, the soles of their feet bleeding, Fraser's men rested at Yale, where the Shuswap Indians received them like "lost relations," and swapped them two dugout boats for two calico nightgowns.

They were also relieved to see the river turn peaceful with a wide brown delta of silt oozing seaward. But, as they paddled near where the future city of New Westminster was to grow, they encountered the Cowichans of whom the Atnah had warned, canoeloads of channel pirates with ferocious Fu Manchu moustaches, cedarwood coats of mail, and arrowheads dipped in rattlesnake poison.

"Howling like so many wolves, and brandishing their war clubs, they appeared mad as furies," Fraser wrote. "Singing a war song, and beating time with their paddles upon the sides of the canoes, they made signs and gestures highly inimicable." With the Indians in pursuit, Fraser and his men paddled up the Strait of Georgia to Musqueam Island. Beaching behind them, the pirates pillaged their dug-outs, snatched a dagger out from Quesnel's scabbard, and tied the hands and feet of one of the guides. Then, wielding moose-horn clubs, with spears and arrows poised, they began a frenzied circling of the palefaces.

Their chief, Blondin, was particularly insolent. Fraser tried not to notice his large belt, garnished with scalps of human hair. "He asked for our daggers, for our clothes, and in fine for everything we had," Fraser reported. "He became very unruly in his impertinence, kicking up the dust." But the Scot outbluffed him. "I pretended to be in a violent passion. I spoke loud my threats, with vehement gestures and signs exactly in their own way. I made him and the others who were closing in upon us understand that if they did not keep their distance, we would fire upon them." They approached so close that the party had to push them away with their gun muzzles. "Perceiving our determination, their courage failed," Fraser wrote. "The Chief spoke to his party, and they all dropped behind, but they still followed and kept us in view."

While his bone-weary men camped and slept, Fraser and Stuart kept guard. A suspicion had begun to gnaw at Fraser. Couldn't Stuart see the seagulls wheeling overhead and smell the salt tang of the air? It was the ocean all right, but how could it be the mouth of the Columbia? Surely the Columbia must meet the Pacific at least three degrees of latitude further south? Had they come, then, on a wildgoose chase down some totally unknown river? Stuart unpacked his sextant to establish their location: 49 degrees; the Columbia was at 46 degrees. "This River, therefore, is not the Columbia," wrote Fraser, his dream of glory gone. It was all the more bitter, because he could not gaze upon the main body of the Pacific Ocean. It was hidden by Vancouver Island looming out of the Strait of Georgia, and Fraser had now no canoes in which to cross.

"I must again acknowledge my great disappointment in not seeing the *main* Ocean," Fraser wrote, "having gone so near it as to be almost within view." He thought of his tired, wet, hungry men, ringed by murderous pirates, and at last a trace of self-pity crept into his diary. "Placed upon a small sandy Island, few in number, without canoes, without provisions, and surrounded by upwards of 700 barbarians, our situation might really be considered as critical. However," he added, in one of his characteristic changes of view, "our resolution did not forsake us." Fraser's only recourse was to try to buy a canoe from the Cowichan chief. "He asked his price — I consented — He augmented his demand — I again yielded — He still continued to increase his imposition. Feeling highly provoked at the impertinence of his conduct, I exclaimed violently — He then ordered the canoe to be brought."

Reluctantly, Fraser turned his expedition homeward, paddling a single leaky canoe, the Cowichans trailing behind like river jackals. On July 6, the pirates, chanting a war song, attacked. "Some were in canoes," Fraser wrote. "Others lined the shore. And all were advancing upon us. At last, it was with difficulty we could prevent them, with the muzzles of our guns, from seizing upon the canoe. They contrived to give us a push with the intention of upsetting us. Our canoe became engaged in the strong current, and in spite of all our efforts, carried us down the rapids. However, we gained the shore at the foot of a high hill. We tied the canoe to a tree with a line. Here I ordered Mr. Stuart, with some of his men, to debark in order to keep the Indians in awe . . . and make them understand that, if the Chief should pursue us any farther, he should suffer severely for his presumption."

To Fraser's horror, his *voyageurs* refused to obey. The Cowichans had frayed their nerves to the point of mutiny. It was too much to face again those dark canyons on the Fraser — "defiles in which a few men might easily annoy an army with stones." All except Stuart and Quesnel wanted to leave the river and cut across the mountains to Fort George. Fraser remonstrated and threatened by turns. "The other gentlemen joined my endeavours. We spoke of the advantages that would accrue to us all, by remaining in perfect union, for our common welfare. After much debate on both sides, our delinquents yielded. And we all shook hands, resolving never to separate during the voyage." Two dozen men, who had altered the shape of a nation, now stood on a rock, raised their hands, and above the river's roar, shouted an oath of defiance that Fraser had just devised: "I solemnly swear before Almighty God that I shall sooner perish than forsake in distress any of our crew during the present voyage."

The circling Cowichans were baffled by this weird paleface rite, by the way they shaved and changed into their best apparel. Then, picking up their paddles, looking neither to right nor left, the mad white men paddled straight ahead, singing their *voyageurs'* ballad:

Behind our house we have a pond,
En roulant ma boule!
Where three fine ducks swim round and round,
Roulez, roulant, ma boule roulant . . .

"The Indians, observing us so cheerful and full of spirits, felt disheartened, and kept their distance," Fraser commented. "Some of them thought proper to paddle downstream and the others desired us to proceed in peace, and they said that no one would disturb us."

Fraser's men paddled upstream, through the canyons, climbed the spiderweb ladders, and without mishap, reclaimed their cached canoes at the Atnah village.

"The Atnah Chiefs were both so overjoyed to see us," Fraser wrote, "that they annoyed us with caresses. They assured us they felt extremely anxious for our safety during our absence. And they had determined that, if the Indians of the sea destroyed us, they would collect their friends and go to revenge us."

Fraser thanked the chief for his friendship and good intention and recorded that "they expressed regret at our departure, and begged that we should return among them as traders. This I in a manner promised." But he could not let it go at that. It was not in the curious nature of Simon Fraser, so uneasy in the show of love, so demanding of fear and respect. "At the same time," he wrote, "I wished to make him and his friends understand that we were not to be easily destroyed. For our nature and our arms were superior to anything we could meet among the Indians."

How the Cities Began

The Hudson's Bay Company post of Fort Garry, at the junction of the Red and Assiniboine Rivers, in the heart of what is now Winnipeg. This is how it looked in 1857, but by 1897 the walls had tumbled, and only the original gateway remained.

This was Winnipeg, thirteen years later, in 1870 . . . not yet a city, but showing signs of becoming the boom town of the West.

The first settlements sprang up around
the early trading posts and
North West Mounted Police barracks.

Present-day Calgary began as the Mountie post of Fort Calgary, built in 1875 and named by Col. James Farquharson Macleod.

Fort Edmonton: trading centre of the North Saskatchewan.

Fort Macleod: the Mounties gave southern Alberta its first town.

The Roman Catholics built this church, Holy Cross, at Fort Macleod. The great Chief Crowfoot often visited the settlement.

Gateway to the Prairie

As a city, Winnipeg is the oldtimer of the plains,
for its history dates back to the 1811 Selkirk Settlement,
first colony in the old Northwest.

On the way west, many settlers paused at Winnipeg to buy their tools, their wagons and livestock. The city boomed as a distributing centre and the coming of the Canadian Pacific Railway in 1881 brought even greater prosperity: in the golden era of grain, the city became the financial capital of the Canadian West. This photograph shows Winnipeg's Main Street, 1880.

At the 'Murky Water'

The Cree called it Win-nipiy, this spot where
the Assiniboine met the Red River, churning up a silt of
reddish-brown. The name meant "murky water."

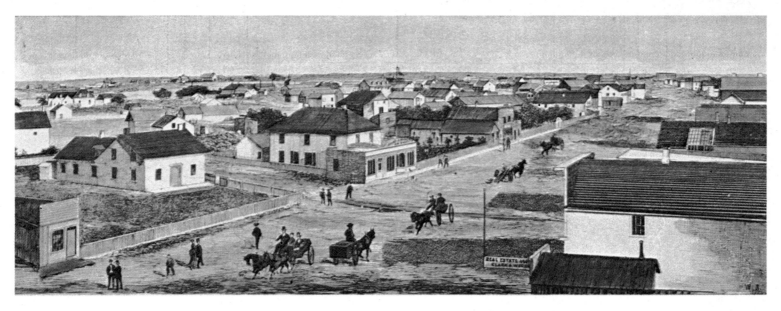

*Three views of early Winnipeg: from across the Red River
(upper left); from the Assiniboine, showing the arrival of
the first group of Mennonites (upper right); and looking
down Main Street (bottom). Across the Red River was St.
Boniface, and to the right was old Fort Garry. The Red
River flows north from Minnesota, through some of the finest
farmlands in the world, and empties into Lake Winnipeg.*

Old Fort Edmonton

The first Fort Edmonton, or Edmonton House, was built by William Tomison of the Hudson's Bay Company, to compete against a nearby North West Company trading post. So fiercely did the two companies vie for trade that several times they depleted the furs of the area, and chased each other up and down the North Saskatchewan River, relocating their forts, until in 1821 the companies united. This shows how the old Fort Edmonton looked in 1873.

Fort Yale, originally a Hudson's Bay Company post built in 1848, sat in the shadows of the tall mountains of British Columbia, at a bend on the west side of the Fraser River. Thousands of miners passed or camped here in the 1860s, on their way to the Cariboo gold-fields. This scene shows Yale in 1880.

New Westminster, seen from across the river, was chosen capital of the new mainland colony of British Columbia, 1859. The town, then called Queensborough, was Governor James Douglas's second choice. He wanted Fort Langley as his capital.

Gastown, 1884: "Gassy Jack" Deighton, a hotel proprietor, gave the name to this lumber town, soon to become Vancouver.

GRANVILLE, 1882. 1. Deighton Hotel. 2. Prov.Gov't building and jail. 3. Telegraph office. 4. Mannion's Granville Hotel. 5. Sullivan's grocery store and hall. (invisible) (invisible) Louis Gold's store. 6. Robertson's saloon. 7. Ben Wilson's store 8. Trail to landing and "Spratt's Ark" (floating cannery)

Officially, Gastown was called Granville. It was incorporated as the city of Vancouver, 1886 — just before it burned down.

This is how Victoria, now capital of British Columbia, appeared in 1860, from a painting of that time by Herman Otto Tiedeman. New Westminster took over as capital when the island and mainland were united in 1866, but only for two years.

*Once a remote H.B.C. fur-trading post, Victoria boomed as a provisioning
base when gold was discovered. This was Yates Street, in 1862.*

*It was from this Victoria harbour in 1858 that the Hudson's Bay Company
shipped 800 ounces of gold, destined for San Francisco.
These nuggets sparked the gold rush that changed the destiny of British Columbia.*

V

The Gentle
Map-Maker

SIMON FRASER, disappointed in the river he had discovered (it was too full of fury to make a supply highway for the fur trade) did not bother to give it a name. It was left to his friend, David Thompson, to name it in Fraser's honour. Fraser, ironically, did christen the biggest eastern tributary "Thomson's River," mistakenly thinking that his friend, whose name he misspelled, was exploring its headwaters. So Thompson was immortalized by a river he never saw. And, doubly ironical, he had charted just about every other major river in the Canadian West *except* the Thompson.

Thompson was the greatest map-maker Canada ever had. He was the first to explore the full 1,200 serpentine miles of the Columbia River. He walked, paddled and rode more than 50,000 miles for the pure delight of surveying the unknown half of a continent, and he left behind a superlative monument: a topographical map that has been the basis for every map of the Canadian West up till the present.

Thompson's friendship with Fraser was odd, for no two men were more unlike. Fraser was fractious and arrogant; Thompson was gentle and tolerant. Fraser was semi-illiterate; Thompson kept 39 voluminous journals that are rich with a sense of poetry and vivid imagery. And no detail escaped the sharpness of his dark binocular eyes. Even when he was resigned to death by starvation – eating the carrion of eagles and slaughtered horses – he still managed to scribble his diary on birch rind with charcoal. His fingers, stiffened by sub-zero cold, recorded his impressions: "I find the meat of the tame horse better than that of the wild horse; the fat was not so oily . . ."

Unlike Fraser, Thompson had a lyric sense of poetry. His Welsh voice was a melodious instrument for story-telling, and he had a flair for painting vivid images. To him, the Piegan Indians in battle with the Kootenays were "harder to hit than a goose on the wing." After travelling across the plains to catch his first glimpse of the Great Continental Divide, he marvelled, "At last

the Rocky Mountains came in sight, like shining white clouds in the horizon." His yarn-spinning gift was described by his American friend, Dr. J. J. Bigsby, who later helped Thompson map out the international boundary line. Thompson, he said, "could create a wilderness and people it with warring savages. Or he could climb the Rocky Mountains with you in a snowstorm so clearly and palpably, that you could shut your eyes and hear the crack of a rifle, or feel snowflakes melt on your face as he talks."

He was a first-class amateur navigator and astronomer, a naturalist who took pains to taste every species of moss, to gauge the speed of an antelope, and to take the temperature of a reindeer's blood. "For the age of guessing is passed away," Thompson said, "and the traveller is expected to give his reasons for what he asserts."

His yearning and his questioning found fulfilment in the precision of his instruments – his ten-inch sextant, his compass, his thermometers and his telescopes – and the birds and creatures of the unmarred wilderness.

"No dove is more meek than the white prairie grouse, with its pleasing cheerful call of *Kabow-kabow-kow-a-e*," he noted in his journal. "I have often taken these birds, with their deep chocolate feathers against a background of beautiful white brilliance, from under the nest. I provoked them all I could without injuring them. But all was submissive meekness. Rough humans as we were, sometimes of an evening we could not help enquiring, 'Why should such an angelic bird be doomed to be the prey of carnivorous animals and birds?' But the ways of Providence are unknown to us."

He noted how the pain of snow blindness differed with the colour of the eyes. "The blue eye suffers first and most, the grey eye next, and the black eye the least; but none are exempt. I have seen hardy men crying like children, after a hard march of four months in winter. Three men and myself had made for a trading post in the latter part of March. They all became snow blind, and for the last four days I had to lead them with a string tied to my belt, and they were so completely blind that when they wished to drink of the little pools of melted snow, I had to put their hands in the water."

Like every great man, David Thompson had his frailties. When another Hudson's Bay Company surveyor, Peter Fidler, was promoted over his head he refused to talk to Fidler when they met deep in the wilderness. When Peter Pond made a rival map of the Athabasca country, Thompson called him "an unprincipled man of violent character."

But where Fraser patronized the Indians, Thompson loved them. He was the only Nor'wester trader who refused to debauch them with rum. He extended them credit and was amused when "several old Indians made a bargain with me. If they should die in winter, I should not demand the debt due to me in the other world – namely, heaven. To which I always agreed."

He respected their individuality. "Writers on the Indians always compare them with themselves, who are all white men of education. This is not fair. Their noted stoic apathy is more assumed than real. In public, the Indian wishes it to appear that nothing affects him. But in private, he feels and expresses himself sensitive to everything that happens to him or his family. On becoming acquainted with the Indians I found almost every character in civilized society can be traced among them – from the gravity of a judge to a merry jester, from open-hearted generosity to the avaricious miser."

He admired the Indian's woodcraft, his ability to navigate through the forest, "his keen, constant attention on everything: the removal of the smallest stone; the bent or broken twig; a slight mark on the ground – all spoke plain language to him. I was anxious to acquire this knowledge, and I paid attention to what they pointed out to me, and became almost equal to some of them." He acknowledged the superiority of their "erect, graceful walk. The Indian, with his arms folded in his bison robe, seems to glide over the ground, light and easy. But the white people walk seldom in an erect posture, their bodies swaying from right to left, and sawing the air with their arms. I have often been vexed at the comparison."

Though they thought it the wizardry of a fortune-teller, the Indians respected Thompson's desire for scientific knowledge. They watched him gaze through his telescope for hours at the sapphire shine of the Pleiades, and they nicknamed him *Koo-Koo-Sint* – "Man Who Looks At Stars." But he could never communicate their meaning. "Once, after a weary day's march," he wrote, "we sat by a log fire. The bright moon, with thousands of sparkling stars, passed before us. The Indians could not help enquiring who lived in those bright mansions and, as one of them said, he thought he could almost touch them with his hand. I explained to them the nature of these brilliant planets. But I am afraid it was to no purpose. The Indians concluded, 'The stars are the abodes of the spirits – of those who have led a good life.' "

With his cherry-red cheeks, his snub nose, his short compact body, and his long black hair in square-cut bangs on his forehead, Thompson looked very like John Bunyan, author of *The Pilgrim's Progress*. Indeed he modelled himself on Bunyan, refused to drink liquor, smoke, swear or gamble. He would seat his *voyageurs* on a riverbank and, in primer French, read to them aloud, with explanations, from his Old Testament.

His simple canoemen, he found, were more concerned with the ways of the flesh. "Each man requires eight pounds of meat per day or more. Upon my reproaching some of them for their gluttony, the reply I got was, 'What pleasure have we in life but eating?' A French Canadian, if left to himself, and living on what he has, will rise very early, make a hearty meal, smoke his pipe, and then lie down to sleep again for the rest of the day. But Jean Baptiste will not think; he is not paid for it."

Thompson acquired his blend of religion and science in a charity home. His Welsh father had been buried in a pauper's grave and the three-year-old boy was brought up in London's Grey Coat School, designed to educate poor children in "piety and virtue." He displayed a precocious mastery of mathematics and navigation. He borrowed books and pored over *Tales of the Arabian Nights, Robinson Crusoe* and *Gulliver's Travels*. His holidays were spent in "venerable Westminster Abbey and its cloisters," reading the monumental inscriptions.

In 1784, when Thompson was 14, the school paid the Hudson's Bay Company five pounds to take him as a fur trader apprentice. The boy arrived at the Bay with a Hadley's quadrant and Robertson's two-volume *Elements of Navigation* "to learn what?", he later asked bitterly. "For all I had seen in their service, neither writing nor reading was required. And my only business was to amuse myself, in winter growling at the cold and in the open season, shooting Gulls, Ducks, Plover and Curlews, and quarrelling with Musketoes and Sand Flies."

At the age of 28 – assured of a plentiful supply of map paper and a new set of drawing instruments – Thompson joined the Nor'westers. They needed a surveyor to tell them whether their posts were in Canada or the United States. The Treaty of Paris of 1783 that formally ended the American Revolution had set out the boundary lines. Thompson was commissioned to mark the line, to explore the Missouri River and, if possible, find the headwaters of the Mississippi.

Taking time every day to pray and write his journals, Thompson carried out all three assignments as though they were ordained destiny. In April, 1797, he discovered the source of the Mississippi, bubbling out of Turtle Lake. It was a "noble River," and he predicted that some day its Anglo-Saxon population would "far exceed the Egyptians in all the arts of civilized life," the Nile being cluttered with "pompous, useless Pyramids." But it was an Indian spearing for fish that most intrigued him. "A low fog hides the Canoe," he wrote, "and only the Indian Man, with his poised spear ready to strike is seen, like a ghost gliding slowly over the water."

His commission ended, he set out to find a pass through the Rocky Mountains. His headquarters was Rocky Mountain House, a cluster of log cabins on the North Saskatchewan River near the mouth of Clearwater River, in the foothills of Alberta. Here he kept his wife, Charlotte Small, the half-breed daughter of an Indian princess and an Irish trader. When she was 14 he had married her *au façon du nord*, and she was to bear him 16 children. Here, too, he vainly tried to dissuade his two Nor'wester partners from peddling firewater to the Indians. One partner, who had married Thompson's wife's sister, was John McDonald of Garth, Scotland, called *Le Bras Croche* because of his withered arm. This handicap did not prevent him from challenging a Hudson's Bay rival to a duel over possession of a well. The other was Finan McDonald, a red-whiskered, violent six-foot-four giant, who once shot 14 Piegans in a raid.

Thompson tried to smoke the pipe of peace with the Piegans, the warriors of the Blackfoot tribe who kept vigilant guard over the passes leading across the "Shining Mountains." They did not want the palefaces to introduce firearms to their foes, the Kootenay Indians, who lived by their bows and arrows on the western side of the Rockies. Thompson sought out their Piegan war chief, Kootenae Appe. Surrounded by his five wives, his 26 children, and his 200 warriors, Kootenae Appe was an imposing figure. "His stature was six feet six inches, tall and erect, of bone and sinew with no more flesh than absolutely required," Thompson described him. "His countenance was manly, but not stern: his features prominent, nose acquiline; his word sacred, both loved and respected."

Kootenae Appe put out his left hand for Thompson to shake. "I gave him my right hand," Thompson wrote, "upon which, he looked at me and smiled, as much as to say a contest would not be equal."

Later, Thompson learned that "the right hand is no mark of friendship. This hand wields the spear, draws the bow, and the trigger of the gun. It is the hand of death. The left hand is next to the heart, and speaks truth and friendship. It holds the shield of protection, and is the hand of life." Despite his initial error, Thompson and Kootenae Appe talked often. Once a band of hungry Piegans was at Rocky Mountain House, praying to the Great Spirit to stop the three-week rains that had swollen the streams and had prevented the tribe from hunting. "At length, the rain stopped," Thompson wrote. "And I was standing at the door, watching the breaking up of clouds, when of a sudden the Indians gave a loud shout. 'Oh, there is the mark of life!' they called out. 'We shall yet live!' On looking to the eastward, I saw there one of the widest and most splendid rainbows I ever beheld, and joy was now on every face."

Thompson had never before heard the Indians call a rainbow the "mark of life," and he asked the chief, "Why did you keep this name secret from me?"

"You white men treat with contempt what we have learned from our fathers," Kootenae Appe said. "Why should we expose ourselves to your laughter?"

"I have never laughed at you," Thompson replied. "Our books also call a rainbow 'mark of life.' What the white man sometimes despises you for is this: One day, you make prayers to the Good Spirit for all you want. And another day, you make offerings to the Evil Spirit. You fear the devil because he is wicked. But the more you worship him, the more power he will have over you. Worship the Good Spirit only, and the Bad Spirit will have no power over you."

"Ah," said the chief. "But the Evil Spirit is strongest."

"If you worship the Evil Spirits," warned Thompson, "you will suffer eternal hell fire."

"You white people, you look like wise men, you talk like fools," said the chief. "How is it possible that anything can resist the continued action of fire?"

Caught between his scientific and his theological principles, Thompson could only shake his head and confide to his diary, "Christianity alone will eradicate these superstitions." He saw a glimmer of hope for them when he learned the *Romeo and Juliet* story of "The Stag and the Beautiful Maiden." Chief Kootenae Appe's son, named *Poonokow*, was called "The Stag." He had been engaged to a beautiful Blackfoot girl. While he was away on a long war expedition, the Snake Indian father of an eligible male had bought the beauty for his son.

The Stag rode to the Snake camp. He passed along a message to the aunt of his beauty, "I am determined to have the bride, though I have to kill the man who now has her." The girl was smuggled out of the camp to join

The source of the Columbia River, painted by Henry J. Warre. David Thompson charted the river from here to its mouth.

him, and she and The Stag set off for Kootenae Appe's home village. But at a trading post on the Saskatchewan River, The Stag was shot in the stomach on the mistaken assumption that he was trying to steal horses. The Stag knew his wound was mortal. He picked up a dagger and held it ready to plunge into the heart of the young girl beside him. "Am I to go to death alone?" he said to her. "Do you really love me?"

She burst into tears and held her head down, but said nothing. "I see you do not love me and I must go alone," The Stag said. "Tell my brothers of what happened and that I die by my own hand." With his dagger, he cut his belly from side to side, and died. The traders buried him.

The Indian maiden rejected all pleas that she flee to escape the rage of her Snake betrothed. "The Stag told me to go to his brothers," she insisted, "and to them I must go." By a borrowed horse she rode and told her story to the sons of Kootenae Appe. They knew the Snake warrior to whom she was given would kill her in revenge, and in pity they asked, "What do you wish to do?"

"I know what I ought to have done," replied the girl. "But my heart was weak then. It is not so now. My true life is gone. If I die by the hand of the man to whom I was given, I shall die a bad death. In the other world, I shall wander friendless and no one to take care of me. Your brother loved me. He is in the other world and he will be kind to me and love me there. Have pity on me and send me to him." An arrow through her heart laid her dead for her soul to rejoin her lover, and they buried her as the widow of their brother. Thompson added in his diary: "Whatever may be the idea of some civilized atheists, the immortality of the soul is the high consolation of all these rude Indian tribes."

It was the rival Lewis and Clarke expedition that finally freed Thompson to cross the Rocky Mountains. By "moccasin telegraph" Kootenae Appe heard that the Yankees had murdered two Piegans on the upper Missouri River. Collecting his sentinels who had been

guarding Howse Pass in the Rockies, he rode with his war party south after Yankee scalps.

In May of 1807, Thompson and his *voyageurs* set out from Rocky Mountain House for the gateway to the Columbia River. With him he took his wife, Charlotte, and their three small children: the youngest, only 15 months old, perched in a cradle on her mother's back. Ten packhorses were loaded with 300 pounds of *pemmican* and goods to trade with the Kootenay Indians. His Nor'wester partners insisted he also take along two barrels of whisky.

"I had made it a law unto myself that no alcohol should pass the Mountains in my company," Thompson wrote in his diary. At Howse Pass, he "placed the two kegs of alcohol on a vicious horse. By noon, the kegs were empty and in pieces, the horse rubbing his load against the rocks to get rid of it. I wrote my partners what I had done; and that I should do the same to every keg of alcohol. And for the next six years that I had charge of the fur trade on the West side of the Moun-

tains, no further attempt was made to introduce spirituous liquors."

On June 22, 1807, he stood surrounded by glaciers on a bluish-white ice field just north of the present city of Golden, B.C. He could see the little green Blaeberry Creek foaming into the Columbia River. He was now gazing upon the river whose headwaters had flowed in and out of the dreams of so many men. "May God in His mercy," he prayed, "give me to see where its waters flow into the ocean."

It took him four years to fulfill that prayer. The 1,200-mile Columbia is the most complex jigsaw puzzle that ever linked two countries. Its source is the deep-blue Columbia Lake, lying among the mountain ranges of British Columbia about 150 miles south of Golden. Thompson had to learn the hard way that the Columbia first flows 200 miles *north* of its source, before looping south at Big Bend Boat Encampment, 50 miles above Golden. For 300 tortuous miles it then flows south through British Columbia toward the forty-ninth parallel. Then it winds for another 700 miles through the present State of Washington before it finally empties into the Pacific Ocean. To make it more confusing, the Columbia's chief tributary – the Kootenay – begins from a separate source about a mile from that same Columbia Lake. It meanders south through the present States of Montana and Idaho, and then twists *north* to empty into the Columbia River back in British Columbia.

In addition to mapping these freakish curves, Thompson had other delays. He had to stop exploring in order to build the first four trading posts on the Columbia and its American tributaries. The furs he got from the Kootenay Indians had to be transported through the mountains back to his Nor'wester partners at Rocky Mountain House *in the East*. And, he had to do it while dodging the Piegans, now hostile because he was selling fire-arms to the Kootenays. That first winter of 1807, Kootenae Appe sent a 40-man war party to lay siege to Kootenay House, stoutly barricaded with lodge-pole pine but short of supplies. "The Indians, who had pitched their tents close to the gate, thought to make us suffer for want of water," Thompson wrote. "For the riverbank we were on was about 20 feet high and very steep. But at night, by a strong cord, we quietly and gently let down two brass kettles. Then we drew them up, each kettle holding four gallons, which was enough for us." After three weeks the besiegers left and Thompson was alarmed to learn that Kootenae Appe was gathering 300 warriors to attack. A *ruse de guerre* was called for. Kootenae Appe's advance scouts had arrived and Thompson invited two of them into the fort. There he introduced them to two enemy Kootenays. "Their eyes glared like tigers," Thompson wrote. "But I told them to sit down and smoke, which they did."

Then Thompson reminded the Piegans that their chief, Kootenae Appe, would be treading on enemy territory if he attacked Kootenay House: and the Kootenays were well stocked with paleface thundersticks. Then he gave them tobacco and a long-stemmed red porphry pipe to take back as gifts to their tribal war council. Later, Thompson learned that Kootenae Appe, "wistfully eyeing the tobacco, of which they had none," had said to his fellow chiefs: "What can we do with this 'Man Who Looks At Stars?' Our women cannot mend a pair of shoes but he sees them with his magical instruments . . . You all know who I am. My knife has cut through enemy tents, and I am ready to do it again. But to fight against logs of wood that a ball cannot go through, and with people we cannot see, and with whom we are at peace, is what I am averse to. I go no further." Then the Piegans filled Thompson's pipe of peace and smoked.

By the fall of 1810, Thompson – back at Rocky Mountain House on the Saskatchewan River – was facing a new crisis. From the east came news that John Jacob Astor had hired four disgruntled Nor'wester partners for his American Fur Company, and intended to send them by ship around Cape Horn to build a fort at the mouth of the Columbia River. And from the west came the news of Kootenae Appe's death. The Piegans were on the warpath again, refusing to let any palefaces enter Howse Pass. If Thompson hoped to beat Astor to the mouth of the Columbia River, he would have to discover a new pass over the Rockies.

He set off through "chill November's surly blasts." He and seven *voyageurs* with packhorses chopped their way north through scrub to the headwaters of the Athabasca River, "a wretched country, full of solitude which is broken only by the loon." His horses, floundering hip-deep in snow, had to be abandoned. His men, whispering of a "mammoth" that haunted the icy peak of Athabasca Glacier, kept threatening to mutiny.

Thompson was buoyant with the spirit of scientific inquiry. Despite January's 26-below-zero cold, he urged his party on. With 16 husky dogs pulling eight homemade sledges, they trudged on snowshoes through what is now Jasper National Park and across the Athabasca Pass. Thompson had discovered the pass that for the next half century would be the British trade route across the continent.

As the dogsleds slalomed down the slope of a 2,000-foot-glacier, Thompson was enraptured by its greenish diamond brilliance. "But to my uneducated men," he wrote, "it was a dreadful sight. Eastward of this glacier was a forest of pines, cut clean off by some avalanche, as if with a scythe . . ."

When they pitched camp, the men tried and failed to measure the snow with a 20-foot pole. "While we have good snowshoes," Thompson assured them, "it is no matter to us whether the snow is ten or a hundred feet deep."

Then, typically, while the *voyageurs* were asleep, he examined the hole made by the pole and "was surprised to see the colour of the sides a beautiful blue. Many reflections came on my mind. A new world was, in a manner, before me. And my object was to be at the Pacific Ocean before the month of August. How many of my dispirited men would remain with me?" His reflections were answered at Boat Encampment, where the tiny Wood River trickles into the Big Bend of the Columbia. Four of his *voyageurs* deserted in the night and returned by the Athabasca Pass. In morose commemoration of what he considered cowardice, Thompson renamed the Wood, "Flat Heart River."

With his three remaining men, one of them snow-blind, Thompson hacked out planks from cedar trees for a 25-foot canoe. Since he had no nails he sewed them together with thongs of pine roots. In April, with three feet of snow on the ground, the men toiled and portaged up the rapids of the Dalles des Morts. A curly-haired Indian, with the unlikely name of Chief Ugly Head, proved a brave guide as their craft heaved and rolled through the chutes and whirlpools near Kicking Horse Creek. A portage across the flats led them to the churning Kootenay River, "full of small whirlpools and violent eddies, which threatened us with sure destruction. We escaped by hard paddling, keeping to the middle of the river . . . We continued under the mercy of the Almighty, and at sunset put up, each of us thankful for our preservation. As the morrow did not promise anything better, and necessity urged us on, my poor fellows, before laying down, said their prayers. They crossed themselves, and promised a Mass to be said for each by the first priest they could see."

Horses, bought from Indians, brought them overland to Kettle Falls, where the Columbia River twists just below the present United States border. Here Thompson could see Indian fishermen hang kettle-shaped baskets on the end of poles close to the waterfall. Many silvery-scaled Chinook salmon, trying to leap the cataracts, tumbled back into these rude traps. "A terrible cataract," Thompson noted, as he and his party, refreshed, and increased by four Indians, pushed off down the Columbia in a new canoe, "with careless gaiety – until rammed by an 18-inch-wide floating tree."

Like a good travelling salesman, Thompson stopped along the route to ingratiate himself with the Indian chiefs. He was greeted warmly by the Nez Percé Indians, their noses pierced with macaroni-like shells, and the Walla Walla Indians, each sing-song sentence in the chief's welcome speech being punctuated by the tribesmen's loud cries of "Oy! Oy!"

As usual, Thompson's observations were sharply detailed: "When the Chief proposed a dance, the men formed two slightly curved lines, with the women close behind them. A man, painted red and blue, his hair stuck full of feathers, sang. His voice was strong and good, but had few notes. I asked why the Indians preferred the curved, to the straight line, in their dancing. The answer was, 'The curved line gives us the pleasure of seeing each other.' " The Shahaptin Indian maidens, who were naked, embarrassed him. "The women would pass for handsome, if better-dressed. But they were all as cleanly as people can be without the use of soap – an article not half so much valued in civilized life as it ought to be. What would become of the beau and belle without it? Take soap from the boasted cleanliness of the civilized man, and he will not be as cleanly as the savage, who never knows its use."

At Pasco, Washington, where the Snake River wiggles into the Columbia, Thompson planted a pole and raised the Union Jack. Here, in the empty wilderness, on July 9, 1811, he nailed a half-sheet of paper, claiming the territory for Britain, adding, "The N.W. Company of Merchants from Canada do hereby intend to erect a factory in this place for the commerce of the country around."

It was a gesture of defiance. A week later, on July 15, as Thompson's canoemen paddled around the Tongue Point bend of the Columbia to the sea, the explorer saw four newly-cut log cabins. It was Fort Astoria. John Astor's crew of ex-Nor'wester traders had rounded Cape Horn on board the *Tonquin* and landed at the mouth of the Columbia four months before.

Thompson's former comrades greeted him exuberantly, and dined him on duck and partridge, regretting that he would not share in a tipple of Madeira wine. If Thompson felt beaten he didn't show it. His first "full view of the Pacific Ocean was an immense pleasure," he wrote. "But my men seemed disappointed. They had been accustomed to the Great Lakes of Canada and their rolling waves. From the Ocean, they expected a more boundless view . . . a something beyond the power of their senses . . . which they could not describe. I

informed them that directly opposite was the Empire of Japan. This added nothing to their ideas. But a Map would."

It took him two years in retirement from the North West Company to draw it. His masterpiece, over ten feet long, delineated in detail the million and a half square miles he had travelled. Since it showed the 78 trading posts of the Nor'westers, he presented it to the Company, and it hung in state in the council hall at Fort William, Ontario.

For ten years Thompson worked as British representative on the commission that mapped the international boundary between the United States and Canada. And for the next 30 years he eked out a living as a private surveyor at Williamstown, in Glengarry County, Ontario, where a group of other impoverished Nor'wester cronies had retired. Here, aged, forgotten, half-blind, the great map-maker spent his winter years of discontent. Nearby at Gray's Creek lived Thompson's brother-in-law, John McDonald of Garth, and a dozen miles away, in St. Andrew's, his old friend, Simon Fraser, now supporting a Scottish wife and nine children.

All three pioneers nursed memories of their shining achievements in taming the West.

In 1846 when the United States was given all rights to western Montana, Idaho and Washington, which Thompson had explored and claimed for British Canada, the gentle map-maker protested the decision. But his appeal to Sir Robert Peel was in vain. Thompson was so incensed that he used what was, for him, a swear word. He cursed the British for their "blockhead treaty." He also failed to raise the money to publish a small edition of his map and journals. The Canadians, it seemed, were not interested in either the geography or the history of their own country.

As his eyesight worsened, Thompson had to sell his sextant and his instruments to buy food for his wife, and 16 children. Finally he pawned his overcoat. Just before he died in 1857 at 87, *Koo-Koo-Sint*, the "Man Who Looks At Stars," made his last entry in his unpublished journal: "This day borrowed two shillings and sixpence from a friend. Thank God for this relief."

In the early 1880s, Dr. Joseph Tyrrell, then a young geologist working in the West, was surprised to find that an unidentified map of the Columbia River was more accurate than any possessed by the Canadian Pacific Railway or the government. When Tyrrell returned to Ottawa, he discovered that the map had been prepared by somebody called David Thompson. Curious, he investigated, located 39 journals, and began the studies that at last brought fame to Canada's greatest geographer.

VI

Saint and Sinner

THE frontiersmen hired by the Nor'westers first came to the Canadian West like buccaneers, then, entrapped by the romance and challenged by the perils of the wild country, they were lured back again and again. They knew they might be murdered by rival fur traders, butchered by natives, unhinged by the great loneliness or lost in the green forests beyond the "Shining Mountains," but they could not resist the call of *le pays sauvage*. Most of them would bitterly complain that for up to eleven months they were isolated within their log-cabin trading posts, marooned like so many Robinson Crusoes. Occasionally the silence of the plains might be broken by the stamping dances and pounding drums of Indians circling their forts, but this would only temporarily relieve their melancholy. To escape the timeless tedium, the traders might snowshoe or paddle hundreds of miles to the nearest fort to hear another English-speaking voice. They would endure anything on their treks – blizzards and flash fires, maddening swarms of mosquitoes, and clouds of grasshoppers that hid the sun.

The isolation often transformed them into eccentric hermits. This oddness was described by Frederick Ulrich Graham, third baronet of Netherby, who, after visiting Fort Edmonton and Fort Pitt on the plains, wrote: "I hate the sight of these forts, strange, tumbledown places, like lumber rooms on a vast scale. All the white men living in them look as if they had been buried for a century or two, and dug up again, and had scarcely yet got their eyes open, for they look frightened when they see a stranger."

Scraps of news from the "Outside" came once a year by canoe and dogsled "Express" from Montreal. Mail came in rawhide pouches which often had to be thawed out before their contents could be pried free. The Express couriers also dropped off year-old copies of the Montreal *Gazette* and London *Times*, which the traders would read and reread as one Nor'wester phrased it, "with greedy voracity . . . a remnant of a newspaper swallowed, an auctioneer's advertisement, a quack doctor's puff."

The news of most interest was anything disclosing moves on the part of the rival fur trading companies. Competitive forts might be clustered a hundred yards away from each other and, on the surface, gentlemanly civilities prevailed. Rivals would drop in at Christmas or New Year's for a friendly dram of rum, but no commercial information was discussed. Efforts to spy out secrets resulted in simmering feuds that might boil over any time into actual clashes. One Nor'wester wrote that the competitors would often be "dusting each other's jackets."

While the Nor'westers were at the peak of their power, they attracted many remarkable men. None were more remarkable than Daniel Williams Harmon who thought himself a saintly idealist, and Alexander Henry the Younger, a sinner unrepentant. So different outwardly, they had certain attributes in common. Each spent at least 16 years in *le pays d'en haut*: as a Plainsman in the Saskatchewan and Athabasca country and Mountain Man west of the Rockies. Each began as a Nor'wester clerk at twenty English pounds a year, working up to become bourgeois wintering partners at about 100 pounds a year. Both died in poverty.

Harmon looks out from his portrait with the primness of a Sunday school teacher, lean, ascetic, his face bracketed by neatly barbered black sideburns. He must have seemed an odd fish in his predatory surroundings, with his lips pursed in disapproval of Sabbath swearing or gambling, his soft brown eyes bathed in tears at news of the death of a loved one. He was a humourless man, addicted to spouting homilies. Without cracking a smile, he could lavish this praise on a fellow fur trader: "He has an even temper and is fond of his mother."

Harmon was a Christian of tender compassion, with a cultivated mind, and he went out of his way to teach Indian children Biblical English and decent conduct. He lived in a state of perpetual conflict within himself:

the sentimentalist warring against the realist, the scholar against the man of action, the moralist wrestling for his soul in a match against the libertine. He acquired a granite-like conscience from his parents, who ran an inn in Bennington, Vermont. They were bastions of the Congregationalist Church. In 1800, Daniel ran off to Montreal to join the Nor'westers as a clerk, largely to escape their confining orthodoxy. Yet he could not shake himself free that easily of his religious upbringing. The wilderness became a testing ground for his faith.

"We passed the afternoon over a few bottles of wine," Harmon wrote in his diary one day, "and some of us (as the Irishman says) got more than two sheets in the wind." The next day, filled with remorse, he would pray, swear to fast and read his Bible every Sabbath, and resolve "to be in the company of the wicked as seldom as possible, and when among such people . . . persuade them from the folly and sin of their unGodly lives."

Alexander Henry the Younger was an engaging rogue, a matador in fringed buckskin, a wenching Lochinvar out of Montreal. His roving eyes glowed at the sight of a comely Indian maid. He was clean-shaven with blond "Buffalo Bill" hair and the picaresque flair for high adventure of his uncle, Alexander Henry the Elder, who founded the Nor'westers. The younger Henry rarely suffered moral qualms. He might comment reprovingly on the midnight merrymaking of the Indians he had debauched if the noise kept him awake in the fort, but he indulged himself with gusto. "Played with J. McKenzie of the H. B. Co. with drum and fife," he noted, "and drank out of a ten-gallon keg of brandy." He was a *bon vivant* who loved company. On his wanderings from fort to fort across the West, he was usually accompanied by his 200-pound Negro *voyageur*, Pierre Bonga; his tame dancing bear; and his huge black dog, a blend of wolf and Newfoundland hound. Henry was genuinely touched by the sufferings of animals. "Found one of my yellow chickens dead this morning, and discovered that the cock had killed it," he wrote indignantly. "I must make a separate coop for him. He is really a brute, tormenting the sitting hens and killing the chickens."

Henry and Harmon both looked at the world with curious eyes, enraptured by all things, whether it was the sight of someone tobogganing down the banks of the Red River on a buffalo-hide sleigh, or a housewife measuring a 25-pound turnip from the kitchen garden. Both kept journals to divert themselves during the lonely nights – Harmon's consisting of 244 pages of foolscap, Henry's 1600 pages, bound in rawhide covers. After watering the "Blackfoot milk" rum of the trading

Indians all day, Henry would pull out his book from behind the counter and scratch down his observations with his quill pen. With a keen eye for geography, Henry's voluminous journals were filled with detailed observations of the countryside he travelled.

The two scribes had a chance to meet at the annual summer Rendezvous, when all Nor'westers from the *pays d'en haut* and Montreal met to talk business and carouse. In 1800, it was held at Grand Portage, at the head of Lake Superior. As the brigades of canoes paddled within sight of Fort William (named after William McGillivray, reigning grandee since the death of his uncle, Simon McTavish), brass cannons on the bastions greeted them with a *feu de joie*. Inside the palisades was uproar. Clerks bustled as they packed bales of beaver skins and cheap trading novelties. The easterners cheerfully gambled and fought with *hommes du nord* canoemen (Nor'wester style: kick, bite, gouge and scratch). Half-breed *voyageurs* squandered their wages on liquor and on Chippewa Indian girls. Wintering partners who had not seen each other for a year embraced with oaths of *camaraderie*. "Toward the evening," Harmon jotted in his diary, "I walked to the other end of the Portage to see Mr. Alexander Henry, who had just arrived and was pleased to see us."

For a week, the "lords of the lakes and forests" wrangled over business matters in the Great Hall. This was a sumptuously appointed room, lined with portraits of the proprietors. A bust of Simon McTavish stood on the mantel over the fireplace, next to the full-length painting of Lord Nelson. A space was left on one wall for the map that David Thompson was to produce of the 78 Nor'wester forts strung across the West. The chief partners sat at the head of a green cloth-covered table. For days and nights they argued about the sharing of profits and decided which clerks were to winter at what forts in the new season. They raged against the "Saints in Parliament" who wanted them to cut down the gallons of rum being ladled out to the Indians, then toasted each other with "bacchanalian Highland songs and brimming bumpers, with old French ditties and Indian yelps and yelling."

The Rendezvous ended with a dance. The palefaces spruced up in their best pea-green breeches and yellow silk vests, while the Indian "Venuses of joy" glistened in white doeskins and beaded moccasins. Fiddles scraped and sleigh dogs howled in a bedlam chorus, while the revellers twirled through the night to *The Reel of Tulloch* an jigged to *The Flowers of Edinburgh*. "This evening the gentlemen of the place dressed, and we had a famous ball in the Dining Room," Harmon wrote. "For music we had the bagpipe, the violin, the

Three Nor'westers carried the name "Alexander Henry."
Above, Henry the Elder. A son and a nephew followed in his footsteps.

flute and the fife, which enabled us to spend the evening agreeably. At the ball, there were a number of this country's *Ladies*. I was surprised to find they could behave themselves so well, and that they danced not amiss."

The gaiety was remembered with fond nostalgia by both Henry and Harmon during the long nights in their separate winter forts in the country now called Manitoba. Harmon's melancholy left when the buds burst pale green in early April, the month the Indians called "Moon of the Goose." In one entry, he noted in his diary: "I took a ride a-horse-back to where our people are making sugar, and my path led me over the Plains and through the woods. There I saw a great variety of birds, straining their tuneful throats to welcome the return of another revolving Spring. I saw also small red deer jumping about in the woods, and squirrels skipping from tree to tree, and swans, bustards and ducks swimming in river and pond. And altogether it rendered my ramble beyond expression delightful." Henry gave similar homage to spring. "Fine warm weather, and the buffaloes are now with the calves of spring . . . Frogs begin to croak, and pigeons are flying north in numbers . . . This morning I saw this season's first turkey buzzard alight on the river . . . Raccoons are coming out of their winter quarters in the daytime, though retiring to their

*Daniel Williams Harmon scorned the common-law marriages
of other traders . . . until he himself felt the loneliness of* le pays sauvage.

hollow trees at night . . . Out of 12 eggs my yellow hen hatched 11 chicks . . . Pierre Bonga's wife was delivered of a daughter – the first fruit of this fort, and a very black baby she is."

The attitude of the two traders toward the Indians differed strikingly. To Harmon, the natives could be divided into good and bad Indians – depending on how they conformed to his flinty code of New England morality. Harmon was enchanted to hear the redskin choirs sing lilting songs, which had been composed by their poets. He encouraged them because "the music greatly resembles the airs which I have heard sung in Roman Catholic churches." Harmon was, however, dis-

enchanted when he had the lyrics of these love and war ballads translated. They were bawdy enough to make a sailor blush. To Henry, there were only bad Indians, Stone Age savages without souls, who had to be pampered and liquored for the sake of their furs. The preliminary ceremony of dressing their chiefs in scarlet-laced coats and ladling out sample drams of rum and listening to their braggadocio was an amusement that soon palled. "Singing and bellowing seems to be their chief pleasure," Henry remarked wearily. "They pester us so that we are heartily tired of our customers."

Both Henry and Harmon wrote that they sternly resisted the many Indian princesses who were thrust upon them as concubines. Harmon, at 24, was distressed by his "natural inclination" to say yes, when a Cree chief offered his daughter. He wrestled with his conscience, and decided it would be sinful. "Thanks to God alone," he thought, "I have avoided a snare laid, no doubt, by the Devil himself." Four years later, Harmon capitulated when offered a 14-year-old half-breed daughter of a Cree and a French Canadian, rationalizing that it was to be a marriage of convenience, strictly temporary. "In case we can live in harmony together, my intentions now are to keep my fair partner as long as I remain in this uncivilized part of the world," Harmon decided. "But when I return to my native land, I shall endeavour to place her in the hands of some good, honest man, who is no stranger to her people's customs and language . . . The girl is said to be of a mild disposition and even-tempered, qualities that make an agreeable woman." His squaw must have had that serene temperament, for she bore Harmon 14 children. Yet nowhere in his diary does he give her a name. It was always "the woman who remains with me," or "the mother of my children." Yet he wept when two of "my darling children" died at birth. Henry posed as a prude, deploring Indian girls for their "licentious nudity." He seemed concerned that, "The Indian women sit down in a decent attitude, placing their knees close to each other." He pretended to be offended when Blackfoot chiefs offered their wives as bedmates, but noted with a lecherous eye that the women were "the handsomest of their six or seven wives." Henry, the marriage-shy bachelor, finally succumbed. After an uproarious New Year's Eve party, he awoke in the grey morning-after to find a Saulteaux chief's daughter cuddled up beside him, and the black-eyed maiden was not easy to jilt. "Liard's daughter took possession of my room," his entry for January 1 read that year, "and the devil himself could not have got her out." He tried to shake her off by going on a buffalo hunt. On his return, he noted: "I was vexed to find my room still occupied, and no sign of her budging." The war of the boudoir raged for three weeks, with Henry using every trickery to oust the girl. At last, on January 30, the entry in his diary read: "I got rid of my bedfellow, who returned to her father with good grace . . . Fine weather." Two days later, he added: "The lady returned . . . A terrible snowstorm."

Acknowledging defeat, Henry cheerfully took to calling the girl "Her Ladyship, My Squaw." He accepted her father, Chief Liard, as his father-in-law and proclaimed the Indian, "My Beau-pere." The relationship ended in tragedy in August, 1805. While Henry was away from Fort Pembina on business, all his redskin in-laws were killed. A few weeping survivors among the Saulteaux told him how a war party of 300 Sioux had swooped down on the Tongue River camp, a few miles from the Nor'wester fort, and butchered 14 Saulteaux, women and children included. With "grief and lamentation," Henry went to survey the mutilated bodies. Only the torso of his father-in-law remained. The skull had been carried off by the Sioux for use as a water dish.

"I gathered up the remaining bones of my *Belle-mere* in a handkerchief," Henry mourned. "Then I gave a party of 300 Assiniboines, Saulteaux and Crees a nine-gallon keg of gunpowder and a hundred musket balls. 'Go,' I encouraged them. 'Revenge the death of my *Beau-pere* and family.' " They accepted the ammunition, and added: "Paleface, you have almost as much sense as an Indian. If you add a few kegs of rum, you will be considered fully as wise as ourselves." When this "war party" of drunks returned from Sioux territory three months later, without having fired a single musket in revenge, Henry reflected bitterly, "Their manner of comparing a white man to an Indian is the highest compliment they can pay. But let no white man be so vain as to believe an Indian really supposes him to be his equal. No – they despise us in their hearts."

Perhaps because tragedy had touched him personally, a twinge of pity for the Indians began to stir within Henry. "The Indians totally neglect their ancient customs," he said, "and to what can this degeneracy be ascribed but to their intercourse with us? We opposing parties of traders teach them roguery, and destroy both body and mind with that pernicious article, rum. What a different set of people they would be were there not a drop of liquor in the country! If a murder is committed among the Saulteaux, it is always in a drinking match. We may truly say that liquor is the root of all evil in the Northwest." Liquor and women affected Henry and Harmon in oddly different ways: Harmon had always rationalized, when doling out diluted rum to the prairie Indians, that "It is in the blood of the Savages to be fond of spirituous liquor." Therefore it was not unChristian to quench that natural need. In 1810, Harmon was transferred to Fort St. James, on Stuart Lake – the New Caledonia outpost hacked out of the British Columbia forest by Simon Fraser. Here, "among lofty summits that appear to reach the sky," Harmon met Carrier Indians who had never before been corrupted by white men. He sermonized about the delight the Carriers took in gambling their last rag of clothes ("the wretches boast they are naked as a dog"), yet he introduced the Carriers to liquor. On New Year's Day, 1811, he noted in his diary: "This being the first day of the year, the Indians desired us to allow them to remain at the fort to see our people drink. But as soon as our people began to be intoxicated and quarrel and fight among themselves, the Natives were apprehensive that something unpleasant might befall them also. Therefore, they hid themselves under the beds, and said they thought the white people had become mad."

Exactly a year later, Harmon made this entry in his diary: "This being the first day of the year, I invited several of the most respectable men among the Carrier chiefs to come into the fort and partake of what we had remaining of our repast. I must acknowledge that I was surprised to see them behave with so much decency, and even propriety, when drinking a flaggon or two of rum. And after their repast was over, they smoked their pipes and conversed rationally on the great difference there is between the manners and customs of Civilized People and those Savages. They readily conceded that ours was superior to theirs."

Harmon's attitude toward Indian women gradually changed. At first he believed it was not unChristian for a white man to discard his Indian wife if she displeased him. This divorce, he wrote, "I think reasonable. For I cannot conceive it to be right for a man and woman to cohabit when they cannot agree, but live in discontent, if not downright hatred to each other, as many do." Sixteen years after writing this, however, Harmon became conscious that the Indians of British Columbia felt love and attachment as deeply as any white man. He was surprised by the grief of a Carrier chief whose wife had died after a lingering illness of several months. "Cheer up," the widower was told. "Do not be so sorrowful. What has befallen you already has happened to many."

"I will do as I think proper," the chief replied. "I have not yet forgotten what my deceased wife told me before her death. She said, 'Accompany me, my loved one.'" A day later, the chief was found hanging from a tree. The villagers placed man and wife on the same funeral pyre. "Many people, who are not well acquainted with the Savages, will not believe that their affections can be so deeply rooted as to make them commit suicide," Harmon wrote. "But they are much mistaken. For such melancholy circumstances happen in the Indian country."

In 1819, when Harmon was preparing to retire from the Nor'westers and to go east to Vermont, he reversed his original decision of abandoning his Indian wife. Elizabeth – as his squaw came to be baptized – was pregnant with another child; and, besides, Harmon had moral and emotional qualms about leaving his "Lizzette" behind. "My intentions have materially changed, since I first took her to live with me," he wrote. "We have wept together over the early death of several children. We have children still living, who are equally dear to us both. How could I spend my days in the civilized world, and leave my beloved children in the wilderness? How could I tear them from a mother's love? The mother of my children will accompany me. And, if she shall be content to remain in that part of the world, I design to make her my wife by a formal marriage. I consider it my duty to take her to a Christian land, where she may enjoy Divine ordinances, grow in grace, and ripen for glory."

Harmon did marry his Lizzette in a Congregational Church ceremony. He then founded the Vermont town of Harmonsville, near the Canadian border, and he and his family tried to run a general store and sawmill. Things did not go well for the Nor'wester away from the western plains. He and Lizzette died on a rented farm on the outskirts of Montreal, so impoverished that his heirs renounced his estate of less than 100 pounds as "more burdensome than profitable." Most of his children died young of smallpox: the last of the 14, Maria, tried to manage a girls' school in Ottawa, then committed suicide by drowning. Harmon's namesake town of Harmonsville was eventually renamed Coventry.

Alexander Henry spent his last trading days at Fort Astoria, at the mouth of the Columbia River. The Rabelais of the Nor'westers set out for this post in 1813, mushing by dogsled through the passes of the Rockies ("a grand sight – rocks upheaved in all shapes, high and craggy and enveloped in clouds, resembling the ramparts of a citadel"). On his arrival in August at the palisade fort, Henry found the Mountain Men in a state of panic. The War of 1812 between the United States and Britain was being used by the Nor'westers as an excuse to grab John Jacob Astor's trading post. The Canadians circled Fort Astoria, warning that a British warship, the *Raccoon,* was on its way to blast the Yankees with cannon. The "Yankees" inside the fort were almost all former Nor'westers – British subjects hired by Astor. Led by the ex-Nor'wester Duncan McDougall, the Astorians were trading under the Stars and Stripes while their own country was warring against the United States. Even more embarrassed were their besiegers, who were short of provisions. The Nor'westers had to beg for handouts from the very fort they had come to conquer.

After bargaining, the impasse was resolved. McDougall decided to sell the fort to the invaders, for $40,000, a third of its fur value. McDougall himself came as part of the deal; having sold Astor out, he became chief factor for the Nor'westers. To increase his influence over the neighbouring Chinooks, McDougall bought a Chinook Indian princess: a flatheaded girl, her pierced nose adangle with sea shells, her hair glistening with whale oil. She was the daughter of the great one-eyed Chief Comcomly, and the man known as the "Mephistopheles of Astoria" drove a hard bargain. Henry was amused to see how the chief haggled 15 muskets and 15 blankets as well as sundry trinkets from McDougall.

When *HMS Raccoon* arrived, her 26 cannons bristling for action, Captain William Black was disgusted to see the Union Jack already flying over Fort Astoria. This meant he would not receive any prize money for conquering the Yankees. "Great God Almighty!" fumed His Majesty's representative. "Is this the fort I've heard so much about. Why, damn me, I could knock it down in a couple of hours with a four-pounder!" Determined not to be robbed of his pageantry, Black demanded that all the Nor'westers be armed with muskets and drilled to serve as guard of honour. Agleam in his gold braid, the ship's commander ordered the Union Jack to be lowered. The Stars and Stripes were raised and then hastily jerked down, then the Union Jack was triumphantly rehoisted. Stepping forward, the Captain broke a bottle of Madeira wine on the flag pole, formally took possession of the fort in the name of His Britannic Majesty, and rechristened it Fort George. "Three cheers were then given by us all, and three rounds of musketry fired," wrote Henry, adding the postscript: "One of the latter men had a narrow escape from shooting himself in the face, his gun having flashed and gone off."

Henry was glad to see the British Navy leave on New Year's Eve. His Majesty's officers consumed prodigious vats of Nor'wester rum. "Famous fellows for grog, they are!" The English sailors attracted hordes of Chinook Indian girls, ready to sell their favours, like "their frail sisters at Portsmouth when attacking the crews of the newly-arrived East Indian fleet." Henry was so morally incensed that he personally drove from the fort's gates "one canotee of prostitutes, who were not allowed to land on pain of being put in irons."

His moral compunctions smack of hypocrisy. In April, 1814 the Nor'wester ship *Isaac Todd* sailed into Fort George carrying the *bourgeois* gentleman who was to take over as governor of their coastal empire. He was Donald McTavish, an irascible Scotsman with a passion for hard liquor and female company. Aboard with him, Henry was astounded but delighted to discover, was a blue-eyed blonde, Jane Barnes, a barmaid whom Mc-Tavish had brought as his mistress from a tavern in Portsmouth, England. She created a sensation. The Chinook braves were also fascinated by her buxom good looks. Chief Comcomly's eldest son came in red paint and daubed with his most fragrant whale oil to ask Jane

for her plump hand in marriage. He offered 100 sea otter pelts as dowry and said he would make her head wife of his harem of four squaws. Never would she have to dig for roots for his royal palate; and, as a special inducement, "You will be allowed to smoke as many pipes of tobacco during the day as you think proper." Jane was flattered, but said no.

She did take a liking to Henry, however, who took it upon himself to protect her from hearing any coarse language aboard the *Isaac Todd*. "Mr. McTavish, Jane and myself partook of a bit of cheese, brown biscuit and a glass of Noyeaux cordial," Henry wrote loftily. "A vile discourse then took place in the hearing of Jane on the subject of venereal disease and Chinook ladies." Jane exclaimed: "Oh, Mr. Mac! I suppose you agree with Shakespeare that 'every woman is at heart a rake'?"

"Pope, ma'am, if you please," McTavish corrected her.

"Pope?" replied Jane, looking puzzled. "Bless me, sir, you must be wrong. Rake is certainly the word. I never heard of but one female pope!" Whatever her literary deficiencies, her physical charms enraptured Henry. His journal becomes full of references to the problem of which gentleman was to take over "protection" of Miss Barnes: McTavish or himself. "I shall make it my duty to make Jane's situation as comfortable as possible," one entry reads. "Not as a lover, but through humanity." This was followed by: "During a walk, Mr. McT. and myself came to an understanding for future arrangements. We differ on some personal points. But my course is clear to me." This was climaxed by: "About sunset the jolly-boat took Mr. McTavish on board alone. Jane, of course, remained, having taken up her lodgings in my room." McTavish consoled himself by buying a Tête Platte girl for one strip of black broadcloth.

A few days later, on May 21, 1814, Henry wrote the last entry in his journal. He and McTavish were preparing to make an expedition up the Columbia River. He ends in the middle of a sentence. . . "Now all is in readiness and order, and a bedstead put up. There has been a misunderstanding on board the ship with Mr. McKay, regarding the bread given out to the crew, and an appeal made to the captain. The weather cleared up – "

The weather did not clear up. Nevertheless, the next morning Alexander Henry and Donald McTavish set out in the little schooner *Jane*, named after the barmaid they both had wooed. While they and their five *voyageurs* grew tipsy on rum, a gale tipped *Jane* over in the Columbia. Henry and his Nor'wester comrades all perished.

From Britain, Europe and eastern Canada, pioneers
pushed west to the plains. The lure: 160 acres for free.
These prairie schooners were Alberta-bound.

THE LAND HUNGER

The loneliness and promise of the prairie
were captured by English immigrant Adrian Neison, about 1877.
A house-painter, he settled in Saskatchewan.

The Hard Sell

The West belonged to everyone – except 6,630,000 acres of the most fertile belt, retained by the Hudson's Bay Company. In 1878, you could get it for $3 per acre, on "remarkably easy" terms.

The settlers detrained at Winnipeg, the "Gateway to the West." After the Free Land Homestead Act of 1872, the gate was wide open.

MANITOBA
AND THE
NORTH-WEST.
FARMING LANDS
FOR SALE.

THE HUDSON'S BAY CO. have very large tracts of land in

THE GREAT FERTILE BELT
FOR SALE,
AND NOW OFFER
500,000 ACRES
IN THE
TOWNSHIPS
ALREADY SURVEYED.

They own two sections in each Township, and have in addition large numbers of farms for sale on the Red and Assiniboine rivers.

Splendid Prairie Farms, Grazing Land and Wood Lots.

Prices range from $3 to $6 per acre, according to location, &c.

Terms of payment remarkably easy.

Pamphlets giving full information about the country, and the lands for sale can be had on application at the Co.'s offices in Winnipeg and at Montreal.

C. J. BRYDGES,
Land Commissioner Hudson's Bay Co.
Montreal, November, 1878.

These contemporary engravings on steel show the paddlewheeler Manitoba, *taking on freight and settlers at Sarnia, 1876.*

The First Task:
Shelter

The end of steel was often the start of the trail: this nervous homesteader made the last lap by ox-wagon. In Winnipeg a wagon sold for $175, a Red River cart, $20.

The first "home" on the treeless plains was usually of sod, like this one at Souris, Manitoba, 1883. One indomitable pioneer woman even hauled her piano to such a shack.

Miss Brown of England visited her
brother, Osborne, at his relatively luxurious
log home on the Elbow River, 1890.
She left this painting as a memento.

OVERLEAF: *Life on a homestead, according to an
illustration in the* Canadian Illustrated
News, *1800, was a happy hustle and bustle,
with pigs in the pen, livestock grazing,
and venison for the taking.*

The 'Luxury' of the Log Cabin

Farther west, plentiful wood solved the housing problem. This cabin sheltered miners in British Columbia, 1872.

This homesteader, posed with family and family pet on their stoop, was rightly proud of his chinked log cabin at Calgary in 1885. It was a long way from the crude sod huts of the first arrivals, and a man could feel he was "here to stay." The rancher (below), at High River, Alberta, could even boast a fence and although his bunkhouse was roughhewn, it somehow suggested a new prosperity, marking the passing of the pioneer era.

The Settlers, Settled

Dressed in their Sunday finest, posed like any English gentlefolk outside a country mansion, these Westerners sat for their portrait in the front yard of their Manitoba "estate."

The West was still a very young land, still sparsely settled when this photograph was taken in 1890, but already the hand of time is visible. The plaster walls are crumbling on the weather side and the little saplings planted to give shade now dwarf the house.

VII

The White Savage

THE Mountain Men who tamed the Indian country west of the Rockies were a gifted breed of yarn-spinners. They could out-brag Cyrano de Bergerac, out-lie Baron Munchausen and out-wench Don Juan. They wrestled grizzly bears that would have tested Paul Bunyan. They shot mountain eagles, cougars and Indians (always in self-defence, of course) as unerringly as James Fenimore Cooper's fictitious *Deerslayer*.

The tall tales they swapped around the campfire at night bolstered the courage of these bearded French-Canadian half-breeds, these flea-ridden Yankee riff-raff turned into "White Indians," these lonely English ex-ribbon clerks yearning for home. Romancing was an escape from the grim realities of mountain life – their starvation diets of roots, rosebuds and boiled moccasins; their arthritis from wading through icy streams to trap beaver; their economic thraldom to the big fur-trading companies.

Most of them seemed to feel a nomad's rebellion against responsibility, a craving for freedom, a hunger for excitement. Some explained it as " fur fever," which meant greed for sudden wealth. Others called it "the itch," the beckoning to the unknown. But whatever they called it, they followed it to adventure.

They had no need to embellish the truth. Their exploits were truly Gargantuan. One of them, Joe Meek, records that on his first sight of four Mountain Men, they were playing poker, using the body of a scalped comrade as a card table. An ex-*voyageur*, Mike Fink, who liked to brag he was "half horse and half alligator tipped with a snapping turtle," and a crony named Carpenter, used to amuse themselves by shooting cups of whisky off each other's heads at 70 paces.

The two mountaineers came to blows over possession of an Indian maid and Fink lost. To reseal their friendship, Fink proposed their usual game. A coin was tossed and Carpenter lost. "You're going to rub me out," he croaked, as he poised the tin cup on his head.

"Don't shake so, old pardner," Fink said. "You'll spill the liquor, and I'll need a drink when I've finished this job."

Fink shot and Carpenter fell with a hole through the centre of his forehead. "Oh, darn!" Fink is reputed to have said, "You've spilled my drink."

The heyday of the Mountain Men was from 1813 (when the Canadian Nor'westers seized the Yankees' Fort Astoria at the mouth of the Columbia River) until 1846 (when the Canadians ceded the country below the forty-ninth parallel to the Americans). Those were the palmy days, as one of them put it, when Canadian fur traders "ruled with bullets and whisky" a Rocky Mountain empire stretching from British Columbia to California.

The territory was loosely called "the Oregon country," or "West of the Rockies." It was a sea of unexplored mountain peaks and craggy gulches, of prickly sagebrush desert and impenetrable fir jungle. These formidable badlands – sporadically gleaming with honeysuckle and the ruby-like orchid called mountain lady slipper – were the central backdrop for contending fur trade interests and nations.

After the War of 1812, the Pacific Coast region became a kind of international no-man's-land. The Treaty of Ghent threw it open to "joint occupancy" by both the Canadians and the Americans. But the Canadian North West Company had already built fur-trading posts there. Their palisaded log forts were strung out from the present states of Montana and Idaho to Washington; they spilled over from New Caledonia in British Columbia down to Oregon. And the Nor'westers were determined to hold their coastal fur bases even at the price – in 1821 – of union with their hated rival, the Hudson's Bay Company.

Yankee fur traders slowly dribbled into this virginal beaver heaven. Their headquarters was a southerly outpost in Colorado, near Taos, New Mexico. But for most of the Yankees, St. Louis was the jumping-off point. From this saloon town (named by a French-Canadian fur trader after King Louis XIV of France), they poled their way up the Missouri River in flat-bottomed keel-boats. Then from "Old Muddy's" headwaters in the Rockies, they fanned out westward.

One of the first big newcomers was the Missouri Fur Company. It was founded by Manuel Lisa, a Spanish American; as early as 1812 he erected Fort Lisa at the mouth of the Platte River. Then John Jacob Astor, chagrined at losing his Columbia River Fort to the Nor'westers for a pittance, bought out Lisa and began again to extend his tentacles northwestward.

The other big rival of the Canadians was the Rocky Mountain Fur Company. As early as 1810 Major Andrew Henry, a Pennsylvania lead miner, had built a fort called "Henry's Fork" on the Snake River. His partner, William H. Ashley, a Virginia gunpowder maker, advertised in the St. Louis *Missouri Republican* for a hundred "Enterprising Young Men." They would "ascend the Missouri River to its source, there to be employed for one, two or three years" trapping for fur on the Yellowstone River. These were the first Yankee Mountain Men: one hundred Nor'wester outcasts, wastrels and thugs from the St. Louis grog shops. There was Kit Carson, the legendary "Kentuckian Killer," a bandy-legged, five-foot-four runt, glorified by dime-novel fictioneers for his feats of strength. There was Jedediah "Bible Man" Smith, said to carry a Bible in one hand and a gun in the other, and who wore his hair over his shoulders like an Old Testament prophet to cover a missing left ear that a grizzly bear had chewed off. There was Joe Meek, who called himself "a harum-scarum, don't-care sort of man," and who taught his infant half-breed son to say "God damn you" as his first words because Meek considered "this prayer the most important one for use hereabouts." And there was the notorious Jim Baker, who would shoot an Indian not just for stealing his beaver traps but for *looking* as if he might steal them.

The Canadian Mountain Men, largely Nor'westers, were scarcely more savoury. Alexander Henry the Younger ladled out whisky to the Indians and wrote in his journal: "Chief Big Mouth stabbed Red Blanket. Chief The Beef stabbed his young wife in the arm. Little Shell almost beat his old mother's brains out with a club. I sowed garden seeds."

Donald Mackenzie, Sir Alexander Mackenzie's cousin, boasted that he attained his 300-pound corpulence by eating rattlesnakes for lunch. When surrounded by hostile Nez Percés, Mackenzie flattened two with his tent pole and then outbluffed them by threatening to light a match to a keg of gunpowder.

Peter Skene Ogden, "M'sieu Pete," led five beaver-trapping expeditions as far south as the Gulf of Cali-

fornia and as far east as his namesake of Ogden in present-day Utah. The son of a Quebec judge, he had given up law at 17 to become the Nor'westers' most lawless beaver hunter. After slashing the breeches off a rival Hudson's Bay Company trader, Ogden solemnly explained: "In this place, King's writ does not run. The custom of the Indian Country – or as we lawyers say, the *Les non scripta* – is our only guide. We must, in our acts of summary legislation, perform the parts of judge, jury, sheriff, hangman, gallows and all."

There was Finan McDonald, "Big Red Chief," a bull-like redheaded Scot who often led Flathead Indians against the Blackfeet. In one raid he killed 68 Piegans and returned with 4,000 pelts.

Then there was John McLoughlin, another six-foot-four giant, called "White-Headed Eagle" because of his piercing grey eyes, prematurely white hair and his temper. A French-Scottish ex-surgeon from Quebec, he once caned a blacksmith for selling three pelts to the Bay Company, who later hired McLoughlin to head their Pacific Coast principality. The Bay's Sir George Simpson described him as "dressed in clothes that had once been fashionable, but were now covered with a thousand patches of different colours. His beard would do honour to the chin of a Grizzly Bear. He was loaded with firearms, and his own herculean dimensions formed a *tout ensemble* that would convey a good idea of the highwaymen of former days."

The Canadian "free trappers" were largely disenchanted *voyageurs*, disgruntled clerks, and footloose Iroquois from the east. They were tired of being eternally in debt to the Nor'westers or the Bay Company. After serving their two-to-five-year contracts they would trap on their own for beaver, or barter for beaver with the coast Indians, then sell their pelts to the highest bidder among the big Canadian or Yankee companies. But though they called themselves "free men," they remained in bondage. All the big fur companies charged them exorbitant prices for steel traps, horses, pack-mules, guns, liquor and other supplies – making as much as 500 per cent profit. Even then the Nor'westers and Bay factors were incensed when these renegade "loners" sold to the enemy for five times as much cash – six dollars for a single "plew," as a beaver peltry or French *plus* was called.

The growing American competition brought two new elements into the far-west fur trade. White men were hired by the Canadian companies and dispatched in brigades to trap for beaver, and the horse and pack-mule displaced the birchbark canoe as the chief means of travel. In short, the Rockies began to be explored by caravans – itinerant bands of Mountain Men looking and often behaving like the Forty Thieves in the tale of Ali Baba.

Most of the Mountain Men were illiterate, but three of them left readable memoirs about their escapades. Except for the occasional purple patches, these journals have a pace and humour unmatched by the writings of any other explorers of the Far West. The trio, born story-tellers all, were British Canadians – one a Scotsman, one an Irishman, and one an Englishman.

The Scotsman was Alexander Ross. Sir George Simpson described him as "full of bombast and marvellous nonsense." He saw the personalities of the Far West as so many absurd caricatures that he drew in words with a dryly satiric, often vinegary wit. His own portrait, painted when he retired from the fur trade to become a sheriff and teacher at the Red River colony in Manitoba, shows him looking down his long, condescending nose, lips curled into a faintly mocking smile, index finger sharply pointing, piercing blue eyes sceptical.

The painting of a dandy in an elegant waistcoat, flowing four-in-hand tie, and immaculately combed sideburns, does not do justice to Ross the Mountain Man. At 22, he emigrated from Nairnshire in Scotland to teach school at Glengarry in Upper Canada. When Astor began recruiting fur traders in Montreal to compete against the Canadian Nor'westers, Ross dropped his Shakespeare and Virgil to sail aboard the *Tonquin* for the Columbia Rivermouth. When the Nor'westers bought Fort Astoria in 1813, Ross became a company clerk, and later switched to the Hudson's Bay Company.

Ross developed a curious love-hate for the fur trade. He resented not being promoted to the full *bourgeois* partnership he felt he deserved, yet he could not bear to leave this savagely lovely Pacific Coast. He had an "irresistible propensity to see more of the Indian country . . . a curiosity never satisfied, until one knows every hole and corner of the country, and every native in it by name." For 15 years he explored from his chief base at Fort Okanagan, at the mouth of the Okanagan River. He also led Nor'wester beaver-trapping expeditions out of Fort Shuswap, at the Kamloops forks of the Thompson River, into the empty wilderness of British Columbia. He was awed by the Thompson River forest. ("Everything here wore the stillness of the midnight hour".) But he was dismayed by what is known in B.C. today as Rossland ("too rocky, hard, and flinty for beaver").

From Fort Nez Percé, at the mouth of the Walla Walla River, Ross roved around present Washington, Oregon and Idaho, and was both repelled by the Indian men whom he saw as oscillating between butchery and beggary, and enchanted by the Okanagan Indian girls.

("No females in the land are so fair to look upon. No damsels could dance so gracefully as they.") He recorded without irony the conflicting values of Indian and white man. When the traders hanged a Chinook Indian on the gallows of his own lodge poles for stealing a silver goblet from Fort Astoria it was "capital punishment." But when the Indians in retribution scalped two Astorians at the gate of the fort, the killings were "barbaric acts of cruelty, calling for white man's revenge."

The avenging Astorians set off in canoes encumbered with six cannons, hand grenades and cutlasses, with umbrellas tucked under arm, and handcuffs ready to clap on the criminals. In the night, the Chinooks pilfered most of the hardware, the umbrellas, and a suit of clothes belonging to the expedition's leader, Donald McLennan. As the embarrassed expedition beat a retreat from the Chinook village at the Columbia River Cascades, McLennan stood up in the canoe and tossed his cocked hat to the tribe.

"Gentlemen," he shouted, "you have got the rest. Now your suit is complete." It was not the only absurdity. The Nor'westers paid the Indians for returning the cannon balls they shot at them. They used the Indians as mailmen for the forts between British Columbia and the Oregon country, which is how the Carrier tribe got its name. With much mumbo-jumbo, in exchange for a few strings of glass beads, Indian runners passed the white man's "magical" documents from tribe to tribe.

Ross etched his fellow fur traders with donnish acid. John Jacob Astor's Columbia River enterprise "promised so much and accomplished so little: like the May fly of an hour, it rose, flittered, and died." He blamed its downfall on his comrades who guzzled like "Hogarth's drunkards in Gin Lane and Beer Alley." And the Nor'wester Mountain Men were "strutting and plumed bullies," committing their acts of "folly and tinsel grandeur, the waggeries of their licentious indulgences . . . their gambling, drinking and foppery, in which they spend in a few hours the fruits of many years' labour.

"It was no uncommon thing," Ross wrote, "for a dashing Nor'wester to parade the streets of Montreal, with his horse shod with silver shoes; nor to be seen throwing handfuls of small coins among the children." He told of a Nor'wester leading his horse into a tea house and ordering for it "a pint of Chinese *samtschu* and a slice of bread." When the horse reared and shattered "a splendid mirror valued at 25 guineas," the Nor'wester called for pen and ink and wrote an order on the company for 50 guineas. There was little incentive to save for any of the Mountain traders. When Ross tallied the death toll he found that sixty-one of Astor's Mountain Men had drowned or been killed by Indians within one year.

The Irishman who wrote of the Mountain Men was Rossenberg Cox, a gauche and clownish young tenderfoot, perpetually homesick, the butt of many practical jokes by the Mountain Men. The only surviving portrait is his self-description: "cropped head, John Bullish face, low, and somewhat corpulent person." He had apparently come to Upper Canada as a journalist. But, at 18, intrigued by Astor's advertisements, he had signed on at $100 a year as a clerk "captivated with the love of novelty, and the hope of speedily realizing an independence in the supposed El Dorado."

Cox found no El Dorado in his five years west of the Rockies. He ascended the Columbia River to its source in B.C. nine times, and spent the rest of his service in Fort George (as Fort Astoria was renamed after the Nor'westers took it over) and Fort Spokane in present Washington, at the confluence of the Little Spokane and Spokane Rivers.

"A land of contrarieties," Cox called it, when he was later Dublin correspondent for the London *Morning Herald*. In summer the air might be aromatic with the smell of iodine from the Pacific seaweed, or steamy as a Turkish bath, or in the mountains, crisp and antiseptic.

Cox enjoyed the informality of the *voyageurs* when William McGillivray, chief partner of the North West Company, formed a corps of Nor'westers to fight against the Yankees in the War of 1812. "It was quite impossible to make the French Canadians amenable to military law," Cox reported. "They generally came on parade with a pipe in their mouths, and their rations of pork and bread stuck on their bayonets. They paraded with naked necks and rough beards, and they could not be got to wear socks. On seeing an officer, whether a general, colonel, or subaltern, they took off their hats and made a low bow, with the common salutation of familiarity, '*Bon jour, Monsieur le Général.*' And, if they happened to know that the officer was married, they never failed to enquire after the health of '*Madame et les enfants.*' When called to order by their officers, one would reply, 'Ah, dear captain! Let us off as quick as you can. Some of us have not yet breakfasted, and it's upwards of an hour since I had a smoke.' "

Cox thought that the coastal Indians were "thoroughbred hypocrites and liars." But he appreciated the dignity of an Indian chief whom that headstrong Nor'wester, Finan McDonald, tried to taunt into fighting a duel. "Come on, you cheating rascal!" jeered McDonald. "Will you fight with pistols?"

"The foaming mouth and violent gesticulation of my Nor'wester companion presented a striking contrast to the calm and immutable features of the chieftain," Cox wrote. "The Indian's inflexible countenance was for a moment disturbed by something like a smile when he told his opponent, 'No one but a fool of a white man would stand before a gun to be shot at.' When we explained to him afterwards this was the *civilized* mode of deciding gentlemanly quarrels, the Indian manifested the utmost incredulity. He shook his head and said, 'I see plainly there are fools everywhere!' "

Cox was revolted by the Chinook Indian men, with their unwashed bodies smeared with whale oil, their noses and ears split and strung with chokers of beads. "Then the women – O ye gods! With the same auricular, olfactory, and craniological peculiarities, they exhibited loose hanging breasts, short dirty teeth, skin saturated with blubber, bandy legs, and a waddling gait in their petticoat quilt."

He censored the "shameless profligacy" of the Chinook mothers for peddling their daughters as prostitutes, and the "barbarous incrustation" of the maidens who poured a cosmetic of salmon oil over their hair. "While in this oleoginous state they are quite unapproachable near a fire," Cox said, "and even the *voyageur*, whose sense of smell is not over-refined, cannot bring his nasal organ into a warm apartment with one of those bedizened beauties."

But, like Ross, he found the girls of Spokane attractive, and the maidens of the Walla Walla, Kootenay and Tête Platte tribes, he said, made devoted wives for the palefaces. A Nor'wester, taking a comely 16-year-old for his squaw, would put her in the hands of a professional "scourer," who would cleanse off her Indian grease and corset the bride in an ungainly hoop-skirt. It was sometimes pathetic, he said, to see these slim, free-striding Venuses, stripped of their gay togas and chic feather headdresses, walking pigeon-toed in a drab Mother Hubbard like self-conscious little girls told by their parents to dress up and show off at an adult party. "They are not allowed to sit at the same table with their respective lords," Cox noted. "For they still continue the savage fashion of squatting on the ground at their meals at which their fingers supply the place of a fork."

The third of these literary mountaineers, and the last to come west, was George Frederick Ruxton, a romantic English poet-explorer. He arrived just in time to record the life of the Yankee and French-Canadian "free men" trapping independently out of St. Louis and Fort William, Colorado.

The only existing portrait of him is a miniature painted on ivory. It reveals a callow youth with a wispy

At the annual Rendezvous of the Mountain Men, beaver skins bought an Indian girl, or jugs of "Taos lightning."

goatee, long carrot-coloured curls, and soft, dark-lashed eyes, his five-foot-ten frame languid in a green-and-plum plaid waistcoat.

The picture does not convey the exuberant spirit of George Ruxton, who crammed a half-dozen careers into 27 years. His father was a wealthy English army surgeon, who had sent him to the Royal Military Academy at Sandhurst. After two years he was expelled.

"Everything quiet or commonplace I detested," he explained. "My spirit chafed within me to see the world and participate in scenes of novelty and danger."

At 15 he ran off to a civil war in Spain and was awarded Queen Isabella's Cross of San Fernando, with the title of Knight, for his bravery. At 19 he was a lieutenant with the Royal Irish Fusiliers. At 23 he was with a camel caravan in the Morocco desert trying to

Canada, but he soon sold his lieutenant's commission because, as he wrote to his brother in Halifax, "The gun has ever been my delight, and my *ardor venandi* has been worked up to the highest pitch by reading the adventures of Natty Bumppo and his friends, the Mohicans, in the admirable romances of Fenimore Cooper. I had always longed to pull a trigger in the woods of America." With a Chippewa Indian named Peshwego as a guide, Ruxton wrote delightful accounts of hunting for game in the unexplored wilds of Ontario near Lake St. Clair, "washing down my snack of *pemmican* with copious draughts of excellent Quebec beer," and sleeping on pine needles wrapped in a blanket "as though I were a mummy."

The taste of the wilderness whetted his appetite for the Far West. Soon he was setting out from Vera Cruz, Mexico, on a roan stallion, Panchito, with a *mulada* of four packmules, on a lonely trip of 3,000 miles through the New Mexico and Colorado Rockies, eating and sleeping with the wintering "free trappers."

They would sit cross-legged around the fire, occasionally taking a "chaw from a plug," or "puffin' away at the cheerin' weed," or swigging from a jug of raw whisky "to gratify my dry," or gnawing at a "buffler hump rib," and trying to outdo each other at yarning. They would listen with Indian gravity to fantastic whoppers, interrupting only to give vent to a corroborative, "Wagh! This child remembers that fix," or, "He one damn good montaigne Man, *Enfant de Gârce*! I see him tickle the fleece of bout hondred brown skins, pe gar, before Blackfeet rub him out, so he gone under *mort*!"

It was magnificent folklore: how Black Moses Harris claimed to have seen in the Black Hills "peetrified trees still a-growin', with peetrified birds on 'em a-singin' peetrified songs."

How Old Bill "Lone Elk" Williams tamed a troupe of Rocky Mountain goats to leap 30 feet down the crags, land on their horns, and give him milk. How Old Hugh Glass – "him with jaws like a nutcracker and carcass wrinkled tough as the *parflêche* soles of his moccasins" – was left for dead after the "Injuns gathered around him like flies on a sugar barrel" and pierced his hide "as full of arrows as a porkypine," and after "Old Ephraim, the grizzly b'ar, ripped the flesh from his bones slick as a cook peels an onion;" and danged if that "hard case Glass" didn't turn up in camp 90 miles away, yelling, "Hurroo, boys! Thought I was gone under, did you? This old hoss ain't made wolf meat yet by a damn site! Wagh!"

The free trappers of the Yankee fur companies bragged of "wiping out" swarms of Blackfeet or "Bug's

find the source of the Zambezi River for the Royal Geographical Society. And, the next year, he contributed a paper to the Ethnological Society of London on the bushmen who existed on locusts and flamingoes in the Karoo desert of South Africa.

Ruxton's reputation as an explorer who wrote from the saddle was capped in North America. The young fusilier was sent to Amherstburg barracks in Upper

Boys" without raising a sweat. Like knights in buckskin, they tied butcher knives to their hickory rifle-wiping sticks as lances and charged the enemy, sometimes dictating oral wills to each other as they rode. They "counted coup" on the Blackfeet whose "fleece had been tickled," hanging their scalps on their rifles. And when a trapper "went under" in an Indian raid, his comrades buried him with his scalp trophies strung around his chest.

Ruxton looked with understanding on the polygamy of the trappers. Owning a harem of squaws had its advantages for a Mountain Man. For 20 years a French-Canadian trapper, Michael Laframboise, was able to travel freely in the most perilous parts of the Oregon country because he had a wife in almost every tribe he was likely to run across. But Ruxton was distressed when a French-Canadian half-breed named La Forey ate his Digger Indian squaw, rationalizing it as, "Meat's meat."

A free trapper had no scruples about abandoning his woman for a prettier face. Nor did he hesitate to "lodge-pole" (beat her) when he wearied of her gabble or her jokes, which could be earthy enough to curl a missionary's hair. But, Ruxton observed, "When the mountaineer does suffer his redskinned wife to gain the upper hand in the domestic economy of the lodge, his better half becomes the veriest termagant that ever henpecked an unfortunate husband."

He records the answer of a trapper named Killbuck when asked by a puzzled tenderfoot how to understand the workings of the female mind. Killbuck sprayed out some tobacco juice and drawled, "At killing meat when meat's a-running, I'll shine in the biggest kind of crowd. But though I'm hell for 'sign,' a woman's breast is the hardest kind of rock to me, and leaves no trail that I can see of."

No squaw man himself, Ruxton had an eye for a girl whether she was a Spokane Indian *jeune fille*, a beautifully limbed Tête Platte, or one of those "houris of paradise with the languishing eye," a Mexican Indian half-breed. He tells of coming across "a bevy of women and girls, 'in the garb of Eve,' tumbling and splashing in the water, enjoying themselves like ducks in a puddle. They were in no degree disconcerted by our gaze, but laughed and joked in perfect innocence, unconscious of perpetrating an impropriety."

Ruxton was at his most graphic when describing that singular institution known as a "Rendezvous." Held annually in the Idaho mountain valley known as "Pierre's Hole," it was a combination of open-air trade fair and saturnalia. Indians and white free trappers would ride whooping into the sagebrush flats to sell

In the days when the Oregon country was jointly occupied by Canadians and Americans, the furs belonged to the man who got there first. Above, Kit Carson, U.S. Mountain Man.

their pelts to rival tents of the American and Canadian fur companies. It was two weeks of jamboree, of feats of horse-racing, revolver-shooting, fisticuffing, bragging, making love *al fresco* with Indian belles, and making whoopee with jugs of "Taos lightning." Both Indians and white trappers often squandered their year's work on gambling. The redskins played the game of "hand" – the opponents betting on which hand clenched a cherry stone. The trappers crouched around buffalo robes to play cards – seven up, poker and euchre. Beaver skins were the common currency, and when the gamblers' furs were gone, their horses, hunting packs, rifles, squaws, even their pants were staked.

"There goes hoss and beaver!" was the mountain expression for a calamitous loss. "And sooner or later 'hoss and beaver' find their way into the insatiable pockets of the company traders," Ruxton wrote. "An old trapper, a French Canadian, assured me that he had received $15,000 for beaver during a sojourn of twenty years in the mountains. Every year he resolved in his mind to return to Canada, and, with this object, always converted his fur into cash. But a fortnight at the Rendezvous always cleaned him out, and, at the end of twenty years, he had not even credit sufficient to buy a pound of powder."

While they were still "flush," trappers laid bets on tests of skill. Ruxton saw two French Canadians compete to see who could swallow most yards of *boudins* – buffalo intestines that when lightly browned over the embers of a fire were considered succulent French "puddings." "The two Canadians commenced at either end of the snake-like coil," he wrote. "As yard after yard slid glibly down their throats, and the serpent between them was dwindling from an anaconda to a moderate-sized rattlesnake, it became a great point with each feaster to hurry his operation . . . at the same time each exhorted the other to feed fair. But every now and then, one would suddenly jerk back his head. Thus he would draw out several yards of greasy *boudin* from his neighbour's mouth and stomach, and greedily snap it up himself."

Bets were made on the best story-teller and the best "fandango" dancer. A guitar would strike up *Meet Me by Moonlight Alone*, or a jew's harp would twang *Buffalo Gals*, and the "bear-like mountaineers" would stamp around the campfire inserting into their leaps the "dyspeptic 'scalp dance' jumps of the Terpsichorean Indians." One of the dancers was Kit Carson, small but "slenderly limbed, with muscles of wire, and an incarnate devil in Indian fight." Ruxton told how Carson led a bunch of trappers from a Rendezvous to snatch a Mexican-Indian bride for young Dick Wooton. The "houri of paradise" was Dolores, a dusky *muchachita* whose coquettish fan, cashmere shawl and red petticoat did not conceal her bosomy charms. Her parents had forbidden her to marry Wooton, so Carson and his comrades held them back with their rifles. "Ho, Dick!" Carson hollered. "That's the gal and thar's the mountains." Dick whirled the senorita onto the saddle in front of him, dug spurs into his horse, and galloped off to celebrate their "hymeneal enjoyment" at the mountain Rendezvous.

The most incredible bet at a Rendezvous was made by a Sioux and a Crow Indian. When the Sioux lost all his belongings in a game of "hand," he bet his scalp. Luck was against him. "Without a murmur," Ruxton wrote, "the Sioux bent his head and the Crow sliced the top of his head off.

"The next day they sat down to play again. This time fortune was with the Sioux. The Crow, in his turn, was stripped to his skin and the Sioux lifted his topknot. Then the Crow staked all he had left: his life against the Sioux's winnings. Again the Crow lost. Quite casually, he thrust out his chest and the Sioux plunged in his knife. The Sioux to this day wears suspended from his ears his own and his enemy's scalp."

It was neither scalping nor rot-gut whisky nor prostitution that ruined the Indians of the Far West; it was a white man's disease, spread by infected supplies poled up the Missouri River. The Indians called it *omikewin* – meaning a scab erupting into a rash. It shrivelled the skin and turned the face blue, and made a brave lurch from his horse and fall vomiting beside the trail, while his family prayed to the *Manitou* or plunged into an icy mountain stream in a vain attempt to cool their fever. It wiped out entire tribes and left the gulches reeking with the sour smell of death. Ruxton, Cox and Ross called it smallpox, or Asiatic cholera, or scurvy, or black leg – meaning it was a mysterious "plaguey disorder," that called for fumigation with sulphur.

The plague had preceded Alexander Ross across the "Shining Mountains" as he left with his Okanagan Indian squaw and his three half-breed "bantlings" for his job as sheriff and schoolmaster for the Hudson's Bay Company in the Red River Colony. On the Canadian plains, he wrote that some Hudson's Bay factors were "cut to the heart" by the sufferings of the Indians, and nursed their stricken children inside the forts. Others insisted that the Indian free trappers pay their debts to the Bay even in death, and they stripped the corpses of even infected beaver robes.

The Nor'westers exploited the Indians' fear of the scourge. Before Rossenberg Cox left Fort Astoria for Montreal and Dublin – where he married an Irish girl named Hannah Cumming – he told how the Nor'wester *bourgeois*, Duncan McDougall, assembled the Indians before the fort, showed them a small bottle, and said it was filled with the dread disease of smallpox. If the Indians caused any trouble, McDougall threatened, he would uncork the bottle, and its black magic would "run like fire among your people." The Indians were so horror-stricken, Cox said, that forever after they called McDougall "Great Smallpox Chief."

Ruxton left the mountains briefly to visit his brother, Augustus, in Halifax, and write his *Life in The Far West* for *Blackwood's Magazine*. Then he left again for the frontier "to pack my 'possibles' on a mule, and mounting a buffalo horse (Panchito, if he is still alive), I shall strike the Santa Fé trail . . . always supposing my hair is not lifted by Comanches or Pawnee on the scalping route." The trail took him only as far as the jumping-off point of St. Louis. There, at 27, the most gentlemanly of the Mountain Men caught smallpox, and died in the arms of a nun of the Sisters of Charity.

VIII

Women of the West

THE first child born to a Selkirk settler came into the world aboard the *Robert Taylor*, while the squalls and sleet of Hudson Bay slashed relentlessly at the colonist ship. The mother, Mrs. Alec McLean, never forgot those hours of August 24, 1812, when she was seized with her pains. She lay in a wooden bunk in the hold, near the big bin of oatmeal used as food by the Canadian Pilgrim Fathers. Sacks of wheat for the Manitoba colony tossed around near her feet. Twenty-one frightened, noisy Spanish merino sheep added to the confusion.

The 71 settlers had been on the high seas for two months. They had been recruited in Scotland and Ireland to farm the Red River Colony, launched by Thomas Douglas, Fifth Earl of Selkirk. As the ship lurched, the 15 children and five "young ladies, ripe for marriage" among the settlers clung together, weeping. The young men tried to keep up their courage by squabbling. Irish "Paddies" fought bare-knuckle with the Scottish youths. The whiskered Presbyterian elders read aloud from an Old Testament, with the words "Lord, teach me to pray" stitched into a brown silk ribbon.

Mrs. McLean, gasping and sweating in the sour-smelling hold, was comforted by the Scottish housewives. Wearing dark shawls and starched white, high-crowned bonnets known as Scotch mutches, tied under their chins with plain black kerchiefs, they clucked about her like hens. With the wisdom of the Hebrides peasant, they lashed a homemade crossbar across the mother's chest, whittled handholds in the bar, and told her to grasp it with both hands and strain against it, and press her bare feet hard, "like a brave lassie," against the end of the wooden bunk. After 20 hours' labour, a daughter was born – one of the first white native-born children in the Canadian West.

When the ship reached the Hudson's Bay Company's York Factory, the colonists celebrated their first wedding in *le pays sauvage*. To mollify the Irish, the couple, though both Presbyterian Scots, had their marriage performed by the Irish Catholic priest, Father Charles Bourke. The "kirking" was highly informal. Father Bourke had been brought over a year earlier by Lord Selkirk's advance contingent of bachelors, but was being sent back to Ireland because he was often tipsy. When in his cups, the Scottish phrase went, he "danced about like a cock on red hot cinders." Nevertheless, the priest sobered up enough to produce a wedding ring carved out of an English shilling. At the wedding, the Presbyterians insisted on standing to pray; sitting down to sing; and sternly resisted any kind of organ music as a "kist o' whustles." The bridegroom, a Lowland Scot named James Fraser, could not speak the Gaelic tongue of his bride, a Highlander. Years later, a granddaughter remembered asking this first Selkirk bride teasingly, "When you and grandfather did not understand each other's language, how did you know what he meant when he told you he loved you and wanted you to be his wife?" The elder smiled and replied, "Wait until your time comes, my dear, and you will know."

There were few smiles, however, as the contingent pilgrims set out from York Factory to paddle the 700 miles southward to the forks of the Red and Assiniboine Rivers. The sheep leapt out of the eleven flat-bottomed York boats and the children wailed at the weird night serenades of this empty land – the howl of a timber wolf, the hoot of a horned owl, the scream of a loon. Mothers tightened their shawls over their shoulders at the spectacle of the dancing purples, greens and violets of the Northern Lights, crackling and shimmering by the wash of a yellow moon. Husbands gripped their muskets when they encountered Indians, bizarre with goose quills pierced through their nostrils and leggings fringed with human scalp hair.

The kilted Scots noted that the Crees and Saulteaux had painted buffalo skins wrapped over their shoulders, "just like Highland plaid." The equally startled Indians stared at the paleface girls, with their Scotch mutches, and whispered, "Squaws with white caps have come."

In late October the string of boats reached the fork of the Red River and pulled up before the cluster of oak and maple shacks, grandly named "Colony Gardens." A piper in the lead canoe skirled a heartfelt *Bonny Dundee* and the settlers stepped out of the boats to a prayer from the Hundredth Psalm. They were greeted with a salute from swivel guns and handed a nip of rum, a ceremony arranged by Governor Miles Macdonell, a United Empire Loyalist with a love for spit and polish. Married couples were each given a 100-acre farm and an Indian horse, and their children soon set to work planting potatoes and Indian corn. Single girls were welcomed with a barrage of marriage proposals.

"The young men and maids were not altogether idle in the matrimonial affairs," Governor Macdonell wrote in a light-hearted mood to Lord Selkirk in London. "Many could hardly wait for your Captain to join them in that humble embrace."

Mrs. Ann Adams remembered the marriage rush. "We had not been at Point Douglas for more than 24 hours before men flocked in, each eager to get a wife," she later wrote. "On finding a maiden that suited their fancy, they would open negotiations at once, either with her or her parents, and would not take any refusal. An eager settler seized a woman by the hand, saying 'I want to marry you.' But he was much discomposed when she told him, 'I already have a husband.' My sister, however, was one who consented to share the lot of a Red River farmer."

A descendant later asked another woman settler, "Weren't you afraid to marry in such a fashion a man whom you'd never seen before?"

"Oh, no," replied the colonist's bride. "I just took a good look at him out of the corner of my eye as we stood to be 'kirked,' and I said to myself, 'I guess he'll do.' And time proved that he 'did' very well."

Inevitably, in the near-wilderness, there was disappointment and despair. A woman wrote after her first glimpse of the Red River Colony: "I leaned my elbows on the wooden table in the dirt hut, buried my face in my hands, and sobbed aloud, 'My God, help me to cleave to thee.' I could not help it. I felt so lonely, so homesick, so isolated."

The women brightened up the bachelors' hewn-log shacks with what they called their "feminine etceteras" – a bit of muslin hung here, a buffalo robe curtain there. Except for an embroidered black kerchief to wrap around one's Bible, few retained any of the Old Country comforts. When Kate McPherson of Kildonan lay dying, she bequeathed her daughter her dearest possession – her white cotton wedding cap with goffered frills – her only concession to a woman's vanity in the Red River Colony.

Young Donald Cameron wanted to marry a girl who brandished a parasol but his father, Hugh Cameron, a Presbyterian elder, shook his head austerely and said: "Aye, lad, she's bonny to look at, but no wife for you when she'll be too proud to let God's sun shine on her head."

The women had to be extraordinarily industrious to clothe their large families from head to toe in home-knit. They knitted when they rose at dawn, while waiting for the fire to start and the kettle to boil and the pre-breakfast prayers to be said. They knitted while they walked to the fields to help children pitch hay and cut the grain with scythes and sickles, and if they dropped their ball of wool, as Mrs. Duncan McCrea once did, they ran a mile to retrieve it. And they knitted at night, after the children had recited their Bible lessons, by the lamplight of a rag dipped in a dish of buffalo fat.

They had to be ingenious to make the wilderness ways their own. They boiled buffalo grease for soap and made starch from potatoes. They adopted the Indians' savoury stew, known as *rubaboo*, sweetening it with wild saskatoon berries. They pounded *pemmican*, flavouring it with sturgeon caviar and the crumbs from Scottish bannock baked each morning. The Scottish "quern" was used by the women for grinding wheat. It consisted of two round stones, the upper turned by hand upon the fixed lower stone. The Presbyterians solemnly informed the Irish Catholics that Jesus had the Scotch "quern" in mind when, as the Bible chronicles: "Two women shall be grinding at the mill: the one shall be taken and the other left." The Irish, in turn, teased the Scots for being so rigorously devout.

Life was not all hard work at Red River Colony. On Christmas Day, Governor Macdonell reported to Lord Selkirk that his colonists had played "hurl," meaning hockey, against a rival team of fur traders from the various forts, on the frozen Red River. Another entry reads: "Gave a dance to the Bag Pipe this evening to the people – very pleasant party. The gentlemen, men and women enjoyed themselves and encroached on the Sabbath."

Of course, the Presbyterian elders railed that dancing on the Sabbath was a damnable sin. For gyrating her ankles too merrily, a girl was condemned as "Lot's wife"; there were tirades against the *Métis* for the "monomaniac fiddle shrieks of their trembling strings, as if a devil was at the bow." But as one Irish colonist put it, "They have fired a few pepper corns from the pulpit, but it is sparrow shot against the bastion. Papas may remonstrate, and parsons may dispense brimstone by the wholesale, but the girls will dance." The mocca-

White apron and starched bonnet in the wilderness? Early artists had a romantic conception of a pioneer's life.

sined feet of the belles of the colony thumped to the beat of the Red River jig; and even the painted Indians were invited to lift their voices in a "Ho! Ho! Ho!" chorus as the fiddle scraped and the bagpipe wheezed the melody of *Here's a Health to All Good Lassies*.

In winter, some of the women found pleasure feeding the snow chickadees, redpolls and juncoes that fluttered around their skirts. In summer, they walked barefoot through the cool grass by the Red River, watching for the *voyageurs* from Lake Winnipeg, whose singing echoed around the river bend long before they were actually seen. Caroline Pruden, one of the most beautiful girls at Red River, used to walk out on the river bank and hold up her apron to the breeze and say, "They must be sailing on the lake today."

In time a Red River dialect sprang up in the colony, a blend of Irish, Scottish, *voyageur* French, and pidgin Indian. The charm of the dialect is preserved in this story told about two children by an Irish settler, Willie Brass: "John Jems Corrigal and Willie Garge Liklater was out sooting in the marse, and the canoe went *apech-e-quanee*. The watter was sallow, whatever, but Willie Garge kept bobbing up and down, calling 'Lard, save me.' Well, John Jems was on topside the canoe, and he souted to Willies, and he sayed, 'Never mind the Lard just now, Willie – grab fer the willas!' "

Despite dire predictions, the Indians at Colony Gardens did not lift their tomahawks against the women settlers. The Crees and Assiniboines were friendly and

the Saulteaux tribal chief, "Peacemaker" Peguis – also known as "Pigwise" because his nose was bitten off by a Sioux – was a rock of support to Governor Macdonell; he was, in fact, more steadfast than either the Hudson's Bay or Nor'wester fur traders. But there was a threat from the scalping knives of the Sioux Indians. When on the warpath, the Sioux rode northward from the Pembina plains of present Minnesota to steal horses and attack settlers who ventured outside the colony. John Pritchard, hunting for buffalo on the Pembina plains, found himself chased by the Sioux and, in desperation, ran to the lodge of a Sioux squaw. Pritchard once had done the woman a kindness and he now threw himself upon her mercy.

"I will hide you," she said.

"But where?" asked Pritchard. ". . . in a skin tent, on the flat prairie?"

"I will sit on you," she said.

Pritchard was a very small man, and she was a very fat squaw. When he burst in upon her, she had been weaving rush mats. She pushed Pritchard under her skirts, resumed her seat on her pile of mats, and placidly squatted on him as she continued her work. She sat on him all day, smoking her pipe, ignoring the Sioux braves running in and out of her tent in their search for the fugitive. At nightfall, the somewhat flattened Pritchard blessed the squaw as he escaped under cover of darkness to the colony.

In spite of the condescension showed by some palefaces, the Indian women were their mentors in the wilderness. They showed the whites how to survive on soup made from white moss clinging on rocks and wild rice growing in the marshes, taught them to brew *tea muskeg* from white azalea flowers, and how to smoke the native mixture of tobacco leaves and bark known as *kinnikinnick.*

The cultural gap between white and redman was bridged best by the traders and settlers who became "squaw men." In exchange for a keg of rum, they took an Indian's daughter as a bedmate, "according to the customs of the country." Sir George Simpson, Governor of the Hudson's Bay Company (known to keep at least two Indian "winter wives") introduced the new Bay policy with a grandiloquent phrase: "Since connubial alliances are the best security we can have of the good-will of Natives, I have therefore recommended the Gentlemen to form connections with the principal Families immediately upon their arrival . . . This is no difficult matter, as the offer of their Wives & daughters is the first token of their Friendship & hospitality."

Yet even in the bedroom the social caste system prevailed, and an Indian bride was frequently regarded as a slave concubine. She was often deserted when her white lover moved on to another fur-trading post, and she was certainly forgotten if he married by bell, book and candle back in Montreal. Rarely did a paleface bother to record in his diary the name of his Indian squaw. It was usually "the little rib," "the little partner," or just "she."

"Her ladyship, my squaw" – as the Nor'wester, Alexander Henry the Younger, called his consort – had to conform to some strange customs. She was sometimes taught to dance to a Scottish piper's skirl of *McLeod's Reel*, keeping her moccasined feet together, and jigging straight up and down in time with her hobnail-booted white master. So enamoured was one Nor'wester that, in imitation of the polygamous Indians, he maintained a harem of squaws at the trading post. Nor'wester Alexander Ross wrote of a comely Okanagan maiden: "Her presence brightens the gloom of the solitary post and her smiles add a new charm to the wilderness."

When a "country wife" died, a fur trader sometimes realized how terribly he missed her companionship. Nicol Finlayson, mourning the death of "my little dearie" at Fort Alexander, expressed it poignantly: "I have not got over the shock of my severe bereavement. My hearth is desolate. I have not even a domestic animal to caress me when I enter my house from a journey . . . I feel greatly the loss of her prattle, as it beguiled me for many a solitary hour."

Some liaisons between white men and Indian princesses were uncommonly tender. The romance between Nor'wester Peter Skene Ogden and one of the "nymphs of Spokane" became legendary. She was the daughter of Chief How-How, and was "a damsel both lovely and fair, the flower of her tribe; her ochre cheeks were delicate, her features incomparable." Ogden named her Princess Julia, and bought her for 50 horses, a dowry fixed by the Princess herself. Ogden sent one horse after another to Chief How-How's lodge, and the daughter increased the price each time. After the fiftieth pony was sent, Julia came riding it back, dressed in white doe skin, with hawks' bells tinkling in her black hair.

Ogden remained faithful to Julia and during their long lives she gave him eight children. She called him "M'sieu Pete," and he affectionately spoke of her in his letters as "the Old Lady." Once, in March, she swam the Snake River to capture a goose for a sick child and trappers saw her return with a necklace of icicles strung where she had held her head above water. On another occasion, Yankee trapper Joe Meek stole her packhorse loaded with beaver pelts, as well as Julia's saddle horse, not realizing her baby was slung in a sack from the saddle. Julia entered the Yankee camp to retrieve her horses and child, quelling with a contemptuous gaze the Americans who threatened to shoot her.

The Indian brides served as translators. The *wawa* ("talk") that the *klootchman* ("wife") taught her white *tillicum* ("friend") enabled the traders to communicate more easily with the Indians. At the height of its popularity in the 1840s, this pidgin-English-Indian tongue consisted of more than 600 words. The palefaces called it "Chinook jargon," since it spread widely through intermarriage and trade with the Chinook tribe on the Pacific Coast. An Indian girl could convey delightful Chinook images to her paleface suitor. If he made her laugh, he was a *heehee tumtum* – a "merry heart." If he protected her, he was a *skookum tumtum* – a "brave heart." The musical word, *tumtum*, came from the sound of his beating heart. Similarly, his clock was a *ticktick*, a cat was a *pusspuss*, a crow a *kahkah*.

The inevitable half-breed children were nicknamed "bits of brown" by Sir George Simpson, of the H.B.C. He sired a good number himself in his love affairs around the Indian country. "Bois-brûlés" was the name the *Métis* preferred. It designated, in French, the scorched-wood colour of the skin. Whatever they were called, the lives of these mixed-blood children were often unhappy. They had to fit into the rigid caste system of the fur-trading companies. The white men – known as "wintering partners" – ruled supreme; the half-breeds handled the boats; the Indians trapped and did menial tasks. At the Nor'wester post dining tables, a rigid tea etiquette was observed. The white gentry sat at the head of the table, drank from a porcelain teapot which brewed the finest grade of China leaf, and genteelly sucked the "refined loaf of sugar." The half-breeds sat below the salt, drank second-grade China tea, sweetened with "common crushed sugar." The Indians seated at the end were lucky to have inferior dregs of tea and inferior brown sugar.

The half-breed's role in this backwoods society was often suspect and shadowy. "They are indolent, thoughtless and improvident," said Nor'wester Alexander Ross of them. "They alternately associate with the whites and the Indians, and thus become fatally enlightened. They form a composition of all the bad qualities of both . . . A sort of outcast from society."

A few of the half-breed children, however, overcame their handicaps. Most famous of all were the eldest son and eldest daughter of Nor'wester Bill Conolly. When he was 18, this Irish-Canadian trader fell in love with the daughter of a Cree chief at Rat River in the Athabasca country. The Indian princess, whom he took as a bride "according to the customs of the country," became known as Susanne *Pas-de-nom* – "Susanne No Name." Their oldest son was John, and their oldest daughter, Amelia. After 30 years of amassing wealth in the fur trade, Conolly left his children behind, but took his Indian wife with him when he retired to Montreal. There, Conolly fell in love again, this time with his cousin, Julia Woolrich, daughter of a well-to-do Montreal merchant. Though his Indian wife was living in the same city, Bill Conolly married his Julia. He obtained a dispensation from the Roman Catholic Bishop of Montreal, and sent "Susanne No Name" back to the Indian country to be placed in a convent where he paid for her support.

Conolly died in 1849, leaving his fortune to Julia. She quietly continued paying "alimony" to her late husband's Indian wife, until "Susanne No Name" died 13 years later. Then the oldest half-breed son, John Conolly – angry at being robbed of what he considered his mother's rightful share of the estate – raised a public scandal, by suing to have his father's will upset. At the trial in Montreal, traders testified frankly about their own amorous adventures in the West; they bared Indian skeletons that had been hiding in the family closets of some of the most renowned Nor'westers. The defendants argued that an Indian marriage was not, even among the polygamous Indians, a binding ceremony. Therefore, John Conolly should be laughed out of court. Justice Monk thought otherwise. The marriage ritual in

the Indian wilderness between Bill Conolly and "Susanne No Name," no matter how unorthodox, was, he found, as legally sound as a wedding by church bell. Consequently, John Conolly and the other half-breed children were entitled to one-twelfth of the Nor'wester's fortune.

Amelia, the oldest half-breed daughter of Bill Conolly, did not participate in the public furore. When her father was chief factor at Fort St. James, on Stuart Lake in British Columbia, she was described as "modest as a wood violet," and because of her fair skin, her pale auburn hair, and her blue eyes, she was called "Snowbird." There, a young Scottish-Creole trader, James Douglas, his skin darker than most Indians, fell in love with her. At 16, Amelia was married to Douglas – just as her father, Bill Conolly, and her mother, "Susanne No Name," had been – "according to the customs of the country."

Soon afterwards, young "Snowbird" showed she was no shrinking violet when her husband's safety was endangered. The fur traders had executed a Carrier Indian named Tzill-na-o-lay for murdering two of the white clerks at Fort St. James. In retribution, Chief Quaw of the Carriers seized the fort, James Douglas was overpowered, and forced down with his back on a table-top. Amelia was horrified to see a warrior holding a poniard at her husband's throat. The brave was shouting to Chief Quaw, "Shall I strike?" Quaw hesitated. Amelia, knowing that the Carriers regarded gifts thrown at them as ceremonial reparation, hurled every trading trinket and gimcrack that she could lay her hands on at the Indians. Quaw, satisfied that his tribe's face had been saved, retreated.

Amelia eventually bore 13 children to Douglas. The only thing that marred her marriage was the snubs she endured when her husband switched to the Hudson's Bay Company post at Fort Vancouver. The Honourable Company's official Church of England chaplain, Rev. Herbert Beaver, sneered at the Bay's paleface traders. He said they were "living in adultery" with "kept mistresses." The missionary's wife, Jane, was "uppish" to Amelia. The Reverend Beaver was once thrashed with his own walking-stick for being so persnickety, but Douglas succumbed and allowed the missionary to perform "civilized" marriage rites on himself and Amelia in 1837. Amelia won sweet revenge over the paleface snobs a quarter of a century later. Her husband was appointed Governor of the Crown colony of Vancouver Island and British Columbia, and was knighted by Queen Victoria. "Snowbird," the half-breed Cree squaw, born in the Rat River wilderness, was now ranked the First Lady of the Canadian West.

THE FUR TRADERS

Fur was the wealth of the West, and to win a share traders feuded and
finagled, racing down the rivers, over mountain paths, and
along woodland trails . . . and in the process, opened up a continent.

"Presents to Indians," by A. J. Miller, a romanticist who in 1837 travelled the domain of the Mountain Men.

They Rode
the Trails
with
Rifles Ready

In the early years of the fur trade, the pelts came easily. After King Charles II granted the Hudson's Bay Company its charter in 1670, the traders simply built their forts – five in all in the first 17 years – on the mouths of rivers emptying into Hudson Bay, and waited for the Indians to come to barter. But soon Montreal interests began to challenge the H.B.C. reign over the fur empire. In 1779 the North West Company was founded, and slowly it began to thrust northwestward to the Athabasca country, up to the Arctic Ocean, and to the Pacific Coast. The Nor'westers in turn found themselves faced with rivals – the XY Company, and in the Oregon country, John Jacob Astor's Pacific Fur Company. To the Far West came the rough and ready Mountain Men, free trappers some of them, owing their allegiance to no company. The traders now hustled for the furs, travelling the continental trails by horse, sometimes with their squaws tagging behind to serve as interpreters, typified by the trader on this page. The Nor'westers absorbed the XY Company, and took over the American-owned Fort Astoria on the mouth of the Columbia, but the Hudson's Bay Company fought back. The frontier became a place of feuds and duels. In 1816, a band of Métis hired by the Nor'westers killed 22 Red River settlers, who were under the protection of the H.B.C. But the Nor'westers were waging a losing war. Facing bankruptcy because of the cost of maintaining their long line of communications, and showing poor profits because of the high prices they paid for furs, in 1821 they were bought out by the H.B.C., the company they had fought so long.

Trappers of the Highlands

Mountain Men set their beaver traps under the surface of the streams. They were baited with castoreum, an extract from beaver musk glands.

Some Indians looked upon white trappers as poachers. A. J. Miller recorded these Mountain Men fleeing from Blackfeet.

Joe Meek, the Mountain Man

It was praise, indeed, when Meek's Indian wife said:"No man can fight like Joe;no man can run like Joe; no man like Joe."

The Stern Face of the Fur Trade

The fur kings came from many clans, tough and unyielding Scots with grim-set jaws and forbidding glances. This was John McLoughlin, who helped the Hudson's Bay Company develop the Oregon country.

A Breed of Iron Men

Simon McTavish: one of the first Nor'wester partners.

John Jacob Astor: founder of the American Fur Company.

Donald McKenzie: he became governor of Assiniboia, 1825.

Peter Skene Ogden: an expert at terrorizing the H.B.C.

Alexander Ross: he helped found Fort Astoria in 1811.

William McGillivray: Fort William was named after him.

Archibald Norman McLeod: a proprietor at Fort Dauphin.

Colin Robertson: chief H.B.C. officer at Assiniboia, 1818.

John Clarke: he built Fort Wedderburn for the H.B.C.

The Ladies They Married

John Clarke had two wives . . . but, unlike many fur traders, not at the same time. He married a half-breed, Sapphira Spence, but when she died he wooed and won Marian Tranclar (above), in 1821. They had four sons and four daughters.

Alexander Ross took an Okanagan Indian for his wife (above), and they had four children. He observed that half-breed offspring alternately tried to belong to the white and Indian societies, only to become outcasts of both.

The Women They Bought

This touching scene was painted by Alfred Jacob Miller, to depict how trappers took Indian maidens as brides. The Indian behind the girl was her father. He asked, and received, $600 in goods for his daughter.

Challenge of the Portage

One of the greatest hardships to the voyageurs, *following the great rivers to the interior fur country, was the constant need to portage. Nicholas Garry, deputy chief of the Hudson's Bay Company, in the 1820s left this account of how the portage was done: "The manner of carrying the Canoe:— She is first turned over. Four men then go into the water, two at each End, raise the Canoe and then two more place themselves about midships of the Gunwhale on the opposite side. The weight of our Canoe was about 6 cwt. The Goods are carried on the Shoulders of the men and in this manner; each Canoe Man is provided with a leather Sling broad in the middle: the Ends he fastens to a Package, this is placed on his shoulders, the broad part of the Sling placed across his Forehead. On this Package a second is placed and in this manner they generally carry two Packages of 90 lbs. each and sometimes a third." At the left, a party of canoemen as they struggled around Hoar Frost River.*

The voyageurs *seldom had tents. When it rained, an overturned canoe would provide them with a roof over their heads.*

Uniquely Canadian was the York boat, brainchild of the Hudson's Bay Company. This one ascended the Mackenzie River, 1885.

Silently the paddles dipped, and the traders' canoes slipped through the fog that clung to the cold waters of Lake Superior. The painting was done in 1869 by Frances Ann Hopkins. Half a century earlier, this largest freshwater lake in the world was the great stronghold of the Nor'westers and it was at Fort William that the wintering partners met each summer to trade their furs for goods.

Reign of the 'Little Emperor'

The fang-and-claw fight for the furs ended in 1821 with the union of the Nor'westers and the Hudson's Bay Company. To preserve the peace, they needed a Governor-in-Chief to administrate Rupert's land. George Simpson won the crown.

With an iron hand, for forty years the "Little Emperor" ruled a domain that stretched across one quarter of all North America. Under the resolute Simpson, the Hudson's Bay Company fur-trading empire flourished; he appeased old rivals, increased the personnel, inspected forts big and small, and encouraged geographic explorations. In 1841 he was created Knight of the Bath, and the illegitimate son of a Scot became Sir George.

Simpson kept a notebook, in which he condemned or praised the character of all personnel. This was John Budden, a trader.

...And the Lesser Lords

On the frozen Red River, the Governor takes his well-wrapped family for a sleigh ride near Fort Garry in 1824.

Simpson kept his winter "court" at Red River, a colony administered by a Governor of Assiniboia, appointed by the H.B.C. Here, fur was king, and the visit of a chief called for pomp and pageantry, with flags flying and gun salutes.

The Prince of Wales's Fort

The Hudson's Bay Company first built a trading post near the mouth of the Churchill River in 1689, but it was gutted by fire before completion. The Honourable Company tried again in 1717, with a small wooden fort five miles upstream, first known as Fort Churchill, but later Prince of Wales's Fort. Possible attacks from French vessels worried the company, and so in 1731-32 the soil was turned to build a great fort with walls of stone – impregnable to a French assault. For forty years the stonemasons worked on the walls, and the painting above shows how the new Prince of Wales's Fort looked when it was finished. It was the pride of the H.B.C. . . . but pride came before the fall. In 1782, French naval officer La Pérouse sailed into Churchill harbour – and the great fort was captured. Samuel Hearne, later to become a famous explorer, was in command of the post at the time and was taken prisoner to France, but soon released. In 1783 the Hudson's Bay Company built a new post upriver, called Churchill. It was only made of wood, but it stayed in business until 1933.

Christmas Far from Home

A magazine illustrator depicted Christmas, 1862, in the Hudson's Bay territory: no plum puddings, only a toast in the wilderness.

A busy day at a Hudson's Bay Company post in the Nineties looked like this, according to artist Frederic Remington. Indian, Métis and Mountie came to bargain and buy, or on some occasions just to pass the time of day. In an unsettled land, the trading store was the hub of social life.

When the West Went Dry

The early fur traders had gone to the West like pirates, eager to exploit the Indians, slow to give anything in return. Where competition was fierce, liquor flowed freely. But dissipated Indians made poor hunters, and soon the traders entered the council tepees, trying to convince the chiefs that whisky was bad for them. Governor George Simpson quoted one chief's reply: "It is not for your Cloths and Blankets that we undergo all this labour and fatigue, as in a short time we could reconcile ourselves to the use of Skins as our forefathers did, but it is the prospect of a drink in the Spring to enable us to communicate freely and speak our minds to each other that carries us through the Winter and induces us to work so hard." Nonetheless, the Hudson's Bay Company soon eliminated the sale of rum – in the Oregon by 1825, in Athabasca and Mackenzie by 1835, on the B.C. Coast by 1842, and throughout all their territory by 1860.

IX

The Fight for the Furs

THE last "war" of Canada's two great fur companies smouldered for half a century, then broke out into guerrilla violence in the early 1800s. Often under a pretence of legality, men murdered for a pack of pelts. They starved and they duelled, hijacked and pirated in feudal loyalty to either the North West Company or the Hudson's Bay Company.

The battleground was the harshest land in all the Canadian West, where stabbing winds and hissing hailstones shrivelled the flesh in temperatures reaching 50 below zero, but it produced the silkiest beaver and silver fox furs, which meant a yearly profit of thirty thousand English pounds.

The Nor'westers guarded it jealously. They called it "Athabasca country," but it took in the entire Mackenzie River basin. Its heart was 200-mile-long Lake Athabasca, straddling the northerly boundary of present-day Alberta and Saskatchewan, on which, in the 1780s, the Nor'westers had built their palisaded bastion, Fort Chipewyan. Its gateway was the Churchill River, where for years the Hudson's Bay Company had tried in vain to establish a fur trade outpost to compete with Fort Ile-à-la-Crosse – a fort named after the game of lacrosse which the Nor'westers played with the Indians.

The Nor'westers who patrolled the Athabasca country called themselves "Northmen," and it was with pride that a *voyageur* took his vow, *"Je suis un homme du Nord."* They looked down on the eastern "pork-eater," who canoed merely as far as Lake Superior. Only a Northman had the right to wear a red turkey cock feather in his wool cap. Only an *Homme du Nord* would decorate a team of four huskies with tinkling bells; tie silver foxtails onto the curved oaken sled known as a *traîneau de glace* or *cariole*, or lash little deerskin shoes to the ice-worn paws of a favourite husky. Only he could *"mouche"* with 500 pounds of furs, across the glare ice 70 miles a day goading his team forward with nothing sharper than the oath, *"Sacré chien mort!* – damned dead dog!"

When starving, a Northman would not hesitate to eat his dogs. If a dog turned vicious or chewed on the deerthong harness, the *voyageur* customarily beat it senseless – a taming known as "sending one's dog to Rome." The same Northman would brag inordinately about the speed of his lead husky. His highest compliment was, "That's a *dog* for you."

In fact, an Athabasca *voyageur* bragged about everything: about consuming two geese for breakfast, gulping a half-dozen whitefish for lunch, eating a "freshwater hog" – a 50 pound sturgeon – for supper. Only occasionally would he grumble (*"Toujours le poisson!"*) at his winter fish diet.

His description of the wonders he had seen were always painted in bold colours. The water of the Athabasca River "was so hard, you had to chew it; better still, spill the water out, and fill your cup with a *régale* of rum." Every animal was a giant; "Athabasca *voyageurs*," it was said, "never see little wolves." But he had no need to exaggerate the Athabasca elk – 600 pounds, branch-antlered, statuesque as a camel, with a mating call like the braying of a donkey.

Above all, the *voyageurs* glorified in mastering the hostile land. "To withstand the cold of the Athabasca," a *bourgeois* trader recorded once, boasting, "one ought to have his Blood compos'd of Brandy, his Body of Brass, and his Eyes of Glass." The wintering partners of the Nor'westers were also Northmen, though Baymen called them rakehells and Highland bandits. Some were thugs hired to harry invading Bay traders. Some spent their time swilling rum and wenching with their Indian harems. Many kept the Slave Indians in a state of economic peonage. The times were cruel, and the fur trade had no place for soft men. The Athabasca made a man or it broke him.

They had their inhibitions and chivalry of a kind. No matter how cussed a man might be, he always spelled "damn" in his diary as "d - - n." Many spent their nights with the King James Bible or Greek verse. Fort Chipewyan, with its library, came to be known as "Little Athens of the North." One week a Nor'wester might duel with a rival, the next he might snowshoe for 500 miles, risking snow blindness or death, to bring him the newest copy of Tertulian or Adam Smith's *Roman Antiquities.*

Many, too, felt a genuine love for the austere beauty of the country. One clerk, a Norwegian named Willard Ferdinand Wentzel, lived in congenial, if verminous, brotherhood with the Chipewyan Indians, playing the flute and fiddle for them, exhibiting his mimicry. In the brief Athabasca summers, when the sunlight lingered till midnight, he grew big crisp cabbages, dined on moose nose, and wrote of how "the rose-tipped columns traverse the sky from east to west as a hand might sweep the chords of some vast harp." And in winter, reduced to gnawing the beaver skin parchment that substituted for glass on Fort Chipewyan windows, he jotted in his journal, "*Cooloo!* It is unimportant . . . I am still alive. So why should I complain?"

Soon after the turn of the century, the Bay sent surveyor Peter Fidler, an Englishman from Derbyshire, to establish Nottingham House, on Lake Athabasca opposite Fort Chipewyan. Fidler survived the winter winds, recording in his notebook that water froze at 32 degrees fahrenheit: English brandy at 26, French brandy at 23, milk at 30, Holland gin at 17, and "blood out of the body" at 25 below zero. But not the two Nor'westers in charge of Chipewyan.

One was Archibald Norman McLeod, a stout Highlander who paraded about in his red uniform, cocked hat and sword from the War of 1812. He was a Nor'wester partner, a martinet, violent, sadistic and not above selling an Indian girl in the slave trade. He ridiculed the men of the Bay as "Petit Potties," and "Stupid Puppies." A fellow Nor'wester had described him as one of those men "who can never think themselves forgiven . . . because they themselves are incapable of forgiving." Yet he was known to nurse a sick Bay rival, read the Bible avidly, and regard the Athabasca war as a sort of jovial gentleman's contest.

The other Nor'wester was Samuel Black, of Aberdeen. Sir George Simpson later described him as "callous to every honourable feeling, and equal to the cutting of a throat with cool deliberation . . . in appearance ghastly, rawboned and lantern-jawed. He is so suspicious of attack from Indians, that offensive preparations seem to be the study of his life. He had dirks, knives and loaded pistols concealed about his person, and in all directions about his establishment, even under his tablecloth at meals, and in his bed."

Actually, Black seems to have been a light-hearted rowdy who regarded the struggle with the Bay as a lark. Though born an illegitimate child, he regularly sent 50 English pounds to his mother in Scotland. And though without formal education, he wrote sensitively of the Indians. ("They are very inquisitive, very acute, and swallow ridiculous stories only because they have never been taught. They are seeking for light, sitting in darkness.") Black was popular, and his partners had given him gold rings engraved: "To the most worthy of the worthy Nor'westers."

On Fidler's arrival, McLeod invited him over for tea, and then gave him a gentlemanly warning that the servants of the Hudson's Bay Company would have to walk over the Nor'wester bodies before they'd allow a single Indian into the Bay with furs. On the following day, Black and a mob of Nor'wester bullies slashed Fidler's fishnets, uprooted his garden, banged on his door and frightened off game by howling all night like wolves. That was the end of Fidler. He abandoned what he now called his "Hungry Hall," and explained in his journal: "We are so very few and they so numerous."

It was 1803 before an attempt was made to introduce a modicum of law and order into the Athabasca, and even this required a *cause célèbre.* According to John ("Crooked Arm") McDonald, he and another Nor'wester bully-boy, James King, were drinking tea in the latest Bay outpost set up near Fort Ile-á-la-Crosse when their host issued a warning: "Take care, Mr. King, of Mr. Lamothe. He will shadow you on your dog-sleigh journey to get furs from the Indians. He will shoot you." King laughed. "To be shot at by Lamothe would be a good joke indeed."

"Next morning in high glee King set off," Crooked Arm said. "He was to be absent three nights."

On the second night, King's six-year-old daughter woke from a dream. "Mother," she told King's Indian wife, "there is my father at the foot of the bed, his neck all red."

"You fool, lie down," the mother said, and the girl went to sleep again.

On the third day a sleigh came back bearing King's corpse. Lamothe had shot the Nor'wester in a scuffle over furs. And just as his half-breed daughter had dreamed, King's neck was caked with blood.

The Nor'westers seized Lamothe and took him to Montreal for trial. The resulting furore caused the British Parliament to pass the Canada Jurisdiction Act. It authorized the Governor of Lower and Upper Canada to appoint a justice of the peace in the Indian country with the power to arrest criminals. The appointed justices were almost all Nor'westers, and "criminals," of course, were mostly Hudson's Bay men. Justice of the peace for Athabasca was Archibald Norman McLeod. He would sign a warrant for a Bay man's arrest and then send over Black and his bullies to pick a quarrel and clap the trader into irons.

The Gentleman Adventurer who finally led the Bay into battle was an improbable character named Colin Robertson. A Nor'wester until he was dismissed from the company in 1809, Robertson was a flamboyant, grandiose man with a long beak nose and long feathery red sideburns, a romantic who, Sir George Simpson once said, "fancied himself the hero of every tale of romance that passed through his hands."

In his memoirs Robertson likened himself to Don Quixote. Although some of his tilts were indeed with windmills, he was a man of action. As a boy in Perth, Scotland, he thought that his father's weaving trade was dull. At 25, he found his milieu in the Saskatchewan country as a fur trader. There he gained a nickname: they called him "Lord Chesterfield," because of his fondness for Shakespeare, Madeira wine and fine china. Six feet tall, with a cutlass at his side, he cut a dashing figure. His hazel eyes under red curls blazed with arrogance. He once duelled with John ("Crooked Arm") McDonald when the notorious Nor'wester, who kept a sword secreted in a hollow cane, "condescended to eye me over the end of his nose, as if I was no bigger than a grain of mustard seed." In anger he would fling a biscuit into the face of a rival: but he seldom uttered a curse more horrendous than, "Oh, sky blue!" or, "For the love of beaver!"

Robertson decided that under him the Hudson's Bay Company could stand-off the arrogant Nor'westers and take the lion's share of the fur trade. He borrowed money for his passage to London and confronted the Bay Committee, headed by Thomas Douglas, fifth Earl of Selkirk, then involved in establishing a colony at Red River in Manitoba. It was time to wrest the fur-rich Athabasca from the Nor'westers. The Athabasca riches couldn't be won by the Bay's present "drones and drivellers. . . . They may as well attempt to take hold of the moon with their teeth! When you are among wolves," he told the H.B.C. governors, "you must howl!" He would lead the wolf pack, at a salary of one English pound a day.

Lord Selkirk adopted Robertson as his protegé, and the battle was joined in earnest. In the summer of 1815, Robertson set out from Montreal in command of 160 *voyageurs* and three former Nor'westers who, like their chief, had turned their coats. When they paddled up the Red River they found that the Nor'westers had burned down Lord Selkirk's colony and scattered the settlers. Robertson felt that his first duty was to rebuild the razed colony, take revenge by sacking the Nor'westers' Fort Gibraltar on Red River, and to send his *voyageurs* to Athabasca under his second-in-command. The leader of the shock troopers was John Clarke, a 34-year-old Montrealer, a handsome redhaired ramrod of a man. He went into every fight swinging a diamond-studded cane, given him by John Jacob Astor for his escapades as a Mountain Man. He would hang an Indian for stealing, or throw a "booze and a dance" to win Indian trade. One minute he would threaten to "toss a little gunpowder in the eyes" of a rival who had dared call him a rattlesnake, and the next he would "crack a flagon and jollify" him. Everyone called him "Bon Garçon." He was one of the few fur traders who took his wives to the Athabasca – one, a blackhaired half-breed named Sapphira; the other, a Swiss blonde beauty of 17 who lived to be 104.

The Bay Committee had handcuffed Robertson with restrictions against "engaging in any contest of manned force. . . . It is enough if one of our officers calmly, and without show of anger, takes hold of the arm, or touches the body of the Northwester master, telling him to come no farther upon the lands of the H.B.CO.". The Committee felt that Clarke was too rash to adhere to its instructions. Robertson, while conceding that Clarke was hotheaded, argued that he was a walking atlas of the Athabasca trails. The *Bon Garçon* was a man after Robertson's heart, and he gave Clarke a salary of 400 English pounds and sent him ahead.

For all his dash, John Clarke ran into some of the toughest men the Canadian West had ever known. He built a string of log cabins opposite the Nor'wester forts on Lesser Slave Lake, on Great Slave Lake, and on Potato Island in Lake Athabasca, facing the Nor'wester bastion of Fort Chipewyan. But at Ile-à-la-Crosse on Lesser Slave, Samuel Black had hired a pack of bullies – Irish soldiers-of-fortune still wearing their scarlet uniforms from the War of 1812. Flourishing his cutlass, Black scratched a line in front of the Bay cabin and dared any Baymen to step across. In the resulting melee three Bay men were "fatally pricked in the body." The post was seized, and the Bay survivors were imprisoned on a frozen island on a diet of rotten fish and the rock moss called *tripe de rocher*.

At Lake Athabasca, Archibald Norman McLeod directed the terrorism. The Athabasca JP sent an Irish sergeant named Hector McNeill to the Bay post, to pick a fight. Sergeant Hector had a face described by a contemporary as "in itself a letter of recommendation as a

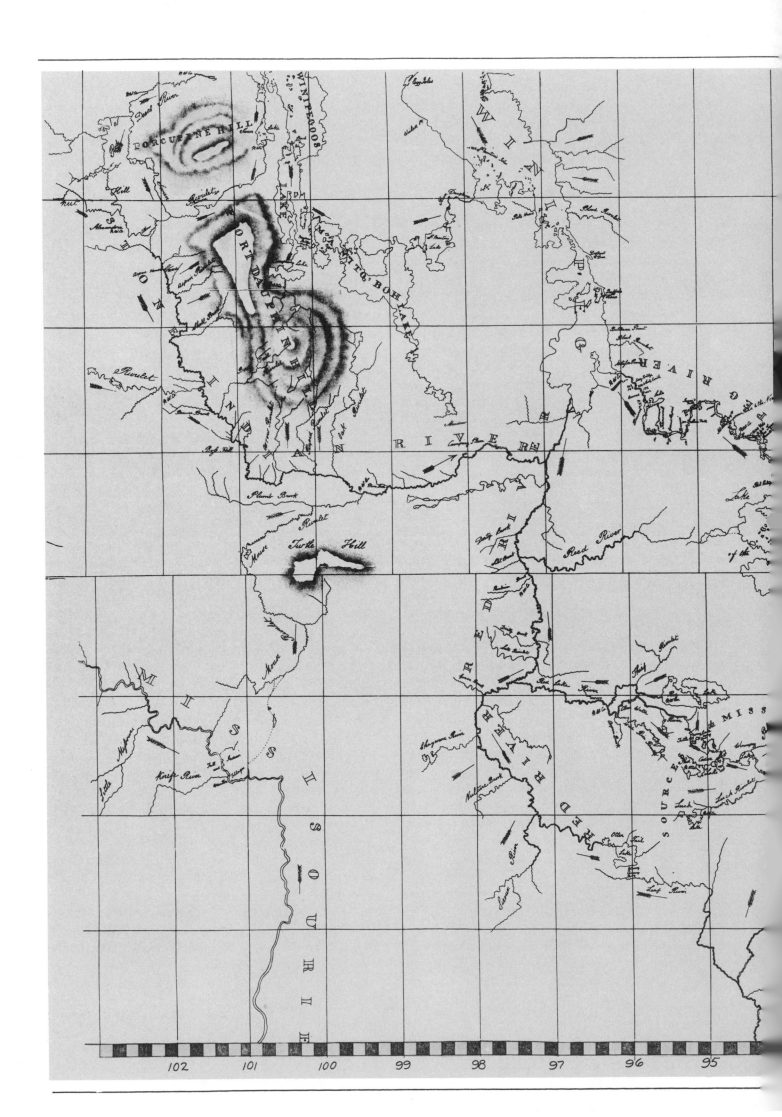

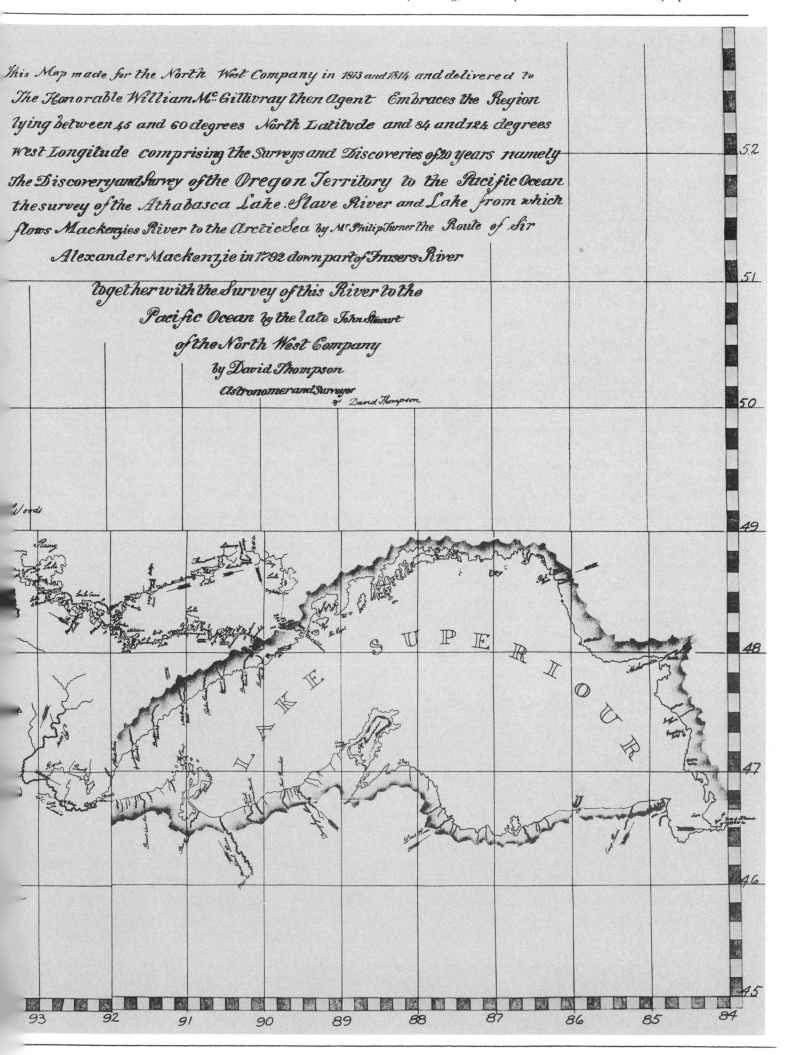

This Map made for the North West Company in 1813 and 1814 and delivered to
The Honorable William McGillivray then Agent Embraces the Region
lying between 45 and 60 degrees North Latitude and 84 and 124 degrees
West Longitude comprising the Surveys and Discoveries of 20 years namely
The Discovery and Survey of the Oregon Territory to the Pacific Ocean
the survey of the Athabasca Lake, Slave River and Lake from which
flows Mackenzies River to the Arctic Sea by Mr Philip Turner the Route of Sir
Alexander Mackenzie in 1792 down part of Frasers River

together with the Survey of this River to the
Pacific Ocean by the late John Stewart
of the North West Company
by David Thompson
Astronomer and Surveyor
by David Thompson

LAKE SUPERIOUR

fighting character. His countenance was a ruddy bronze, with a noble nose of the Nassau cut, a superb pair of full-blown Cossack whiskers, and an interesting transverse sabre wound over his right eye." Hector duelled with an Irish swordsman from the Bay named John McVicar, with both sides cheering for their champion. The Nor'wester Irishman disarmed the Bay Irishman and was poised for a fatal thrust when McVicar's Indian wife charged Hector, scratching and biting furiously until he dropped his rapier, crying that he had been wounded in his thumb.

Naturally, Justice McLeod held "English court" at Fort Chipewyan and charged the entire Bay party with disturbing the public peace. John Clarke refused to submit and was fined 30 bales of furs worth 3,000 pounds – a humiliation that cost him face with the onlooking Indians.

To regain status, Clarke led fifty canoemen up the Peace River to establish a Bay post beside the Nor'-westers' Fort Vermilion. It was a grim fiasco. He refused to take any supplies, convinced that he could shoot all the game he needed. But the Nor'westers drove the moose away from their path, and Indians who tried to feed the Bay men were roughed up. Some *engages* ate the *pemmican* that the Nor'westers had deliberately planted in their camp in order to arrest them for theft. Others survived by chewing the deer sinews of their snowshoes. But sixteen, including a woman and child, died of starvation. Clarke staggered back to Fort Wedderburn to find all his Bay posts captured, all his men under oath to Justice McLeod to stay out of the Athabasca country for three years, and himself under arrest by Samuel Black.

"Indelible infamy!" cried Robertson on hearing the news. And he promptly began negotiations with the Hudson's Bay Company to outfit another Athabasca campaign. The Company would still not let him hire ex-Nor'westers who had offended the Bay's traders, but he was allowed to recruit some mercenaries from the War of 1812. And though the Bay wanted John Clarke, now liberated by the Nor'westers, fired for lack of "caution and circumspection," Robertson kept him as second-in-command, arguing that "No *voyageur* will attempt to disobey his orders; few Indians can resist his entreaties. He cajoles, condoles, and seems to command every string that can touch the heart of a *Canadien*."

Robertson was pleased to hear about the new Governor-in-Chief appointed by the Bay Committee to rule the territory. Governor William Williams was a man after Robertson's style, a former sea captain of the East India Company. True, he was reputed to be a man with the heart of a lion and the brains of a goose, a blustering, profane disciplinarian, full of gold-laced glitter and ostentation. But at least he was resilient about the law. He boasted that he would make the Nor'wester pirates walk the plank: "I shall use every means in my power to drive out of the North country every d – – Nor'wester it contains, or perish in the attempt."

Colin Robertson embarked for the Athabasca country in the summer of 1818. He commanded an invasion force of ten officers and 100 handpicked *voyageurs*. His flotilla of ten yellow birchbark canoes was stocked with hampers of smoked tongues and tinned hams, baskets of eggs and plum cakes, kegs of Madeira wine and French brandy, with fine chinaware for drinking. It was so regatta-like that Robertson wrote in his diary: "The lady with the ring in her nose is now holding a plum cake and with her delicate brown fingers is picking out the fruit."

At Thunder Bay on Lake Superior, where wooden crosses marked the graves of so many drowned comrades, his canoemen faced "truly appalling waves with perfect composure. The *voyageurs* are natural water dogs," marvelled Robertson. "However dismal the prospect, they followed their *bourgeois* master. They sing while surrounded by misery, and the toil of the day is entirely forgot in the encampment. They think themselves the happiest people in existence, and I do believe they are not far mistaken."

At Norway House on Lake Winnipeg, Robertson was joined by John Clarke. His *voyageurs* had absolved themselves of their oath to Justice McLeod, Robertson wrote, by crossing themselves and asking "pardon of their Maker for having taken a false oath to a heretic." Robertson now had about 190 men in 27 canoes. "We descended the current," he wrote as his brigade paddled up the Athabasca River, "firing our guns at intervals while the men kept singing their *voyageurs'* songs, so that the natives might be aware of our approach." When they spotted a Chipewyan Indian scout behind a blackberry bush, Robertson plied him with Madeira wine to draw his tribe's fur trade away from the Nor'westers. His tactics were so successful that when they reached Fort Chipewyan, they were met at the waterside by Samuel Black, shouting: "Mr. Robertson! Let me speak to our Indians before you land. You are an honourable man – give justice!"

"Justice be d – – d!" bellowed John Clarke, his anger shaking the canoe. "When did *you* give justice?"

To avoid an immediate fight, Robertson quartered his men on Potato Island at the former Bay post of Fort Wedderburn. He dispatched Clarke, well-provisioned this time, with a winter brigade up the Peace River to found Fort St. Mary's and Fort Colvile (named respectively in honour of Lord Selkirk's birthplace and his wife's maiden name, Wedderburn-Colvile). Meanwhile, Robertson's Madeira wine proved a more potent trade item than the Nor'westers' diluted rum. Within a week he was trading with 40 Indian chiefs. Black and his bullies, he wrote, "come over every evening in a body, calling out our men to fight pitted battles. But one of their principal hair-pulling heroes got a most unmerciful thrashing from a little man of ours of the name of Bouche."

The Nor'westers now summoned their most eminent wintering partners: Simon McGillivray, Jr., the half-breed son of the reigning grandee, William McGillivray: and two descendents of Nor'wester founders, Benjamin Frobisher, Jr., and John George McTavish. They had to do something quickly, McGillivray, Jr., decided, because the Nor'westers were losing "character, reputation and fame."

One October morning in chapel, while Robertson read the funeral service over a Bay servant perforated in an "accidental" shooting, McGillivray, Jr., burst in. While Robertson, scandalized, protested this was no fit time for a quarrel, Samuel Black and a party of Nor'westers crept in from behind and seized him. He was dragged struggling into a canoe and with Black's pistol pressed to his head, he was taken to Fort Chipewyan on the mainland.

When they landed on the beach, Robertson broke free and dashed to the Nor'westers' trading hall and began to harangue the Indians, partly in French, partly in Chipewyan. Black rushed up and the action that followed was later described by Robertson: "By grabbing hold of a fork which lay on the table, I kept the vagabond at a distance. Loading him with every abuse, I then turned round to address the Indians: 'You must not abandon our houses. There are more brave men I have left behind to defend our property and protect the Chipewyans.'" Pointing his fork at Black, Robertson shouted, "That fellow was not brave enough to *take* me, but he *stole* me. We will revenge this trick, but not like wolves prowling among the bushes. We will take them as we took them at Fort Gibraltar, with the sun shining on their faces.

"At this moment," Robertson said, "one of their chiefs, Mandvelle, came up. Taking me by the hand, and giving it a gentle squeeze, he whispered, 'Never mind. All will be right. We are not afraid.' This short but soothing address relieved me a good deal, and this turbulent scene closed when I was called into a small apartment." The apartment was Fort Chipewyan's log

privy. For the next eight months it was Robertson's prison and his headquarters. From here, guarded day and night, this Don Quixote of the West commanded his Athabasca campaign, the most richly comic episode in the fur trade war.

He did it with a keg of Madeira wine, a volume of Shakespeare's plays, and a secret code. Since Robertson was compelled to state all his wants in a formal open letter to the Bay fort, he requested that his captors send a courier under a flag of truce to the Bay to bring him a barrel of Madeira wine. The Nor'westers obliged, perhaps pleased at the prospect of their prisoner befuddling himself. Robertson then concocted a cipher of 600 numbers, each number keyed to some jargon of the fur trade. He wrote out the code on long strips of paper, rolled up the strips tightly enough to waterproof them and sealed the ends with wax. He knocked the bung from the wine barrel, tied one end of a piece of twine to the papers, the other inside the plug, and dangled his message inside the wine. Then, rubbing in dust to conceal his handiwork and to make the wine keg smell musty, he complained in his next open letter that the polluted barrel should be well scoured.

To his disgust, instead of taking the hint, his Bay comrades sent over a *new* keg. It was obvious his friends had not discovered Robertson's master code. He then requested a copy of Shakespeare's plays. Opposite Falstaff's name, he pencilled: "Examine – the – first – keg." The volume of plays was returned to the Bay and a week later Robertson's open letter stated: "To amuse myself, I am attempting to throw into rhyme some of Jack Falstaff's good sayings. There is one expression where he blows out, 'I am not a wit, but the cause of wit in others.' This sounds harsh in my ears. Please send a copy of the sentence as it stands in the play."

The Nor'wester partners passed the letter. Back came a message from Wedderburn. Not only had Robertson's men deciphered the code, "but they also conveyed the pleasing intelligence of John Clarke's movements in Peace River." From then on Robertson maintained a continuous flow of coded messages revealing inside information about the Nor'westers' activities. He then dispatched a letter to Governor William Williams on how to trap the Nor'wester brigades when they ran the Grand Rapids of the Saskatchewan River that June with furs for Montreal. But a sentinel, peering through a crevice in the privy, caught Robertson scribbling a message, and McGillivray decided to transport Robertson to the east with his fur canoes. At the Bay's Cumberland House, John George McTavish allowed Robertson to say goodbye to his friends at the post on condition that Robertson gave his word of honour not to escape. Robertson inclined his head slightly. But no sooner was he inside the fort than the gates were bolted shut. Shaking their fists in anger, the Nor'wester partners had to push off down the Saskatchewan River without him.

But it bothered Robertson. "However my friends may applaud the act, my conscience tells me I have not acted right," he wrote.

Robertson and his Bay friends now canoed to the trap set at Grand Rapids, a two-mile rocky bottleneck where the Saskatchewan River boils into Lake Winnipeg. Robertson knew that the Nor'wester traders were accustomed to stroll along the portage smoking their pipes and drinking from silver jugs while their *voyageurs* shot the rapids. At the foot of the rapids Governor Williams had gunboats mounted with three-pounder cannons, blocking the river. And behind the gooseberry bushes and aspens were 120 uniformed ex-soldiers headed by *Bon Garçon* Clarke, who was thirsting for vengeance.

As seven Nor'westers, including Frobisher, McTavish, and John ("Crooked Arm") McDonald strolled down to the foot of the rapids, Clarke's men charged, "with muskets, fixed bayonets, pistols and swords & whooping and hollowing like so many demons." Frobisher and McTavish loudly demanded to see Williams' warrants for the "arrest." The Governor roared back, "Legal proceedings are all d – – d nonsense in the North country! . . . Lord Bathurst, d – – him, is bribed by Nor'wester gold, and the judges of Canada are a set of d – – rascals. For our part, we shall act independently of the rascally government of Canada."

The Nor'westers were jailed in a shack on a small mosquito-ridden island. One partner, pleading privacy for a call of nature, eluded the guards and escaped on a homemade raft. He left a suicide note, declaring melodramatically, "I have drowned myself, having tied a stone round my neck to keep me at the bottom." Lake Winnipeg in this area was no deeper than two feet. Benjamin Frobisher also escaped but died of starvation at Bourbon Lake, after having eaten the heels of his European shoes.

The next winter, Colin Robertson commanded the Athabasca operation from Fort St. Mary's on the Peace River. That season, the rival forts faced each other in a state of armed neutrality more concerned about the "famine that stalked the land." The Indians, spoiled by the high prices paid by the rivals, were slack in hunting.

"Our opponents have given me no trouble this winter, but starvation nearly obliged me to abandon the post," Robertson wrote. "My people ate two of our horses. As for myself, from November until February, I lived principally on a few dried berries and water with a few ounces of flour . . ." He kept his morale up with Don Quixote: "What a vein of humour runs through this admirable work!"

In the summer of 1820, he left for the east with 60 haggard Bay men. As he strolled to the foot of Grand Rapids he found himself surrounded by Nor'westers. It was tit for tat, and Robertson could not help smiling. "This," he said, "is certainly following up my blow with a vengeance." At Fort William, the Nor'westers' headquarters, Justice Archibald McLeod demanded that Robertson sign an oath not to return to Athabasca for one year.

"I eyed the fellow with perfect contempt," Robertson said. Then he demanded to know where the brazen fellow derived his authority.

"I assure you, Mr. Robertson, I have *very* extensive powers."

"I suppose, McLeod, you mean Athabasca powers?"

"I don't admit of that familiarity!" McLeod said. "I call you *Mister* Robertson!"

"Tut, tut. I presume you have not forgotten the handsome epithets you bestowed upon me in the Athabasca country?"

"That I have denied, Mr. Robertson, upon affidavit. I never called you a rascal. I never thought you one." He ordered his prisoner to be sent under guard for trial in Montreal. At a portage near Lachine on the St. Lawrence, Robertson seized a biscuit and hurled it in the face of his Nor'wester guards. Then he levelled a captured pistol and dared the whole company to take him. His captors refused the challenge.

To avoid arrest in Montreal, Robertson crossed the U.S. border and took a boat to London from New York. The war he had launched in the Athabasca, he noted, was nearing its conclusion. "Our opponents talk now of conducting their business upon amicable principles. If they are serious, O what a change!"

It was the end of an era of piracy and romance. Now a realist was stepping onto the stage, a practical businessman of a kind the Canadian West had never seen before. He would apply his "pruning hook" to all extravagant swaggerers and rule the Athabasca as if it were a fur-factory and the Nor'westers and the Gentlemen Adventurers both as if they were factory employees.

X

The Little Emperor

O N an icy October morning in 1820, George Simpson, the new charge d'affaires of the Hudson's Bay Company in the Athabasca country, was busy with his account books in his log-cabin office at Fort Wedderburn on Potato Island. It was so cold that the ink in his quill froze four feet from the fireplace, a far cry from the London counting house where he had been eight months before. But whether cozy in London or freezing in the sub-Arctic, business was business with the 28-year-old Scottish orphan. Already he was displaying the demonic ambition, the machine-like precision, the blowtorch energy, that would make him the Little Emperor of half a continent.

He was five feet seven inches tall, built, as one associate said, "like one of those short, square, massy pillars one sees in an old country church." A tall beaver hat in an oiled silk cover concealed the bald patch in his red hair. He wore Beau Brummell cravats and Royal Stuart tartan cloaks of scarlet or black with collars of soft Genoa velvet. He aspired to a gentleman's status, though he always claimed his finery was designed to impress the Indians. Meticulously clean-shaven, he had a blunt nose and a blunter tongue. When the situation demanded it, he could be smooth enough. As an enemy later phrased it, he had "all the craft and subtlety of an intriguing courtier, lavishing his bows and smiles and honied words." His lips were tight, his blue eyes glistened as frosty as the hoar rhime that covered the shores of Lake Athabasca.

As he sat scratching at his ledger, a Bay Company labourer rushed in with news of the latest harassing tactics of the Nor'westers. In addition to Fort Chipewyan a mile and a half away, the Nor'westers had built a blockhouse 12 yards from the Bay fort. From their back window they could see which Indians brought beaver pelts to Fort Wedderburn. Simpson had ordered his workmen to erect a high fence, and now Simon McGillivray, Jr., leading half a dozen armed bullies,

was demanding that Bay labourers stop digging post holes on Nor'wester property.

Simpson told his officers to cover him with rifles and rushed out to order the workmen to go on fence-building. Then he turned to face McGillivray and his rowdies, each brandishing a dirk and a brace of pistols.

"My name is Simpson," the lone clerk said crisply. "I presume yours is McGillivray?"

McGillivray was a handsome six-foot half-breed, the 30-year-old son of the reigning Nor'wester partner, William McGillivray. He had fought valiantly with the Canadian Chasseurs in the war of 1812, and was reputed to have killed at least one Gentleman Adventurer in a duel. He looked down at little Simpson in surprise, and replied, "It is."

"I intend erecting these stockades from the corner of our bastion in a direct line to that stump," declared Simpson, pointing to the stump of a jackpine. "Pray sir, what are your objections?"

"I understand you intend to run them beyond the boundary line," McGillivray said, "which I shall not permit."

"We have no intention to encroach on what is understood to be the line of demarcation," Simpson said. "Nor shall we tamely submit to any encroachment on our rights. We are inclined to be quiet, orderly neighbours, if permitted to be so. But we are determined to maintain our privileges with firmness."

"Time will show," the Nor'wester leader replied.

Just then Simpson's little Scotch terrier ran across the Nor'wester line and laid a stick at the feet of one of McGillivray's bullies. The bully eyed the dog, uncertain whether to play with it or kick it.

"Come here, Boxer," Simpson called with a smile. "You do not seem aware that you are committing a trespass."

"We have no intention to molest your dog, sir," McGillivray protested, concerned that he should be thought unchivalrous.

"Nor shall you his master with impunity," Simpson said, and in his version, "McGillivray and his bullies retired somewhat crestfallen. Two hours afterwards, the fence was completed."

It was the first skirmish in the cold war for the Athabasca country, the beginning of a new epoch in which brains would count for more than brawn. Both the Gentlemen Adventurers and the Nor'westers, for all their strut and swagger, were threatened by economic paralysis. The Hudson's Bay Company, with its caste system, offered no incentive for enterprise. The individuals of the North West Company squandered their profits and both were suffering from the cut-throat competition. A virtuoso of corporate management was needed – a man to slash at overlapping waste with "the broom & the pruning hook," as Simpson later expressed it.

At the very beginning of his fur trade apprenticeship in the Athabasca country, Simpson wrote in his diary of "my star," meaning his destiny to rule. It was a strangely portentous figure of speech for a clerk born a bastard on the desolate moors of Loch Broom in Ross-shire, Scotland. He came of a family long habituated to illegitimacy, and he was to perpetuate that tradition by fathering all across the Canadian West his own "bits of brown," as he called his half-Indian illegitimate children. But, in later years, after Queen Victoria knighted him at Buckingham Palace, Simpson tried to hide his illegitimacy, refusing to reveal any details about his birth to the editor of Dodd's *Peerage, Baronetage and Knightage.*

Simpson never knew the name of his mother but his father, George, was the eldest son of a Calvinist minister, Rev. Thomas Simpson. Abandoned by both parents, the orphan was raised in the manse at the parish of Avoch by his grandmother, Isobel Simpson. At the village

school, young George so excelled at arithmetic and book-keeping that his uncle, Geddes Simpson, made him a countinghouse clerk in his London firm of Messrs. Graham, Simpson & Wedderburn.

Fortune smiled on the youth. In true Horatio Alger tradition (though climbing onward and upward by methods that would have horrified pious Alger), the clerk was to return one day to marry his employer's daughter, Frances Simpson. More important, young Simpson's zealous penny-pinching caught the eye of the third partner, brother of Lady Jean Selkirk and financial adviser to her husband, Lord Selkirk. Andrew Wedderburn-Colvile, to grant him his full handle, was also a director of the Hudson's Bay Company Committee. He was just 13 years older than Simpson and the orphan boy seems to have regarded him as a substitute father.

It was a curious relationship. His many personal letters to Wedderburn – marked "private" and always signed, "Your faithful and obedient humble servant, George Simpson" – seem more obsequious than loving. "This mark of your good opinion and kind patronage," he wrote in one, "has laid me under a thousand weighty obligations to you . . . I shall ever entertain a grateful sense of the interest you have been pleased to take in me, and I fondly trust you will find that I am not unworthy of the confidence thus reposed. To you I feel that I am solely indebted for my advancement in life."

In early 1820, the Nor'westers had warrants out for the arrests of the Hudson's Bay Company's Governor-in-Chief, William Williams. They were threatening to "drag the Governor out of the country" for ambushing them at Grand Rapids. The Bay Company Committee needed a reliable man as Acting Governor in case the threat was carried through, and they needed him in a hurry. Wedderburn called in his protegé. Was Simpson game to seize this main chance at advancement on just five days' notice? He would get a salary of 600 pounds a year, but in case Williams did not require a substitute and Simpson had to return, he would get paid just 400 pounds.

Simpson would have grabbed at the offer if he were not being paid a ha'penny. He sailed in March aboard the *James Monroe*, with an attitude revealed in one of his first letters home: "I will show my Governors that I am not wanting of Courage, if necessity puts it to the test. There is a possibility that I may be obstructed in my Rout, as the North West Company, a band of unprincipled lawless marauders, stick at nothing however desperate to gain their ends. I am, however, armed to the Teeth. I will sell my life if in danger as dear as possible."

With enthusiasm he prepared himself for his trip into the interior, "a serious undertaking" in "a canoe pulled by ten stout fellows. My cloak will answer all the purposes of a bed, and the canoe turned bottom upwards my chamber. The first part of my journey I expect to accomplish in forty days, and my future proceedings will be regulated by the state of things in the Interior . . . Travellers, you know, meet with extraordinary adventures. I shall therefore have some wonderful Tales to relate."

At Fort William, the Nor'wester citadel on Lake Superior, Simpson gained entry by waving His Majesty's Proclamation, which commanded all warring fur traders to respect the law and keep peace, and once inside, delivered a confidential letter from London to a cabal of 18 Nor'wester partners. The Bay had heard that these men were worried about their company's precarious finances, that they wished to break with the reigning Nor'wester grandee in Montreal, resenting their status as "McGillivray's Geese," in the pecking order. The letter was destined to promote dissension.

Simpson then paddled up to the Hayes River Rock Depot, near York Factory headquarters on Hudson Bay, where the H.B.C. outfitted its expeditions to the Athabasca country. Here he was discomfited to discover William Williams still free and still Governor-in-Chief. But in the absence of Colin Robertson, Williams desperately needed somebody with Bay Committee authority to manage the Athabasca campaign and he greeted Simpson gladly.

Simpson thanked Williams profusely for his "polite and friendly attentions." He said he was deeply grateful for this secondary office that the Governor-in-Chief was bestowing upon a mere *mangeur de larde*. He was dissembling. Later, after Simpson had usurped the Governor-in-Chief's job, in letters to Wedderburn he expressed puzzlement as to why Williams was "full of ire toward me . . . abusive, vulgar, foul-mouthed . . ."

For his 15-canoe expedition to the Athabasca, Simpson hired 68 persons. As his combined valet and interpreter, he took Tom Taylor, the half-Indian son of a Bay servant who ran the schooner at York Factory, making no mention in his reports of picking Tom's sister, Margaret, as his cook and mistress. Only a year later was it revealed that Margaret had given birth to the first of Simpson's "bits of brown." For his personal secretary and accountant, he selected a young clerk named Robert Miles, who had helped Colin Robertson plot the previous Athabasca invasions. Robertson had frankly acknowledged that young Miles had written his Athabasca journal, but nowhere does Simpson acknowledge Miles' help with either his journal or his formal report to the Bay Committee. Simpson's Athabasca journal shows a grasp of detail about the fur trade extraordinary in a greenhorn. Miles kept his own diary, and it is at least coincidental that the words and ideas expressed in it for the first 20 days of the voyage are identical with those found in Simpson's journal. Apologists for Simpson have claimed that a captain of industry has the right to pick the brains of his hirelings. Simpson did praise Miles' accountancy. Of Colin Robertson, a possible rival for the executive hierarchy of the Bay, Simpson reported: "He is, without exception, the most trifling, frivolous man I ever saw."

Simpson as ruthlessly undercut another potential rival, John (*Bon Garçon*) Clarke. Even if he had not been Robertson's protegé, Clarke, with his diamond-studded cane and his extravagant *bonhomie*, would have grated on Simpson's nerves. On the present expedition, the *Bon Garçon* was assigned to accompany Simpson until they reached the Churchill River, where Clarke was to take charge of the Bay's Fort Ile-à-la-Crosse. But Simpson made sure the Committee knew that Clarke took the *ladies* into his own canoe, turning the gentlemen into the other, leaving the cargo behind at Cumberland House. "The Committee may well be displeased when they learn that one of the Officers deliberately puts them to an expense of 500 English pounds, *merely for the accommodation of an Indian Mistress!!!*" (The exclamation points are Simpson's.)

For the present, Simpson thought it was prudent to be affable with Clarke. "It would not, in my opinion, be judicious to quarrel with him as yet," he wrote to London," unless means are found to keep him out of the Country, while the heat of the opposition continues." Then, turning the screw a little, he added, "For I believe he is sufficiently mercenary to change sides immediately, and from his influence with the *Canadiens* and the Indians, and his indefatigable zeal in the cause of revenge, he would be a very dangerous Enemy." But when the season had ended he wrote in his final report that "this man should be got rid of without delay. His folly (which is almost too mild a term) is more dangerous than the malice of our avowed Enemies."

Simpson's methods of dealing with the Indians he met on his trip were simple: cajole them and bribe them. He enjoyed the former: the speech-making ("Made a speech in great form to the Indians; they look upon me as the greatest man who ever came into the Country"), the awarding of specially-made medals for their services (silver pieces with a bust of King George III stamped on one side and the Hudson's Bay Company coat of arms on the other). He sometimes displayed an incisive wit. After taking his fellow fur traders to task for think-

George Simpson's giant canoe at Fort William. After he became Governor-in-Chief of the Hudson's Bay Company, Simpson regularly made ceremonious inspections of all the trading posts in his "domain," often accompanied by a Highland piper.

ing that their mission was to "emancipate the Indians," he intoned, "it has occurred to me that philanthropy is not the exclusive object of our visits to these Northern regions." And he never lost sight of what he considered his main duty: to debauch them. ("A little rum, you know, operates like a charm on the Indians. They cannot resist the temptation, and if the bait is properly managed, every skin may be had from them.") He drove his men unmercifully but no more than he drove himself. Every morning, no matter how icy the water, he would strip and plunge in for a swim, and he expected others to be as hardy. Beneath his civilized manner he was as primitive as his men, noting laconically in his journal that "The Bustard's wife died this morning. More properly speaking, a termination was put to her sufferings, as she was actually buried before the vital spark was extinguished."

When a woman in his party was unfaithful to her Chipewyan husband, Simpson posed as an oracle: "The Indian, whose Wife Committed the '*faux pas*,' entreated I would inform him whether she would remain faithful to him during the winter. After the necessary ceremony, I set his mind to rest on that subject. Then I gave a private lecture to the Lady, threatening to transform her into a dog if she repeated the sin. She appeared very penitent, and promised to conduct herself in a more becoming manner in future."

His magic, he assured the Committee in his reports, served a very practical function: "I have persuaded the Indians that I can discover every skin that is privately sold to the N.W. Company." Then, blandly ignoring his own dubious tactics, he pretended to be shocked at the way the Chipewyans succumbed to the blandishments of the Nor'westers, "who made a parade of generosity and juggle the Indians out of Packs originally intended for us."

Simpson's attitude toward the half-breed and French-Canadian *voyageurs* was equally ambivalent, or, as they put it, he spoke with a forked tongue. He flattered his half-breed guide, La Mallice, who though paid an annual salary of 20 English pounds by the Bay, traded privately in beaver tails and moose skins with the Nor'-westers. "I must curry favour with him," Simpson said. "His wife (a thrifty Amazon, who is our best interpreter) is much respected by the Indians. It would, therefore, be highly impolitic to have any misunderstanding with him. But a day of reckoning would come," he wrote, when he would "shake off this nest of vipers."

He regarded these "Mongrel Half-Gentry and North West renegadoes" as "the very dross and outcast of the human species . . . but a useful class of people if kept at a respectable distance. If humoured in trifles," he

advised a fellow fur trader, "anything may be done with them. But if treated with uniform severity, they will mutiny to a certainty. As flattery is a very cheap commodity, I would recommend your bestowing a sufficient quantum on them."

At 12-mile Methy Portage, the entrance to the Athabasca country, he "indulged the people with a bottle of rum" as "it is usual for the *Bourgeois* on his first visit, to this Portage, to treat the men with an extra dram." He joined ten *voyageurs* in devouring 25 geese at a simple sitting, and a few days later at the entrance of Lake Athabasca, he allowed them to wash their purple capots and their scarlet sashes, so that they could "appear in good feather" when making their grand entrance into Fort Wedderburn.

From his headquarters on Potato Island, the little general dispatched directives to the English officer in command of the Bay forts along the Peace River and Great Slave Lake. He goaded them to action with sugary words and subtle threats, posing as a humble tenderfoot, bowing before their superiority, professing to hope he might win "some little credit, altho' yet a 'pork-eater.' " Privately, he felt them "a useless burthen, nor worth their Victuals." And to the Bay Committee, he reported: "I must endeavour to purge Athabasca of such useless drones."

Simpson's most immediate problem was the redoubtable Simon McGillivray. One day Amable Grigon, a Bay constable-clerk (who could neither read nor write), arrived from Montreal with a warrant for the arrest of one "Simon McGillivray." Simpson noted without comment that the warrant was for McGillivray Senior. He informed the constable that he would have to act on his own responsibility, but of course, if he had to ask bystanders for assistance, "in the King's name," it would be their duty as honourable British subjects to comply. As Grigon left the fort to make his arrest, Simpson and ten officers went with him, leaving gunners standing by their cannon.

"Mr. McGillivray," Simpson called, cocking his double-barrelled musket and pistols. "I shall be glad to have some further conversation with you on the subject of this boundary line."

McGillivray, Jr., stepped forward, his hand on the hilt of his dagger. Grigon rushed up with his warrant. "I arrest you in the King's name," he cried. When the Nor'wester protested that Grigon had the wrong man, the constable shouted to Simpson's bystanders: "I demand your assistance in the King's name!" The Bay men dragged McGillivray, Jr., struggling into Fort Wedderburn. Simpson shrugged off his enemy's outrage, claiming that "The Officer acted on his own responsibility, and alone is liable for the consequences." But to the Bay Committee he confided how glad he was to have removed this "troublesome thorn in our sides during the winter."

On McGillivray's "word of honour as a gentleman" that he would not try to escape or have private communications with his Nor'wester fort, Simpson allowed him "parole" to stroll about under guard. When Constable Grigon charged that the guard was too chummy with his prisoner, "pistols were called for a duel," Simpson wrote. "But the guard showed the White Feather, and submitted to have his nose twisted by the constable."

Simpson tried to pump his captive, but as he said, "He very likely perceives that I court his society for the purpose of eliciting information from him, than out of respect, and to avoid the risk of committing himself prefers solitude."

When McGillivray complained of being lonely, Simpson allowed his Indian wife and two children to visit, but only after Simpson's own mistress had carefully searched them for messages. Simpson also permitted his prisoner to send open letters back to his fort. But McGillivray's accusations disturbed Simpson so much that he would insert his answers in the letters.

Simpson soon became convinced that McGillivray was using a code and that his men in the nearby watchtower were plotting some sly *ruse de guerre*. He ordered a higher watchtower built so that he could spy on the spies, and he bribed an Irish bully with grog to slip him notes through the Nor'wester's post hole.

At ten o'clock on a December night, Simpson went to sleep gloating blissfully, "For once, I believe, we have got to the blind side of these Argus-eyed Gentlemen." At one a.m. his watchtower woke him to report torches blazing in the Nor'western watchtower. Simpson dressed in his warmest caribou-skin *capot*, armed twenty of his best men, and stationed them to repel any attack. At three a.m., "being bitterly cold," he said, "I gave my people a dram, and they danced a few reels in the Hall for the sake of the exercise. The noise about the Fort, I conceived, had roused the Prisoner, for there was a fire in his room, and his Woman and Children were heard walking about." At seven, Simpson went back to bed, convinced that it was a false alarm. At ten, two Nor'westers, waving a flag of truce, came over to collect McGillivray's coat and pants. During the excitement, the Nor'wester had escaped in his squaw's nightgown. The *ruse de guerre* had succeeded.

But the comedy ended. Winter and starvation had arrived. The snow crusted and crackled an alarm when the Indians tried to creep up on the caribou herds.

Simpson tried to reconcile his men to "fast days," a diet of putrid white fish, singed beaver skins and the rawhide thongs of their snowshoes. When they were reduced to boiling their dogs, he half-jestingly suggested that reindeer could pull their sleighs. When frostbite froze his officers' noses, he gave it a nickname, "the Company's mark."

Simpson's spirits never seemed to flag. He was nevertheless profoundly relieved to record "charming weather" in late April. "The first goose of the season made its appearance for dinner today. This sapient bird is the harbinger of spring."

Spring brought Chiefs Cut Thumb, Lazette and Rabbit's Eyes with their tribes, loaded with fine pelts of beaver and silver fox, and clamorously "brandy hungry." Simpson greeted them by hoisting the flag, firing cannon, and with gifts of medals, but he had only a scanty supply of adulterated rum.

When his customers threatened to take their furs to the Nor'wester fort, Simpson stripped off "a full suit of my own clothes" and ordered "every Gentleman in the fort to part with their wardrobe." In a long harangue he told the Indians how lucky they were to receive the magical robes of the palefaces. And for next season he promised the best firewater made. As the beaver piled up in his warehouse, Simpson was "much pleased with our few Indians. They have not only been very industrious, but are staunch and true to our cause."

When he left the Athabasca that May, he was a different man to the "pork-eater" of a year earlier. The H.B.C. officers looked upon him with respect. He had proved himself more than a match, both in courage and wits, for the Nor'westers. He could report that his rivals were "daily getting more feeble, have become sick of the contest, and in another year will be beaten out of the field. The Honourable Hudson's Bay Company, on the contrary, is daily gaining ground . . . The campaign of 1821 to 1822 promises to be a memorable era in the North West Chronicles."

When he arrived at Norway House that June, 1821, he learned that, in fact, the long bitter fight for the furs of the West was over. Impending bankruptcy had forced both companies to amalgamate.

The only remaining fight was for the leadership. The new Governor had to be able to smooth out differences. He had to be commercially shrewd. And who was shrewder than George Simpson, who had turned loss into profit in the Athabasca, and who, in reports to his patron, had eliminated all possible competition? Under his stovepipe hat, in the stern of the fastest canoe of the great fur brigade, he already sat like the "Little Emperor" he was destined to become.

New Advertisements.

STEAM TO CARIBOO !

The British Columbia
GENERAL TRANSPORTATION COMPANY

Will place Four of THOMSON'S PATENT ROAD STEAM-
ERS on the route between Yale and Barkerville in the First
Week in April, and will be prepared to enter into Contracts for
the conveyance of Freight from Yale to Soda Creek in EIGHT
DAYS. Through Contracts will be made as soon as the condition
of the road above Quesnelmouth permits.
    Rates of Passage will be advertised in due time.
                              BARNARD & BEEDY,   anagers.

OFF CE—Yates Street, next door to Wells, Fargo & Co.'s

When Gold Fever Hit the Far West

The Cariboo gold rush of the 1860s
was the zaniest, bawdiest, biggest
boom to rock the Canadian West. The
nuggets in the gravels of the Fraser
River lured fortune hunters from everywhere – London, Melbourne, San
Francisco – and sent them swarming
up the B.C. canyons with bullteams,
packponies, even camels. One group
tried to launch a steamer tractor service (top, left), but the idea never
struck paydirt. Before the wagon roads
were built, miners followed the Indian
trails, clinging like crabs to the cliffs.
Some didn't make it – dozens of
miners' bodies came floating down the
Fraser . . . with arrows in their backs.

◁ *Wise men rode the Cariboo Road with a tight
rein. The $1¼ million wagon route linked
Yale to Barkerville. This was China Bar Bluff.*

Guarded by gunmen, stage coaches raced the gold out of the Cariboo.
Their iron safes were booby-trapped with explosive powder.

This was Great Bluff, at 88 Mile Post, edging the Thompson River.
It was 1865, shortly after the completion of a telegraph line (center).

A Nugget 'the Size of a Dinner Pail'

The Mucho Oro claim on Stout's Gulch near Williams Creek more than lived up to its name. In 1863, 4,000 miners were shifting the gravel and blue clay of Williams Creek, and the yields far surpassed those of the earlier bonanzas in California. One of the biggest nuggets of the Cariboo was found in this district, and the richest shovelful: a gleaming 96 ounces.

Many Panned But Few Prospered

Essentially loners, long of beard and patience . . . this is how English painter W. G. R. Hind in the 1860s saw the British Columbia prospector. After the placer mines petered out, enough settled to help change a colony into a province.

Fort Yale was an isolated Hudson's Bay Company post on the lower Fraser until gold fever struck B.C. This was the deadend for steamers – beyond, churning whirlpools made navigation impossible. The Cariboo Road began here, following the Fraser River north to Quesnel, then swinging eastward to Barkerville.

Sir James and Lady Douglas. His main worry as governor was to keep the "British" in British Columbia. The flood of Americans alarmed him.

Amor De Cosmos. Born plain Bill Smith, he changed his name in California, then headed north. He became British Columbia's second premier.

They Tamed the Gold Seekers and Forged a New Province

Sir Matthew Baillie Begbie. He became chief justice of B.C. in 1870; the prospectors knew him as "The Hanging Judge."

John Robson. This fighting editor founded the B.C. mainland's first newspaper, the New Westminster "British Columbian."

John A. Cameron. He struck it rich in the Cariboo. When his wife died, he hired men to carry her pickled body out.

Barkerville

City of Gold

A line of squat shacks and timber shanties, but the gold miners called Barkerville "the biggest city west of Toronto." There was booze, bar-room belles and billiards, and the gold dust panned at the lonely claims slipped quickly through the prospectors' fingers into the pockets of flower-vested gamblers. For many, like Billy Barker (below), it was a story of rags to riches . . . and back to rags. The town that bore his name fared little better: in 1868 a drunken prospector chasing a hurdy-gurdy girl upset a stove, and a fire all but destroyed the flamboyant capital of the Cariboo.

Luxury, Cariboo style, was a bed with linen at the Hotel de France.

Champagne flowed in Barkerville saloons. The price: 4 oz. of gold a quart.

The Barkerville boom. The town boasted a tin shop, bakery, drug store . . . 13 saloons and three breweries, lined along a main street only 18 feet wide due to a drunken surveyor's error. Residents scrambled for the sidewalks when cattle were driven through town.

The Bank of British Columbia, Richfield. Its safe was a 2½ ft. high iron box, often so full the lid was hard to close.

Richfield, B.C., looked like this in 1862. Typical of Cariboo communities, it was just a single street of shacks.

"Scotch Jeannie" ran the Pioneer Hotel at Mosquito Creek. One roll of the dice here once cost a miner more than $1,300.

XI

Canyons of Gold

On a summer day in 1856, a Shuswap Indian squaw was drinking from one of the muddy tributaries of the Fraser River when she spotted a gold nugget as big as a pigeon's egg. She brought the yellow bauble to Donald Maclean, factor of the Hudson's Bay Company trading post at Fort Kamloops. Restraining his excitement, he gave her some iron spoons and suggested, casually, that she and her tribesmen look for more of the pretty pebbles.

Two years later, the nugget arrived in San Francisco for minting in a shipment of 800 ounces of gold brought by the Bay steamer, *Otter*. The news leaked out, and the stampede was on.

Ultimately, thirty thousand Americans left California's played-out gold camps and set out for Canada with their pans and picks, pistols and bowie knives. The San Francisco *Bulletin* sardonically printed "a full vocabulary of Chinook jargon, as used by the Indian tribes on the Fraser and Thompson Rivers." The newspaper could not understand why the Golden State was suddenly being depopulated of all its tinhorn gamblers, saloon keepers, hurdy-gurdy girls, "bummers, bankrupts, and hangers-on at auction sales." The *Bulletin* felt that only boobs would seek gold in the Cariboo, but to those it could not dissuade it bid farewell: "None too poor and none too rich to go. None too young and none too old: even the decrepit go."

It was the biggest, maddest gold hunt to convulse the Canadian West. An estimated $50 millions worth of gold was unearthed from the sand bars and creeks along the Fraser River. And such are history's caprices that it was the invasion of the American sourdoughs that converted the H.B.C.'s fur preserve of New Caledonia into the Canadian province of British Columbia, which in turn ensured the future building of the Canadian Pacific Railway to link the new nation from sea to sea.

The Cariboo country was and still is a 200-mile-wide plateau of lodgepole pine, spiked devil's club, and sagebrush ringed by the ramparts of the Rockies and the British Columbia Coast Range. Slashing its length in the shape of a butcher's hook 850 miles long is the Fraser River. The river begins at Buffalo Dung Lake, near Yellowhead Pass at the British Columbia-Alberta border. Yellowhead, the main gateway from the east, is named for a yellow-haired fur trader, Jasper Hawes, who over-awed the Nazko Indians by threatening to set the cottonwood trees ablaze with his flame-like locks if they did not bring him beaver furs. From the Yellowhead, the Fraser loops northward and then lunges down to Quesnel, the heart of the Cariboo country. It continues down through gorges 5,000 feet deep, through box canyons of perpendicular red rock: it boils with murderous rapids and whirlpools until it reaches the sand bars at Yale. Then it twists west for 130 miles, past silt banks exotic with Indian paint brush and white-starred dogwood and hoary junipers bearded with Spanish moss, to empty into the Pacific.

When the gold rush began in 1858, New Westminster and Quesnel were not yet born. Fort Yale, the head of navigation, was one of the eight Hudson's Bay posts then perched on the Fraser River banks. Fort Victoria, a ten-hour boat ride across the Strait of Juan de Fuca, was the Bay's headquarters. There, on the southern tip of Vancouver Island, 600 Britons nurtured their rose gardens, played cricket, wrote literate — though nine months' belated — letters to the London *Times*, and desultorily dreamed of making their colony a little England on the Pacific.

The Governor of the colony was James Douglas, 55, Chief H.B.C. Factor of New Caledonia. "Black Douglas" was the son of a Glasgow merchant and a Jamaican Creole. He had luminous agate eyes in a swarthy face. He was six feet tall, deep-chested, straight-backed, and he kept in trim by skipping rope every morning. He disliked Americans, having just seen their settlers snatch the Oregon country away from the Bay Company with their political battle cry, "Fifty-four forty or fight!" The last thing he and his colonists wanted was an American gold rush.

Some people considered Douglas cold and pompous. Sir George Simpson, whom Douglas served as second-in-command in the Oregon, described him as sound and able, but "furiously violent when roused."

He was, in short, a blend of St. George and St. Vitus; nothing roused him more than disloyalty to the Company or the Queen.

On Vancouver Island, these godheads were practically synonymous. After losing the Oregon country, Simpson had entered into an arrangement with the British Colonial Office to keep the Yankees out of New Caledonia. Vancouver Island, a border bulwark against Yankee trading ships, was to be regarded as a Crown colony. But the company, by paying the Crown seven shillings a year, would still "own" the island. In theory, the Company would colonize the island, but this, too, was a farce, since settlement was an anathema to the fur trader Simpson.

To ensure the success of his plans, Simpson had managed to install Douglas in the dual role of Governor and Chief Factor.

Douglas loved ceremony and uniforms. He did not mind wearing two hats. And though he was the Governor of a colony without colonists, he insisted on being paid a salary of 800 pounds a year. "One must live in a manner becoming the representative of the Crown," he said, "and I could never consent to represent Her Majesty in a shabby way."

On assuming office on November 19, 1851, Douglas tried to take his job of governing seriously. He suggested to Simpson that the Company bring in 20 British families, totalling 100 persons, free of charge. Simpson slapped him down. And Douglas conceded he had "probably exceeded the mark," and restricted himself to governing the company servants sent over from England to mine coal at Nanaimo and work the company's Puget Sound farms.

Coming from church one April Sunday in 1858, Governor Douglas was alarmed to see the San Francisco steamboat, *Commodore*, glide into Victoria Harbour with a load of 450 brawling Argonauts. It was followed by a fantastic flotilla of 67 other sternwheelers, resurrected from the boneyards of the Barbary Coast. Their hulls had been patched and their names changed to *Gold Hunter, Queen of the Isles* and *Live Yankee* to hide their reputations as floating coffins. Each boat disgorged a rabble of Yankees with wide-brimmed hats, red flannel shirts, iron-cleated gunboots, and pistols slung from their belts.

Victoria was soon white with tents and swarming with sourdoughs waiting to travel up the Fraser as soon as the spring waters receded. San Francisco merchants set up about 50 shops, and within weeks Douglas had $2 millions in the Company safe. Though he had no real jurisdiction over the mainland, Governor Douglas had proclaimed that no Yankee could "disturb" its soil without paying a license of $5 a month to Her Majesty's Government. Putting on his Chief Factor's hat, Douglas ruled that all ships entering the Fraser without a license from the Company would be liable to seizure. No goods could be carried except the Company's. And each passenger must pay the Company a two-dollar head tax. With a flourish, he signed his proclamations, "His Excellency, James Douglas, Governor of Vancouver Island and its Dependencies, Commander-in-Chief and Vice-Admiral of the same."

Douglas wrote to the Colonial Office in London that he had taken these drastic steps to combat Yankees who might have "a hankering in their minds after annexation to the United States." To collect taxes, he was stationing the Admiralty ship *H.M.S. Satellite* at the mouth of the Fraser. Thus the gold-fields would be "as secure from foreign intrusion as the fabled garden of Hesperides."

The American prospectors, unlike the settlers who had come to Oregon in covered wagons, were not interested in land or Manifest Destiny. Their sole interest was to lead the pack up the Fraser to the gold-fields. Some went by leaky wood-burning paddle-wheelers held together largely by paint. With drunken laughter, they helped Captain "Gassy Jack" Deighton, who boasted he could "run her on heavy dew," toss his cargo of bacon into the boiler of the *Henrietta* to get up steam. Gassy Jack collected money enough to set up a saloon at "Gastown," which later had its name changed to Vancouver.

Others battled the current in wooden *bateaux* lashed like pontoon rafts, six abreast to carry mules and Newfoundland dogs. At the slippery trench cliffs, the more foolhardy took off their boots and tried to climb barefoot. Wiser souls strapped their 100-pound packs of "Cariboo turkey" (bacon) and "Cariboo strawberries" (beans) to their dogs and mules and took the Indian trails along the bank.

One enterprising Arizonian, Frank Laumeister, paid $6,000 to import 28 camels. Each, he figured, would carry 1,000 pounds as compared to a mule's 300 pounds. He had not figured, however, on his camels' aroma. The mule teams belonging to "Dirty Harry" Strouse stampeded at the first whiff. Harry himself was ready to take the pledge when he saw them. When the rocks cut the camels' spongy hoof pads to shreds, Laumeister abandoned his plan. He let the camels run wild in the Cariboo and the last of them died in 1905.

Two Swedes, Andrew Olson and John Yorston, won fame of a kind by trundling along the trail a one-wheeled barrow. It had shafts fore and aft, and supported a 2,000-pound pack in the middle. But balancing the weight between the pusher in back and the puller in front was a feuding matter. Tempers snapped like fiddle strings on the trail, and the "push-me-pullya," as the rickshaw was called, went the way of the camels.

The Argonauts found their paystreak between Fort Hope and Fort Yale. While squatting around the fire on a sandbar, frying "Rocky Mountain deadshot" (flapjacks) a prospector named Ed Hill noticed yellow sand in the moss between his boots. In his frying pan he washed out granular gold worth $50. Soon every stretch of sand near "Hill's Bar" was thronged with miners rolling their "rockers" – a cradlelike device that allowed them to filter out the black gravel and catch the free placer gold on a blanket beneath. The names of the claims reflected their stakers: "Yankee Doodle Bar," "Fifty-four Forty Flat," "Boston Bar," "Texas Bar," "Stranger's Flat," "Murderer's Bar."

Inevitably the miners clashed with the Nazko Indians. One prospector, C. C. Gardiner, of California, reported: "The Indians here can beat anything alive stealing. They will soon be able to steal a man's food after he has eaten it." After the miners sold them "hayou," a vile concoction of whisky and bacon grease, the inflamed redskins nicked miner Ned Stout with an arrow, and at Yale a mass meeting of miners drafted a petition to Governor Douglas: "Decapitated, denuded corpses of unfortunate adventurers are daily picked up on the river. Take steps, sir, to check the effusion of blood, and restore law and order."

Douglas arrived to hold a conclave, or *wawa*, with the Indians. He pacified them by dispensing "a keg of treacle, a box of dainty English biscuits, and some speechifying." Actually, he was less disturbed by the Indians than the Yankees. Never had he seen "a crowd of more ruffianly-looking men." But he found that the "Yankee scamps seem in favour of English rule on Fraser's River. They have a degree of confidence in the sterling uprightness and integrity of Englishmen, which they do not entertain for their own countrymen." By sheer force of character and a bit of bluffing, Governor Douglas persuaded 500 prospectors to build a pack-horse trail across the canyons near Fort Yale. He not only got them to work for nothing, each put up $25 as a good conduct guarantee. With the guarantees he built a toll road from Harrison Lake and Lillooet, and collected enough to feed his 500 labourers. Nevertheless, the Yankees worried him. His work gangs "took it with bad grace" when he commanded them to deliver three rousing hip-hip-hoorahs for the Queen. "The Americans will require constant watching," he warned in a report to the Colonial Secretary in London, Sir Edward Bulwer Lytton.

Sir Edward was the author of *The Last Days of Pompeii*. When Governor Douglas wanted to name the new port of New Westminster at the mouth of the Fraser River "Queensborough," Sir Edward recoiled: "Queensborough is not only prosaic, but the quintessence of vulgarity." When Douglas begged for hairy-chested British he-men to stem the hordes of Yankee roughnecks, Bulwer Lytton sent him genteel writers of *belles lettres*. As a consequence, the Americans dredged the most gold from the Fraser River and the British produced the most literate diaries.

The journals of Billy ("Cariboo Yank") Cunningham contained such off-hand items as "Making from two to three thousand dollars a day." The journal of British Dr. Walter Butler Cheadle was full of such entries as "Oh dear! One-eighth inch of ice in our tea cups this morning." Cheadle's journal sold nine editions under the title *North-West Passage by Land*, which was fortunate, since Cheadle did not mine a single nugget.

At the Colonial Office, Sir Edward came to the conclusion that Douglas could no longer serve two masters. He sent a stinging note in which Her Majesty rebuked Governor Douglas for allowing Chief Factor Douglas to favour the Bay Company. The two-dollar head tax was "disapproved and disallowed." The Company had exclusive fur-trading rights with the Indians; it had no right to profit on the Queen's gold-rush trade. Douglas, horrified at the thought of offending Her Majesty, apologized, but Bulwer Lytton was adamant. Her Majesty, he wrote, had decided that the gold business was so lucrative that she was taking over the whole coastal mainland as a Crown colony. Douglas could be Governor of British Columbia – at a salary of 1,800 pounds – if he severed all connections with the Hudson's Bay Company. It was a hard decision, but Queen came before Company. Anyway the coastal fur trade had gone to pot. Clerks were leaving the posts, Indians their traplines to pan for gold.

When "Black Douglas" resigned, it marked the end of Sir George Simpson's plans to control the coast. Douglas made no bones about it: henceforth the Colony of British Columbia would give no preference to the H.B.C. Even though the Bay's new Chief Factor, Alexander Dallas, was Douglas's son-in-law, he would be treated as just another commercial representative. When a man like Douglas changed loyalties, Simpson learned, there were no half measures.

Lytton was delighted with Douglas's forcefulness. When the Governor-elect requested a "naval or military force," the Colonial Secretary immediately sent him a detachment of 165 Royal Engineers. "Wherever England extends her sceptre," he said, "she pledges the defence of her sword." When the Governor-elect requested an Attorney-General who would impress the

The Neversweat mine, Williams Creek. The tunnels were damp and dangerous but a miner could make $8 to $10 a day.

commoners with the majesty of the Queen's law, Sir Edward promptly sent him a man "who could truss a murderer and hang him to the nearest tree."

The new custodian of the law in the colony was a 39-year-old lawyer named Matthew Baillie Begbie. Lytton liked him, because Begbie had gone to Cambridge University and came from a family of novelists; further, Begbie could quote from Sir Edward's favourite authors, Milton and Horace. Douglas admired the new judge because of his arrogance. Even the prospectors approved because, as one said, "He was the biggest man, the smartest man, the best-looking man, and the damndest man that ever swaggered up the Cariboo trail." Six-feet-five-inches tall, with a grey-streaked Van Dyke beard and moustachios waxed to needle points, a black cape tossed theatrically over his broad shoulders, Begbie looked like a Spanish aristocrat. He had been an amateur boxer, singer and actor at college.

On Begbie's arrival, Douglas took him up the Fraser to Fort Langley for what Douglas called the "solemnity" – the formal inaugural of British Columbia, on November 19, 1858.

Cold rain slanted down from a leaden sky and a sharp wind sighed through the ponderosa pine. Bright touches of colour were contributed by the Shuswap Indians huddling in their scarlet blankets, and the blue-jackets saluting aboard the steamboat *Beaver*, and the Royal Engineers in their gold-laced uniforms. The British troops formed a guard of honour for the dripping gentry entering the cedar-log fort. A mace was lacking for the ceremony, so an engineer hurriedly clipped an arrow-shaped slice of metal with a pair of tin shears from the engine room of the paddlewheeler. While about 100 onlookers cheered, and the cannon fired an 18-gun salute, Douglas swore in Matthew Bailley Begbie as Chief Justice, and then Mr. Justice Begbie administered the oath of office to His Excellency, Governor James Douglas.

Governor Douglas commemorated the birth of British Columbia by building another toll road – the "Dewdney Trail" – from Fort Hope into the Okanagan Lake area where Americans from Oregon had scooped out $1,300 worth of nuggets in six weeks. Passing laws by his own proclamation – he disdained representative government – Douglas offered land at ten shillings an acre to Yankee ranchers and farmers who would swear allegiance to The Queen. Without immigrant agriculturists, he shrewdly observed, the Gold Colony would forever remain "a desert – drained of its wealth, dependent on others for its daily food."

Chief Justice Begbie rose to his high office as ably and autocratically as did Douglas. Riding to trouble spots on horseback, Begbie would don his wig, empanel a jury of Yankee prospectors, and hold court in the middle of the camp. When the jury men balked at condemning a friend, he grew furious. He once shouted at a jury in his high tenor, "You, gentlemen, are a pack of Dallas horse thieves. And it would give me great pleasure to see you hanged, each and every one of you, for declaring a murderer guilty only of manslaughter." When a jury acquitted a prospector who had obviously sandbagged a companion, Begbie declared, "Prisoner at the bar, the jury have said you are not guilty. You can go. And I devoutly hope the next man you sandbag will be one of the jury."

Some called him "The Hanging Judge"; some thought him "The Personification of British Justice." But in 18 months the mining camps had only three murders – by drunken Indians. Once, while sunning himself on the balcony of a saloon hotel, Begbie heard some ruffians below on the road plotting to shoot him. He went into his room for his chamber pot, emptied it on their heads, and resumed his siesta.

Begbie's harshness brought him in conflict with two gold hunters turned weekly newspaper editors, and both later to become British Columbia premiers. The editor of the Victoria *British Colonist* was a fortune hunter from Windsor, Nova Scotia. He sought gold in California with a revolver in each boot until the vigilantes chased him out for dallying with "surplus" Mormon wives. He was born plain Bill Alec Smith, but changed to Amor De Cosmos – "*Amor*" from the Latin, "*De*" from the French, and "*Cosmos*" from the Greek. It meant "Lover Of The Universe." The way he drank, some thought he should have called himself *Amor De Bacchus*. The feud began over John Butts, Victoria's tippling town crier. As steamers were leaving for the Fraser, Butts would cry out the announcement and conclude with the prayer "God Save the Queen." One day he bawled, "God Save John Butts," and Begbie had him put in jail. De Cosmos called the judge "a tyrannical nabob." He hinted that Begbie and Douglas were members of a Family Compact, whose policy was "you tickle me and I'll tickle you." De Cosmos was forced to apologize but in his following issue he roasted the "muzzlers of freedom" who wore the toga of Cato the Censor: "It is vain, puffed-up, short-witted mummies and numbskulls that fear the press and strive to gag it."

The editor of the New Westminster *British Columbian* was another flamboyant character, John ("Honest John") Robson, one of 16 children of the first jailer of Sarnia, Ontario. He directed his windiest blasts against Douglas. The Governor was a "feckless and effete buffoon" whose one-man government was full of "foul air, redolent of H.B. peltry and salmon." Begbie, the "Tyrant Judge," he charged, "had accepted twenty acres of land as a bribe for reversing a court decision." Douglas ignored his slander; but not Begbie. Though Robson offered a qualified apology next day, the Chief Justice tongue-lashed him in court and tossed him in jail. The next issue of the *British Columbian* carried a front-page editorial titled "A Voice from the Dungeon": "Fellow colonists! We greet you from our cell, startled by the wild shrieks of a dying maniac on one hand, and the clanking of the murderer's chains on the other . . . "

To administer law throughout the vast territory of Columbia, Begbie imported 15 Irishmen and made them magistrates. They were known as Gold Commissioners. Some kept order with a shillelagh; some with a rope. When miners were feuding over a shooting at Wild Stud Creek, Magistrate Peter O'Reilly ended it with a celebrated line: "Boys, if there is shooting in Kootenay, there will be hanging in Kootenay."

Judge Begbie looked on the Fraser gold as "a perfect nuisance. The miners have to carry it from their cabins to their claims every morning. They have to watch it while they work. Then they have to carry it back again (sometimes as much as two men can lift) to their cabins at night, and watch it while they sleep."

Actually, no more than half a million dollars' worth of gold was panned from the sandbars of the lower Fraser in the first six months of the stampede. And, by 1860, it seemed to be petering out. Thousands of Yankees were returning home to San Francisco in disgust, calling the "River of Gold" the "River of Humbug." But paddling downriver, they could not convince the new hordes paddling upriver. The hardiest prospectors sought the mother lode 200 miles further inland. Crossing the chasm at Spuzzum by cable and bucket, they yanked boats by towline up to the fork of the Quesnel and the Fraser, then fanned out east for more than 60 miles. They explored the creeks wriggling out of Horsefly Lake, Jack of Clubs Lake and Cariboo Lake, until in 1861, in the blue clay of the creek beds they found it.

Lightning snaked across the sky as Ned Campbell picked up yellow pebbles from the claim that he later called Lightning Creek. Dick Willoughby, a violin-playing Indian fighter from Missouri, dug 3,037 ounces (at $11 an ounce), from his Discovery claim on Lowhee Creek. Within six months, John A. ("Cariboo") Cameron, from Glengarry, Ontario, had panned $385,000 worth of paydirt from Williams Creek, including one nugget "the size of a dinner pail." Within twelve months, Billy Barker, a bowlegged black-whiskered Cornish sailor, had $600,000 in his poke. Bill ("Dill Pickle") Diller, a 240-pound barrel-shaped

Bostonian, said he would not stop digging until he could take out his own weight in gold. He took out his own weight in gold and that of his 120-pound Newfoundland dog, and was still excavating $10,000 worth a week. A short Vermont baker named H. F. Davis managed to sneak in a 12-foot claim between Bill Diller's and Billy Barker's claims; it gave him $15,000 and the nickname of "Twelve Foot" Davis. At the claims called Mucho Oro, Neversweat, the Fountain, and Prairie Flower, their owners sluiced as much as 170 ounces of gold in a day. J. C. Bryant of the Ne'er Do Well claim boasted that he dug the richest shovelful ever seen in the Cariboo: 96 ounces. "I dug off a piece of bedrock," he said, "and it was soft and came off like cheese with the shovel . . ."

News of the Cariboo bonanza drew adventurers from London, Melbourne, Hong Kong and Boston. In New York one would-be gold hunter had to stand in line all day to reserve space on the next ship for Victoria. A caravan of 150 tenderfeet from Ontario, known as the Overlanders, set out by oxcart from Red River.

Overnight, the lower Fraser camps became ghost towns. The river was clogged with gum-booted prospectors and flower-vested gamblers, scrambling north to the gold camp called the "Cariboo Elephant." They arrived to find that the best claims were already staked. Newcomers had to dig down 60 feet to bedrock. They had to buy water-wheels, hydraulic pumps and flumes to keep their pits dry. Still they came, were grubstaked, made partnership deals, until their wooden ugly shacks were strung along Williams Creek on the slope of Balding Mountain, for five miles.

The ten thousand citizens of Barkerville called it "the biggest city west of Toronto." It was certainly the most preposterous. Its 13 saloons, its myriad gambling halls, three breweries and one opera house all teetered on four-foot stilts above the sluices and mud. The sawed-lumber buildings and shanties were perched along one thin mud road whose width, due to a drunken surveyor's error, was a mere 18 feet. It was so narrow that, when a rancher drove some Texas longhorns through town, it was claimed that all the citizens ran upstairs to avoid being gored.

Opportunists flocked to Barkerville to cater to the *nouveau riche.* A Quebec postman, Frank ("Jonesy") Barnard set up a mail delivery at two dollars a letter and walked 500 miles on foot on his first delivery. He made so much money that he later launched the B-X Cariboo Pony Express, his red-and-yellow stage coaches each carrying an iron burglar-proof safe (with exploding powder loaded in the interstices to discourage robbery).

The four-page *Cariboo Sentinel,* published each Saturday on a hand press, sold for one dollar. Muleskinners charged a dollar a pound to freight in billiard tables, costing $18,000, kegs of *pâté de foie gras,* and grand pianos. About the only thing they didn't bring in was a bathtub.

The new millionaires had their leg-o'-mutton whiskers trimmed and perfumed in the shop of Washington D. ("Mr. Dixie") Moses, an ex-slave who signified his trade by a pine pole wrapped in red flannels; he also filled teeth with pure gold nuggets. They paid $5 for a pat of butter, $50 for a pair of boots, and $700 dollars for a pot-bellied stove. R. Byron Johnson, author of *Very Far West Indeed,* had to pay 50 cents to sleep on the floor of a billiard saloon with 40 sourdoughs – and was asked to supply his own blanket. "I remonstrated gently with my host," the Englishman wrote. "But all the reply I could get was that he 'reckoned any man that 'ud raise a growl on such an occasion was darned small pertaters.' "

The status symbol of the time was imported French champagne. At Wake-Up Jake's, the Miner's Rest and Big Teepee saloons, bartenders, weighing out gold dust (four ounces for a quart of champagne) would wet their fingers with bubbly and wipe the adhering gold off into their leather pockets. The more dexterous let their fingernails grow, cleaning them frequently. In his best-selling diary, Dr. Cheadle told of a miner who, "having treated all the Company in the bar room, and finding no more, had all the glasses of the Establishment filled up with champagne on the counter. Then he swept them off with his fist. Another, unable to find enough people to treat, opened a hamper of champagne and jumped into it with his bare feet. Major Downie, formerly of Downieville, California, set up champagne bottles in the ten pin alley and bowled at them!"

The miners trickled gold dust down the necks of the hurdy-gurdy girls for the pleasure of seeing them wriggle for the loot. These voluptuous German girls, under Madame Mamie Bendixon of San Francisco, charged $10 to dance to one tune on a hand organ, or "hurdy-gurdy."

Aghast at the thought of all these millionaires in the clutches of such hussies, the Baroness Angela Burdett-Coutts arranged with the Bishop of London to send over a "bride ship." The *Tynemouth* arrived in Victoria with its petticoated cargo of what the *Colonist* called "sixty maidens meditating matrimony – ages varying from fourteen to uncertain." The maidens walked down the gang-plank through a lane of eager whiskered faces. All found mates.

The Duchess of Somerset attempted to bring culture

to Barkerville. The sight of her riding side-saddle, exposing her woollen petticoats, "caused two shy mule teams so much alarm," she wrote in her memoirs, *Impressions of a Tenderfoot*, "that in order to pacify them, and prevent the wagons from leaving the trail, I had to conceal my objectionable self behind some bushes until they had passed."

A British barrister, Clement Francis Cornwall, stocked a ranch named Ashcroft Manor, to teach the sport of the English fox-hunt, using (since there were no foxes) coyotes. He imported English hounds at a cost of 65 pounds each and dressed his pupils in the traditional pink coats, and taught a Shuswap Indian named Henry to sound a silver horn. But he could not get them to shout "Tallyho!" Every time they saw the coyote they forgot their carefully taught instructions and whooped "There goes the son of a ———!" Cornwall closed his school and became Lieutenant-Governor of British Columbia, which entitled him to more gold braid than even Douglas had coveted.

Another English uplifter, the Reverend John Sheepshanks, later Anglican Bishop of Norwich, founded the Cariboo Literary Institute, which ultimately stocked 437 volumes. His librarian, Miss Florence Wilson, started the Cariboo Dramatic Society and later opened, to the Reverend's dismay, the flossiest saloon in Barkerville.

The time-honoured combination of wine, women and song ruined most of the Barkerville millionaires, but they at least went out singing. Billy Barker left and came back with a bride, a London widow. When she refused to stay home with him, he spent his fortune in the saloons. He died broke in the Old Men's Home in Victoria, where he was known to perform a little jig and sing:

> *I'm English Bill,*
> *Never worked, an' never will.*
> *Get away girls,*
> *Or I'll tousle your curls.*

John A. ("Cariboo") Cameron left when his wife Sophie died, offering $12 a day and a $2,000 bonus to any man who helped him convey her body to the coast. It was 50 degrees below zero but seven volunteered. They pickled his wife in alcohol in a 450-pound lead-lined box, put it on a toboggan, with a keg of rum and a bag of gold dust, and slid it to New Westminster for shipment. Eventually Sophie was buried in Glengarry County, Ontario. Cameron plunged his millions in a gold-mining venture in Nova Scotia to seek another fortune but returned to Camerontown penniless, and died of a stroke one week later.

Barkerville, the golden city, went up in flames. The fire was touched off September 16, 1868, when a drunken miner tried to kiss a hurdy-gurdy girl ironing her petticoats in the canvas-covered shed at the back of Barry & Adler's Saloon. True to form, she demanded payment and in the ensuing struggle, the urgent lover knocked over the cast-iron stove. In less than two hours Barkerville was charcoal. But by then prospectors were calling Williams Creek "Dutch Bill's Humbug Creek," and deserting it for the new gold discovery at Big Bend on the Columbia, which, in turn, was soon repudiated as "Big Bilk."

It was the two great figures of the Cariboo, the two Britons who kept a firm restraining hand on the Yankee invasion, who profited most in the end from the stampede. Matthew Baillie Begbie, the terror of the rowdies, was knighted by the Queen and became Chief Justice of British Columbia. He built a house in Victoria, with rose gardens and cherry trees. His lawn tennis soirees and his Saturday dinners became famous. He surrounded himself with cronies from gold rush days to play whist and drink claret, and encased himself in an English atmosphere already reflecting a time that had passed. He died in 1894, at 75, asking in his will that the inscription on his grave read "Lord be merciful to me, a sinner."

Governor James Douglas was also knighted by the Queen for his road-building, which had laced the colony together at no cost to the Crown. The 385-mile Cariboo Road along the cliffs and canyons of the Fraser, blasted from rock by Her Majesty's Royal Engineers, paid for by the gold dust of the Yankee travellers, was his monument. A half century later, road-builders marvelled at the soundness of its construction and continued to use it as a base. His title was heady wine to the half-breed Douglas. In postscripts to business letters, he would write: "Letters to me should be addressed as follows: Sir James Douglas, K.C.B., Victoria, Vancouver Island." Even in his private diary he referred to his own half-breed wife as "Lady Douglas." He retired in 1864 and lived 13 years in retirement among his rose gardens in Victoria.

He lived to see the colony he had tamed and saved from the restless Americans join Canada in 1871. When he died aged 74, the *Colonist*, which had once flayed him as despot, wrote: "Today a whole Province is in tears . . ." He died the richest man in British Columbia, having had the foresight to buy land in Victoria at one English pound an acre, which he sold for as much as $10,000 an acre. Nobody mentioned it at the time, but the man most distressed by the Cariboo gold rush was the man who had made the most money out of it.

Whisky Ruled the West... Until the Mounties Rode In

When the whisky traders came, the days of the "noble barbarians" were numbered. Once-proud warriors prowled the land, craving rum or rotgut; they'd sell their furs or their daughters for a bottle. On the grassland of Alberta known as Whoop-Up Country, traders in the 1870s laced whisky with chewing tobacco, red pepper, ginger and molasses. They called it Whoop-Up Wallop.

When American whisky runners gunned down a lodge of Assiniboines at Cypress Hills in 1873, the Canadian government was pushed into recruiting and dispatching the North West Mounted Police to bring law to the frontier. An artist on the trek drew this picture of the Mountie column snaking westward across 1,000 miles, much of it through badlands, toward the Sweet Grass Hills.

Crude Capital of the Brawling Empire

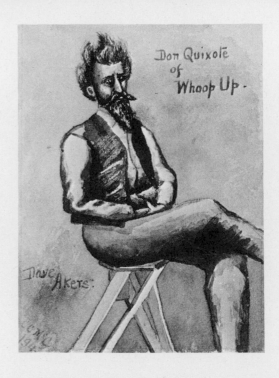

The Whoop-Up Country, ruled in its heyday by American frontiersman Johnny Jerome Healy, stretched 200 miles across the grasslands from Fort Benton, Montana, into southern Alberta. Fort Whoop-Up became the Canadian capital of this violent frontier, and here Indians would trade away even their horses and guns for a few cups of rotgut – then their families faced starvation without the means to hunt. Chief proprietor was Dave Akers, mockingly called the "Don Quixote of Whoop-Up." The portrait of Akers (right) is by Charles C. McCaul, who was a lawyer at Fort Macleod.

Fort Whoop-Up had Jim Crow rules. Indians were not allowed in this bar, but were served outside the stockade walls.

These rare photographs show what Fort Whoop-Up looked like when a fast gun was the only law in the West. The fortress, guarded by cannon, was on Canadian territory, but the traders ladled their liquor under the Stars and Stripes.

The Order Was 'Westward!'

Before these Mounties began their epic 1,000-mile trek westward from Fort Dufferin, their advance guard reported it would be "an easy and agreeable march of a few weeks duration." In reality, it took three months of slogging, starvation and thirst. The Indians and the outlaws marvelled at the dogged determination of the newcomers in scarlet.

George Arthur French, first commissioner of the N.W.M.P. His mission: with 274 Mounties, to bring peace to the riotous Northwest.

James F. Macleod, assistant commissioner, expected a fight when he stormed Fort Whoop-Up, but the Yankees had deserted the fort.

On the Long, Long Trail

Henri Julien, artist for Montreal's Canadian Illustrated News, *went along on the trek and sketched one of the 114 Red River carts in the Mountie caravan.*

On September 8, 1874 the Mounties hunted buffalo for meat. At one point, each Mountie was rationed to 14 ounces of flour and a slice of dried potato per day.

Métis entertained the police with the Red River jig. One half-breed carried a door in his cart to provide a platform to dance on: one of the few luxuries.

Drama at night: the Mounties' horses were broncos, so nervous that even a distant wolf howl would spook them. In a lightning storm, they stampeded.

The trail took a terrible toll of livestock, as this scene in Dead Horse Valley reveals. The men began to call themselves the "Dismounted Police."

On sick parade. Despite the hardships, a constable's pay was 75 cents a day. All the pictures on these pages were from sketches drawn on the spot.

The Law Enforcers

Face to face with the Sioux – this tribe terrorized the American plains, but the warriors bowed to Mountie justice.

The American whisky traders were incredulous, then furious, when the tenderfoot Redcoats dragged them to trial – even this "court" was only a general store at High River, Alberta.

XII

Law and Outlaw

JOHNNY JEROME HEALY, proprietor of Fort Whoop-Up, the rowdiest of all the trading posts peddling rotgut whisky to Alberta's Blackfoot Indians, looked up from his log counter into the barrels of nine rifles. They were in the hands of a reckless gang known as the High River Wolfers.

That summer of 1872, the Wolfers had already browbeaten Healy's agents in the whisky forts called Spitzee, Slideout, Robber's Roost, Standoff, Kipp, Conrad, Sheep Creek and Whisky Gap. At gun point the Wolfers had forced each of his traders to sign a pledge not to barter guns with the Indians in the 200-mile territory straddling the Montana-Alberta border; the Wolfers wanted that trade for themselves. But Johnny Healy was a man of different stripe. With his Buffalo Bill goatee, his brown cowlick and impudent Irish grin, he calmly puffed on his black cigar and blew smoke in their faces. "Speak up, gentlemen," he said. "What's eating you?"

"Mr. Healy," began John Evans, the leader of the Wolfers, "there is a serious charge preferred against you of selling guns to the redskins. We have come down to see about it."

Healy took his cigar from his mouth and held it over a keg on his counter. "Gentlemen, if you don't skedaddle out of here, I'll plunge my cigar into this gunpowder and blow you all to hell – myself included."

The Wolfers lowered their rifles and Healy soon convinced them that they were all in this business together. Their fire-arms and firewater all came from the same source: Montreal's I. G. Baker Company in Fort Benton. Their customers were the same Indians. Why not sign a pact to promote and share the business of bilking the Indians out of their furs and buffalo robes?

Putting his arm around Healy's shoulder, Evans laughed. "I move we all go down to the Oldman River and wash some of the wool out of our eyes."

Thus Johnny Healy became overlord of the whisky trade along the Whoop-Up Trail. It began at Fort Benton, a clutter of log stores, saloons and bordellos on the north bank of the Missouri River. It snaked north 200 miles past the alkali badlands of Yeast Powder Flat, crossed the Milk River near the Canadian border, and wound around the grassy coulées and wind-scoured buttes into Healy's Fort Whoop-Up, at the junction of the St. Mary's and Oldman Rivers. From there the bulltrain tracks cut the Rocky Mountain foot-hills as far northwest as the present site of Calgary, where Healy delivered whisky to Fred ("Slippery") Kanouse's Old Bow Fort on the Elbow River.

It was a time of anarchy in the Canadian West. The rule of the Hudson's Bay Company had weakened with the death of Sir George Simpson in 1860, and there was no Canadian law until the arrival of the North West Mounted Police in 1874.

Into this power vacuum stepped Johnny Healy, a bootlegging frontier gangster, important today mainly for his role in the birth of the Mounties. And, if it had not been for the arrival of those Scarlet Riders of the Plains, Alberta and Saskatchewan might well have been annexed to the United States. As one American politician wrote in the 1860s, the Saskatchewan Valley was "maturing like ripe fruit in autumn ready to fall into our expectant lap."

Healy was a man of raffish charm, cool and courageous, a six-foot-two Dubliner who went west in 1858 with the Second United States Dragoons. He was almost as good with a bow and arrow as with a rifle. "I'll fight anything from a grizzly bear to a circular saw," he once said. While panning for gold in the untamed Indian country near Fort Edmonton, Healy noted that the Blackfeet gave the Hudson's Bay Company traders as much as two beaver pelts for a pint of diluted brandy.

Healy went to Isaac Gilbert Baker, the merchant prince of Fort Benton. "Yankee federal law won't allow the sale of Injun firewater, by the act of 1832," Healy said. "But you stake me on the sly, and I'll set up a dozen trading posts on Canadian soil, all flying the Stars and Stripes."

"How can you snare the redskins away from Hudson's Bay rum?" Baker asked.

"You leave that to me," Healy said. "I'll fix up Injun

'coffin varnish' so strong, you'll be able to shoot the Injun through the brain or heart, and he won't die till he's sobered up."

In 1869, in partnership with Baker's nephew, Alfred B. Hamilton, Healy built his first whisky fort on the Oldman River – eleven log huts encircled by a crude picket fence. As he promised, his brews had strength. One recipe called for a quart of whisky, a pound of rank chewing tobacco, a handful of red pepper, a bottle of Jamaica ginger, and a quart of molasses. When sprinkled with water "ad libitum" and heated to the boiling point, the mixture lived up to its label of "Whoop-Up Wallop." Another consisted of mixing whisky with a painkiller medicine, Hostetter's Bitters, Castile soap, and blackstrap chewing tobacco. Healy laced it with red ink, served it hot, and then got out of the way. In his first year his inflamed customers burned the fort down.

The rebuilt Fort Whoop-Up, six miles from present-day Lethbridge, was more elaborate. Thirty men worked for two years erecting its pointed log stockade. Loop-holes in the mud-chinked walls provided openings for muskets in case of attack by Indians. A muzzle-loading brass cannon was mounted on one bastion. A second bastion supported a six-pound mountain howitzer. A big bell, hung over a well, sounded the alarm and iron bars on the store room chimney prevented uninvited redskins from dropping in. For trading there were three small wickets beside the cottonwood log gates. "The trader stood at the wicket, a tub full of booze beside him," Colonel Sam Steele of the Mounties later recalled. "And when an Indian pushed a buffalo robe through the hole, the trader handed out a tin cup full of some poisonous concoction. A quart of the stuff bought a fine pony. When spring came, wagon loads of the proceeds of the traffic were exported to Fort Benton, south of the border."

Healy collected about him the rag-tag-and-bobtail of the frontier. The Bay Company, whose nearest posts were at Rocky Mountain House and Fort Edmonton, estimated that he had an army of five hundred "border banditti." He probably had about two hundred: de-serters from the army, American free traders, Canadian *voyageurs*, Montana prospectors out of a stake, bull-whackers, muleskinners, and the Wolfers. The latter were despised by Indians and whites alike. They sprinkled strychnine on buffalo carcasses, and collected the skin of the wolves who ate the poisoned bait, often poisoning dogs and starving travellers as well.

Healy's men were characterized by such nicknames as "Waxy Weatherwax," "Slippery Dick," "Toe String Joe," and "Spring Heel Jack," who had to show his heels when his whisky post was set afire by the burning arrows of dissatisfied Indian customers. Another was a full-blooded Indian, adopted by Healy as a boy when white men massacred his parents. He was called Blood Chief Healy as a joke on Johnny Healy.

Blood Chief Joe ran whisky for Healy from Benton to Fort Whoop-Up where the traders would welcome his wagon train with a cannon volley. Joe recalled that the Indians liked Whoop-Up. "There was a lot of life there. The camps outside were alight with dance, and the white stayed within for days while the drunken Indians fought without." A famous letter written by a trader in Fort Whoop-Up to a friend in Fort Benton went like this:

> "*Dear Friend: My partner Will Geary got to putting on airs and I shot him and he is dead – the potatoes are looking well. Yours truly, Snookum Jim.*"

The Blackfeet called Whoop-Up, "*Akiy-een-esko*," meaning "Many-Chiefs-Died." The fort was christened by one of Healy's "bug juice" runners, Harry ("Ka-moose") Taylor. He was a chesty, bantam cock of an English parson from the Isle of Wight, who had found a more lucrative profession than preaching. His nick-name meant "Squaw Thief," bestowed after he had stolen a Blood Indian squaw as a concubine. Kamoose, telling Healy how he evaded the cavalry which enforced the liquor laws in Montana, said, "You've got to whoop it up for the border." The name stuck.

The other whisky forts had equally appropriate names. Fort Standoff, on the Belly River, was named one day in 1871 when Joe Kipp and a band of whisky runners stood off pursuit by a U.S. Marshal. Fort Spitzee was a corruption of the Blackfeet word *ipitsi*, meaning "high." Its stockaded trading cabins were built on High River in 1869 by John ("Liver Eating") Johnson and Dave ("Don Quixote") Akers, two flamboyant Healy lieutenants.

Johnson was a short, skinny Mountain Man, who claimed to have scalped and killed 23 Indians and eaten their livers. Akers was a six-foot-three Kentuckian with a brown, trowel-shaped goatee who claimed to have married 31 Blood Indian squaws, whom he bought for whisky. Their trading with small Indian camps in out-lying districts has been described by Phillips Weinard, first High River settler. "They would pitch nearby, then invite trade by giving the chief a bottle of firewater. It was no easy task to keep a squaw from stealing back the robes her lord and master had parted with for a little whisky. It was a common occurrence to have the squaws gathered around the pile of robes, grab one, and then escape in the darkness. It would often happen that the

A whisky trader and an Indian haggle over a deal. The curse of the West, these traders debauched the tribesmen.

same robe would pass through the trader's hands twice in the same night."

Fred ("Slippery") Kanouse, who ran Healy's Old Bow Fort on the Elbow River, the site of Calgary, insisted that Indian squaws took a far more dominant part in the trading. In 1912, the retired whisky trader told a Calgary *Herald* reporter, "A head wife would come to the post with a party of Indians and dicker for what flour and blankets she wanted. And when she was through, she would hand something to her man, and he would buy whisky. In order to compete," he piously declared, "we *had* to have whisky." As Healy grew rich on bootlegging, he bought the Fort Benton *Record*, ran for sheriff of the county, and swore in Kanouse and other henchmen as deputies.

In spite of his conflict of interest, Healy, as editor of the *Record*, was a good-natured arbiter of etiquette. He thought it vulgar when someone posted a sign on Benton's muddy main street: "This street impassable, not even jackassable." Bachelors bathing nude in the Missouri River were urged to go further upstream, because, Healy wrote, "They don't look well with their clothes off, and might be mistaken for catfish." He editorialized that "making love to a squaw in broad daylight is something that even the broad-minded proprie-

tors of the Overland must condemn."

Healy staunchly upheld the propriety of his whisky trade. When the Reverend John McDougall, Alberta's gun-toting Methodist missionary, came to Benton to preach reform, Healy argued that his "business" had kept the real outlaws out of Canadian territory. "For instance, there was So-and-So," Healy argued. "He came in and was going to run things. He now lies under the sod at Standoff. And there was So-and-So. He went wild, and we laid him out at Freezeout, and some more at Slideout . . . No, Parson John, we did not let any really bad men stay in this Whoop-Up region."

Rev. McDougall decided to visit Fort Whoop-Up and see for himself. He was greeted by "a wild-looking lot," shooting off their flintlock rifles. When he told them he had come neither to drink nor to trade but to preach against it, they eyed him as though he were a "curio," and muttered, "Well, I'll be damned!"

After supper, the bar was cleared off, and the drunks were given an old-fashioned evangelical "love feast." McDougall led them in hymns, preached a sermon, and offered prayers to mothers everywhere. "Tears stood in some eyes," he wrote, "and all observed the best decorum, and as one of them said, 'It was the ————— best thing he had been at in many years.' "

McDougall hoped that perhaps he had redeemed the souls of a few sinners, but on his next trip he found a troop of horsemen shooting drunkenly at each other and one poor fellow "breathing through holes in his back."

In the summer of 1873, the reign of terror reached its climax in a creek bottom in the Cypress Hills, in southern Saskatchewan. Thirteen of Healy's whisky runners, headed by ex-Wolfer Evans, inflamed by their own *hootch*, shot and killed at least 30 Assiniboine Indians. The H.B.C. made the "Cypress Hills Massacre" a *cause célèbre*. Prime Minister Sir John A. Macdonald rose in the House of Commons to condemn the "whisky-sodden" American brigands. To preserve western Canada for Canadians, he said, a corps of mounted militia was needed.

On August 30, 1873, an order-in-council was passed. Three hundred "able-bodied men of good character" were recruited at a salary of seventy-five cents a day. Candidates had to have "good antecedents." Those who indulged in "low language" and drank anything stronger than milk were rejected. Constables wore a pillbox cap; officers, a spiked white helmet with a horse-hair plume. (The familiar broad-brimmed Mountie hats were a later development.) The rest of the North West Mounted Police uniform consisted of a scarlet tunic, breeches edged with yellow stripes, a blue overcoat and riding cape, and high polished-leather boots. An Adams pistol and a sword were carried in a goldbraided belt, and while riding, a Snider carbine was tucked in a boot. The crest of the corps was a buffalo head and its motto (to be misspelled for more than 30 years) was "*Maintiens le Droit*" or "Maintain the Right."

The motto was undoubtedly coined by the two men in charge, martinets of rigid dignity and calculated showmanship. One was Commissioner George Arthur French, a 32-year-old Irishman with a waxed moustache. The other was Assistant Commissioner James Farquharson Macleod, a bushy-bearded Scotsman of 38, who had graduated in law from the University of Toronto. The men who flocked to the recruiting centre were not the legendary Supermen in Scarlet. They were ribbon clerks, carriage builders and school teachers, attracted by the prospect of adventure in the West. It was a group of green recruits that set out on July 8, 1874, from Fort Dufferin, Manitoba, on a 1,000-mile trek to Fort Whoop-Up.

In a monumental understatement, the Government's advance scout, Colonel Patrick Robertson-Ross, had reported that "an easy and agreeable march of a few weeks' duration would suffice to establish them in the respective posts of occupation." The march west was to take three months, and end with hardships more staggering than marching. As one of the "originals," Sir Cecil Denny, recalled, "It is curious today to remember what a vague idea we really had of the long journey ahead."

The police cavalcade stretched out for two miles, led by "A" Troop on dark bay horses, followed by "B" Troop on dark browns, "C" Troop on chestnuts, "D" Troop on greys and buckskins, "E" Troop on blacks, and "F" Troop on bays. Behind them screeched a caravan of 114 Red River carts, 73 lumbering freight wagons, two nine-pounder field guns and two brass mortars, portable field kitchens and grass-mowing machines. Henri Julien, staff artist for Montreal's *Canadian Illustrated News*, came along on a mustang named Old Rooster, and his sketches and prose made the expedition seem like a serio-comic version of the Ride of the Six Hundred at Balaclava. There had only been one experienced civilian policeman in the force, and he had deserted with thirty others at Dufferin. The quartermaster was a school teacher from Quebec who knew no English and had to depend on his English-speaking sergeant. Rockets had to be fired each night to guide back into the camp the tenderfeet lost while trying to collect buffalo chips for fuel. Prairie thunderstorms blew down their bell-shaped tents. Black flies clogged their nostrils. *Métis* drivers fell asleep behind their oxen, which then devoured their harnesses, made of buckskin strings, and their collars stuffed with hay.

The horses were troublesome. A flash of lightning or the howl of a wolf stampeded them. "Most of our horses had been bought for their good looks," Colonel James Walker explained later. "Some of them even objected to harness. Some fiery teams, with inexperienced drivers, would start kicking across the prairie with loaded wagons. The circus was on every morning." The men tried to joke about their hardships, calling themselves the "Dismounted Police." Constable E. H. Maunsell, a well-bred Englishman, wrote light-heartedly of the fleas they picked up: "In a week every man from the Colonel down was infected. It takes only a short time for that insect to become a grandparent." Some of their sentiments would have astonished Healy's hooligans. Constable R. Burton Deane recorded in his diary: "The prairie was carpeted with wild roses, and for a time I tried to avoid stepping on them. But they were so plentiful that the avoidance of them became irksome, and I hardened my heart and walked on."

Each Sabbath was a day of rest and Julien has a cartoon that shows the bewhiskered constables at an outdoor church parade, their helmets off in the bitter cold, their voices lifted in prayer. "I was pleased," Commissioner French noted in his diary that Sunday, "to hear many of the men singing hymns in the afternoon and evening."

By mid-September, ice was forming nightly over the prairie pools, and at times a below-zero wind howled over the caravan. His men were limping and ragged. Behind them were dead horses and broken-down carts and frozen oxen. Food was running out. The men were rationed to 14 ounces of flour and a dried slice of potato. They were drinking brackish water from the buffalo sloughs, which, after being boiled and filtered, was "still the colour of ink." Worst of all, their six half-breed guides had not found them pasturage as promised. Of Morriseau, the chief guide, whose sense of direction seemed as mixed as his ancestry, Commissioner French wrote bitterly in his diary, "I am not certain whether his actions are due to ignorance or design. He is the greatest liar I have ever met, and is suspected as a spy of the Whoop-Up villains . . . I begin to feel very much alarmed for the safety of the Force."

The truth was that the Mounties had begun their career by getting lost. At the confluence of the Belly and Bow Rivers, where Colonel Robertson-Ross had mistakenly located Fort Whoop-Up, they found neither building nor pasture. Commissioner French looked at his bedraggled column of men pushing their shoulders against bogged wheels and lifting fallen horses that "looked skinny as hatracks," and noted in his diary: "And so we were at last at our journey's end, the Bow and Belly Rivers, where there was supposed to be such luxuriant pasturage, a perfect Garden of Eden." French led his worn column of men on to Three Buttes in the Sweet Grass Hills, where he left them to rest their horses and delouse their clothes while he set out with Macleod and a small party for Fort Benton.

French did not want the Americans to know the shape he was in. "I gave out only that I wanted to purchase horses," he wrote. He need not have worried. Isaac Baker had known he was coming. Healy's secret partner sniffed richer profits for I. G. Baker Company in legitimate trade with the Mounties and the settlers they would encourage. He welcomed French and Macleod, and solemnly urged them to clean out Healy's blackguards.

From Baker, French bought at a fair price all the food, boots, harness and axle grease he required and had it loaded on bulltrains to accompany them back to Three Buttes. Most important, Baker commended Jerry Potts to them as a guide, the son of a Scot fur trader and a Piegan squaw. He was a bandy-legged runt with a droopy moustache and a 2B shot pellet lodged in the lobe of his left ear. For the next 22 years he was to serve the Mounties as tracker, Indian interpreter and guide. In the dusk of October 9, Potts pulled up his pony on the slope overlooking the Oldman River and pointed ahead. "Whoop-Up down there," he grunted.

In full uniform, with his heart pounding, Assistant Commissioner Macleod, accompanied by Potts, rode down the slope to the gates. He dismounted and knocked. A hollow echo answered. He rapped again. The outer gate opened. A head popped out, displaying a trowel-shaped goatee. It was Dave Akers, the "Don Quixote of Whoop-Up." The lanky Kentuckian and three of his Blood Indian squaws were the only ones left in the fort. John Jerome Healy had pulled his men out, and Fort Whoop-Up was dry as a temperance hall.

"Come on in and stay for dinner," said Akers, extending his hand to Macleod. The march on Whoop-Up had ended without the firing of a shot. Over buffalo steaks, Macleod bargained with Akers for the fort. "In the name of the Canadian Government," he said, "I'm willing to offer you ten thousand dollars. Our troops need a garrison."

Akers shook his head. "No deal. You'll have to go as high as twenty-five thousand. It cost Johnny Healy that to build Whoop-Up." That was too rich for Macleod, and, on an island in the Oldman River, his men built their own mud-and-log barracks. They called it Fort Macleod.

A village with three trading posts, a log billiard room, a blacksmith shop, a drugstore, an inn, and other appurtenances of civilization quickly sprang up around Macleod's barracks. Two ex-Mounties – Charles Edward Dudley Wood, a former master at Trinity College School, Ontario, and Elias Talbor ("Si") Saunders, a former printer – borrowed $150 from the I. G. Baker Company to establish a newspaper. Until an engine could be installed for their cylinder printing press, the power was supplied by 12 Blood Indian braves; stripped to their breech-clouts, each took a turn at rotating the handle. Their newspaper, the Fort Macleod *Gazette*, was soon battling editorially with Healy's Fort Benton *Record*. Within a year, Inspector A. E. Brisebois was dispatched to build a second barracks at the confluence of the Bow and Elbow Rivers, where Fred ("Slippery") Kanouse had been ladling out whisky to the Indians. Overruling the inspector's choice of "Fort Brisebois" as a name, Commissioner Macleod christened it Calgary, which in Macleod's native island of Skye meant "clear running water."

One hundred and thirty miles east of Fort Macleod, in the Cypress Hills of Saskatchewan, Major James M. Walsh built a third fort, named for himself. Major

Walsh was a spit-and-polish disciplinarian. The stockade of Fort Walsh had to be whitewashed regularly; and after a constable was impeccably prepared for inspection, his comrades would sometimes carry him flat as a tailor's dummy to the parade ground to make sure that his uniform would not get wrinkled. Yet when Sitting Bull, who took refuge in Canada, demanded special privileges, Walsh seized the great Sioux warchief by the seat of his breech-clout and threw him out the door.

The police forts signalled the end of Johnny Healy's whisky traders. Healy had to smuggle his *hootch* across the border via bulltrains in kegs surreptitiously marked "kerosene," "varnish" and "barn paint." The crowning insult came in Fort Benton when the Cypress Hill murderers were arrested for extradition to Canada. Healy's Fort Benton *Record* protested: "What's the idea of trying to hang good Montana citizens – thirteen Kit Carsons – for shooting of a few Indians?" Charges were dropped. Benton celebrated the decision with a torchlight parade and John Evans opened the new "Extradition Saloon."

To Healy, the Mounties were "grabbers of the spoil." He accused them of merely pretending to confiscate booze from his persecuted runners. When tapping the kegs and draining the liquor into the snow, he contended, the Redcoats actually had tin containers secreted underneath. And later, Healy moaned, they would guzzle the bug juice in barracks while singing:

> Pass the tea and let us drink
> To the guardians of our land.
> You can bet your life it's not our fault
> That whisky's contraband!

One by one, Healy's whisky runners were put out of business. A Blackfoot chief, who thought himself cheated by Kamoose Taylor, tipped off the Mounties, who confiscated the buffalo robes and fined Taylor $250. Thereafter, whenever the onetime missionary saw a Mountie wearing a buffalo robe, he would curse, "Look at that damned yellow-legged Redcoat! He's wearing one of the buffalo robes he stole from me!" Kamoose opened a two-storey wooden hotel near the Fort Macleod barracks. When Healy arrived by stagecoach from Fort Benton to visit his old friend, he pulled up before a bizarre hotel sign: a revolver pointed at a man's skull and the cryptic wording, "No Jawbone." It was Kamoose's rendition of "In God we trust. All others cash." In the hotel bar, the proprietor presided with a derby perched on his head and a bung-starter firmly grasped in his hand to thwack unruly cowboys who imbibed too much of his potent raisin brandy.

The hotel rules pasted in the lobby were indicative of the times:

Guests are forbidden to strike matches or spit on the ceiling, or to sleep in bed with their spiked boots and spurs on.

Meals served in rooms will not be guaranteed in any way. Our waiters are hungry and not above temptation.

To attract attention of waiters or bell boys, shoot a hole through the door panel. Two shots for ice water, three for a deck of cards, and so on.

No tips must be given to any waiters. Leave them with the proprietor, and he will distribute them if it's considered necessary.

All guests are requested to arise at 6 a.m. This is imperative as the sheets are needed for tablecloths.

Dogs are not allowed in the bunks, but may sleep underneath. Insect powder for sale at the bar.

Crap, Chuck-luck, Stud Horse Poker and Black Jack games are run by the management. Indians charged double rates. Special rates to Gospel Grinders and the Gambling Perfesh.

The bar in the annex will be open day and night. All day drinks, 50 cents each; night drinks, $1.00 each. Only regularly registered guests will be allowed the special privilege of sleeping on the barroom floor.

A deposit must be made before towels, soap or candles can be carried to rooms. When boarders are leaving, a rebate will be made on all candles, or parts of candles, not burned or eaten.

No kicking regarding the quality or quantity of meals allowed. Those who do not like the provender will get out, or be put out. Assaults on the cook are strictly prohibited. Quarrelsome persons, also those who shoot off without provocation guns or other explosive weapons, and all boarders who get killed, will not be allowed to remain in the house.

When guests find themselves, or their baggage, thrown over the fence, they may consider that they have received notice to quit.

Johnny Healy rented Fort Whoop-Up to Dave Akers as a ranch and at the end of the 1880s he quit the country to seek fatter pickings in Alaska. His parting editorial in the Fort Benton *Record* read: "Things are so quiet about these parts that one of the town's fair but frail citizens fired a pistol just for fun on Main Street."

XIII

Mighty Men of God

FATHER ALBERT LACOMBE, a Roman Catholic priest from Quebec, and Rev. John McDougall, a Methodist minister from Ontario, came into the Canadian West as trail-blazers and peace-makers. Lacombe wore a black robe and a black-and-gold crucifix dangling from his neck and McDougall fringed buckskin and moccasins, plus – on formal occasions – a black coat.

Some historians have painted these two missionaries as saints, but they suffered from the same frailties as do all men. They were not turn-the-other-cheek Christians and, when goaded, their tempers could be as explosive as any man's, white or red. Nor were they meek, but were capable of bold and decisive action when the need demanded it. In the wild land that is now Alberta, the need came often.

Before leaving Lower Canada, Albert Lacombe had been a *habitant* farmboy, short, clean-shaven, strong as an ox; he was the oldest of a family of seven children raised in the village of St. Sulpice, on the banks of the St. Lawrence. He boasted he had Saulteaux Indian blood in his veins, and he liked to be called *le petit sauvage*. Albert had long yearned for the unfettered life of the Canadian West, for his great-uncle, Joseph Lacombe, had been a *voyageur* for the North West Fur Company, and had filled the boy's ears with romantic tales of the frontier. His parents, Albert and Agathe Lacombe, wanted him to become a parish *curé*, but he was determined to be Christ's "vicar of the *tipis*."

After graduating from L'Assomption College, he joined the Oblate order and was ordained in 1849. On his way westward, on a steamboat out of Lachine, English crewmen jeered at his long blond hair and black cassock: "Hey, there! Look at the man in the petticoat." Lacombe barely restrained himself from punching them in the nose. He recognized the hard core of pride within himself. The Blackfeet tribes of Alberta later named him *Arsous-kitsi-rarpi* ("Man-of-the-Good-Heart"). But the priest referred to himself as the "humbug old Indian."

"Ha, I am stu-pide, stu-pide!" he once cried. "What petty pride! Is it not sad to see so much self-love in the old Indian – a blockhead as he is too!"

If Lacombe was quick to fly into a rage, he was equally quick to give sympathy. "You know that I weep easily, and that the fountains of my eyes flow often in abundance," he once confided to a friend. "Many times during my long life I have wept with grief, in hardships, contradictions and embarrassments; as likewise I have shed tears in moments of joy and satisfaction. Voyez-vous," the old priest concluded with his usual touch of drollery, "I have lachrymal fluid for all occasions."

The Rev. John McDougall similarly possessed an unbridled spirit and an over-mastering pride. He was proud of his muscular strength to the point of bumptiousness. When he left Collingwood in Ontario to go west, he was a backwoods evangelist of 17. Short, barrel-chested, with acquiline features, he wore a black beard and moustache which, he fancied, made him look like a frontiersman. Like Lacombe, McDougall was also the oldest of a family of seven; he was the first white child born in the log-cabin village of Owen Sound, on the shores of Georgian Bay. He was nicknamed "the Indian fellow," because he spoke Ojibwa before he could speak English. He was not ordained until 1874 because he couldn't afford more than one year at Victoria College, in Cobourg, Ontario. There, he admitted he was "no slouch" in athletics; he had out-jumped, out-raced, out-wrestled everybody and thus "cleaned out the crowd."

The uplifting phrases of the mid-Victorian novelists came easily to him: tears were a sign of "unmanliness"; the noblest virtues were "pluck and grit." His hero was his parson father, the Rev. George McDougall, a two-fisted, black-whiskered prophet of the old school. At 39, the father had already won a reputation as "Big Black Coat," because of the austere fundamentalism he preached at Ontario camp meetings. The son never forgot one demonstration of the father's "pluck." In 1860, the elder McDougall, appointed chairman of the Methodist missions in Rupert's Land, was taking his family to the headquarters at Norway House. En route, a drunken

Ojibwa pointed the muzzle of his gun at them. The Reverend merely unbuttoned his black coat and dared the Indian to shoot. The man fled.

The Indians named young John McDougall *Aha-yua-me-ha-we-ye-neese* ("The Young Man-who-talks-to-Him"). The preacher sharpened his evangelism by his feats of marksmanship and horsemanship. "I gained a reputation as a crack shot," he said, "and many a man and his whole family came to hear me sing and preach because I had won their admiration by my handling of their pet horse in the buffalo hunt." One sinner who used blasphemy was dumped into an icy creek and McDougall then threatened to thrash him unless he apologized for his language.

In the great empty spaces of their pioneer parishes, it seems strange that the Catholic and the Methodist, with so many unsaved souls to share, were not able to work with tolerance toward each other; in fact, from the beginning anyway, the two sects often clashed. Dr. Walter Cheadle, a young Church of England Oxonian, visited Fort Edmonton in 1862, and in his diary, he recorded the rivalry between Father Lacombe and Mc-Dougall's predecessor, the Rev. Thomas Woolsey: "Priest catches a convert & baptises him. Woolsey hears of it & baptises him over again, & so on *ad infinitum*, it being with great difficulty that convert knows whether he was made Papist or Protestant last."

Lacombe used the "Catholic Ladder," on which a buffalo skin parchment was nailed onto a pole in the middle of a Blackfoot camp. Then, with charred wood, he would draw lurid pictures to illustrate Bible stories, with the Protestants shown tumbling into a fiery pit. His primer version of Christ being nailed to the cross seems to have been misinterpreted by the Indians. In his diary, Cheadle told of the embarrassment it caused a Methodist divine: "I was told story of missionary preaching about crucifixion. Indians delighted. Wished him to give diagram showing how it was done. Missionary fled in terror."

Not until years later did Lacombe begin to understand that Methodists were as sincere in their religious convictions as he was. One day he showed a printed version of his "Catholic Ladder" to Archbishop Manning, a Protestant who had been converted to Catholicism. The Archbishop urged the priest to pray for Protestants. "For I was one of them once," he said, "and I know how they believe in their souls they are right. So there is no blame for them that they do not see the Truth."

"Of course, I have prayed for them before," Lacombe said, "but that was the first time I truly understood the Protestant, and I began to love them – not only a few, like my good Hudson's Bay Company friends, but all of them: to pity them and pray for them, because I love them."

John McDougall never loved his Catholic neighbour, but he did learn to respect him. The code of the wilderness – to help a fellow pioneer in distress – brought McDougall and Lacombe together. One blizzardy day McDougall and his Indian guide, Jacob Bigstoney, were breaking a trail between Victoria and Fort Edmonton. Victoria (now called Pakan) was the first Methodist mission station build by McDougall in Alberta. Suddenly the Methodist noticed that Lacombe and another priest were riding in the same direction. McDougall respected any frontiersman who could battle the elements without "whining or crying," and in his memoirs he paid Lacombe what he regarded as the supreme compliment, calling him: "one of the pioneers of this country."

Each missionary developed his own showmanlike technique for bringing the "Word of Light" to the natives. Lacombe restricted himself to the Blackfoot confederacy, and used pomp and ritual. "For these are warriors," he said, "and they love ceremony." The priest would enter their camps, holding a white flag emblazoned with a red cross. His *Métis* runner, Alexis, would herald his arrival by ringing a little bell. Then the Blackfeet would glide into the priest's travelling tent-chapel of buffalo hides, which could hold as many as fifty warriors. "After each one has taken his place according to his rank, I intone in my finest voice a hymn, then the sermon," he wrote. "We pray, we sing, and at last we pass about the calumet, whose smoke, like incense, crowns this religious service."

McDougall's parishioners were mostly Crees and the Assiniboines (or "Stoneys," as the Assiniboines were locally called). He carried a Union Jack, a New Testament and hymn book, written in Rev. James Evans' Cree syllabic characters. One of his Indian guides, Mark or Peter or Jacob, would introduce him to the camp chieftain. "I would then go from one chief's tent to that of another," John wrote, "and the respective followers would crowd the lodges while I did my best to tell the pagan and barbarous people the old, old story of Jesus and His Love."

Each missionary learned the language of his parish, and compiled dictionaries. Lacombe wrote, "I feel like a king here, a new Moses in the midst of this new camp of Israel. A nobleman's palace is not as precious as my *poétique* tent in the wilderness, where I wrote on my knees my sermons in Blackfeet."

To reach their nomadic parishioners, the two missionaries travelled incredible distances, breaking new trails which radiated from Edmonton like the spokes of a wheel. On the rim of their circuit, sometimes hundreds of miles from Edmonton, the wilderness was dotted with their mission stations. Facetiously called "Canterbury Cathedrals," these were mud-chinked, floorless log cabins, with the stump of a tree serving as a chair, a buffalo parchment as a window. In the Athabasca country to the far north, the Oblates built a mission at Lac La Biche in competition with the Methodist station, which had been erected at White Fish Lake by the full-blooded Ojibwa convert, Rev. Henry Bird Steinhauer. Fifty miles east of Edmonton, Lacombe had Lac Ste. Anne mission, founded by Father Jean Baptiste Thibault; and McDougall built the Woodville mission on Pigeon Lake. To the south, McDougall built Morley mission on the Bow River, 50 miles upstream from present Calgary; and at the junction of the Bow and Elbow Rivers, Lacombe constructed a rival log shack roofed with spruce bark. To the east, on the north arm of the Saskatchewan River, McDougall's Victoria mission competed with Lacombe's St. Paul des Crees (now called Brousseau). Only Lacombe's St. Albert station, nine miles from Fort Edmonton, was not wrapped in primeval isolation.

Lacombe travelled 1,500 miles a year, in temperatures often as low as 40° below zero. He packed his chapel in a cariole, and, in storms, he would run ahead of his dog team to beat a trail, screening his eyes with deerskin mitts against the snow glare. If there was "a sweet zephyr blowing," he could do 50 miles a day. On one memorable trek, when he was determined to meet a visiting bishop, Lacombe ran for 65 miles behind his dog train. He rafted as far as 150 miles down the Saskatchewan River, rejoicing in the *voyageur's* proverb, "You never know what you will meet around the next bend." He loved to mount his pony, Prince, and join a band of *Métis* on the buffalo hunt. "What a scene!" he wrote. "The story of combats of Spanish bulls furious at their adversaries conveys a feeble picture compared to this magnificent attack. I can never express how good these *Métis* children of the prairies were. In that Golden Age, when they hunted the buffalo and practised our Christianity – with the fervour of the first Christians – their lives were blameless. They were a beautiful race then – those children of the prairies."

John McDougall, too, knew the misery and the rapture of being a frontier circuit rider. It was not uncommon for him to cover 3,000 miles in six months. Though he called it the "Jordan of the West," he found paddling around the bends of the Saskatchewan River least satisfying. The back-breaking portages made him think, "Verily, by the sweat of his brow, man earns his *pemmican*." He had married Abigail, the Indian daughter of Rev. Henry Bird Steinhauser and, for companionship on his canoe trips, he often took one of his three baby daughters with him, talking to her while she lay cradled in a black shawl slung over his back.

When he rode after the herds of buffalo, which he called "God's unbranded cattle," he woke before dawn, when the dew still pearled the grass, and his band of *Métis* would sing hymns and kneel in prayer. He would mount his "A-1 buffalo pony," a sorrel named Scarred Thigh because it had once been torn on the horns of a mad bull. The missionary carried a double-barrelled percussion-lock muzzle-loader. Around the neck of his buckskinned jacket was slung a pair of binoculars and a .42 Smith & Wesson revolver. He led his cavalcade on a canter across the grasslands, "my nostrils filled with the rich smells of the earth, my lungs inflating at every jump. Ah, those early morning gallops on the plains!"

Both the Catholic and the Methodist, being ex-farmboys, turned their hands to the axe and the plough until they had tiny colonies fenced off around their wilderness missions.

With the aid of 20 French *Métis* families, Father Lacombe built the first bridge in Alberta – a 300-foot spruce log structure arching over the Sturgeon River. He launched the first horse-powered flour mill, and set creaking the first cart train of "Red River chariots" which freighted in supplies over the thousand-mile trail from St. Boniface. Three young Grey Nuns – Sisters Emery, Alphonse and Lamy – crossed the plains to the Lac Ste. Anne mission in 1859, and helped Lacombe found Alberta's first hospital, boarding school and orphanage. The trio of "blessed pearls," as he called the women, trimmed the wooden chandelier hanging over the priest's chapel altar with pieces of tin and coloured birds' eggs. They kept the priest's newspaper "post office" in chronological order – each paper stacked on the shelf, though a year late, to be read in proper daily sequence.

The sisters offered prizes to the *Métis* settlers who harvested the biggest crops of potatoes, cabbages and corn, but the Blackfeet parishioners could not be bribed easily into becoming farmers. "Essentially a wild, lawless roaming race," Lacombe reported, "they possessed at the same time a savage and a wild love of freedom of their own." The Blackfeet also resisted the Catholic's denunciation of polygamy. One patriarch, when instructed to disband his harem and keep but one wife, asked, "When I love all equally, which one shall I retain?"

It was through an Indian woman that Lacombe won the friendship of the greatest of the Blackfoot chieftains. Lacombe learned that a Blackfoot princess had been

The pioneer missionary, as depicted by Frederic Remington.
They came like voyageurs*, carrying a muscular Christianity by canoe, dogsled or on foot:*
Roman Catholics, Anglicans, Presbyterians, and the Methodist James Evans,
who gave the Cree an alphabet and a Bible printed on birchbark.

enslaved by a Cree war party and the priest bought her for a horse and 25 beaver skins, then returned her to her kinsmen; in gratitude, he was allowed to preach in the Blackfoot camp of Chief *Natous* ("The Sun"). This, in turn, led to his life-long friendship with *Sapo-maxikaw* ("Crowfoot").

One snowy December night in 1866, Lacombe was sleeping in a Blackfoot lodge when a dog put his head inside. It was a Cree dog. A second later, 800 Cree marauders opened fire, and the cry rang out throughout the camp: *"Assinow! Assinow!* The Crees! The Crees!" Lacombe put on his long black soutane and threw his white surplice over it. He said a prayer, kissed his crucifix, and holding aloft his white flag with the red cross emblazoned on it, walked into the battle. "With

the first volley our lodge had been completely destroyed," wrote Lacombe. "Smoking gunwads fell at my feet and the sinister flash of musketry lit the tragic scene. I tried to walk towards the enemy to stop them, but my voice was lost in the confusion. The groans of the dying, the yelling of the warriors, the harangues of the chiefs . . . all mingled, forming a kind of hell." The carnage continued until early morning. Half the Blackfoot camp was butchered by the time Chief Crowfoot galloped into the fray, shouting *"Ekakimak"* ("Courage!"). In beaded buffalo skins, wearing a silver fox headdress trimmed with eagle feathers, and shooting from behind his eagle feather fan, the 39-year-old chieftain fought "like a bear"—according to Lacombe's record. Again Lacombe walked out in the snow toward the Crees. He held his crucifix in one hand and waved his red cross pennant with the other, entreating the attackers to stop firing. But the bullets flew, and the priest toppled over, wounded on the shoulder and forehead. Crowfoot called out: "Dogs! You have shot the Black Robe. Haven't you done enough?"

The Crees retreated, having slaughtered 35 Blackfeet; Chief Natous was severely wounded. "Since that meeting, a true friendship was established between Crowfoot and myself," Lacombe wrote. "He was always advising his people to respect Sunday and the practices of Christianity."

The Rev. McDougall was equally enterprising. His mother and four sisters – aided by a Miss Elizabeth Barrett from Ontario – started the first adult-education night classes in Alberta. His father – taxing the colonists 75 cents monthly for the upkeep of their one-roomed, buffalo-skin-walled hospital – instituted the first hospital insurance scheme. McDougall claimed to be the first amateur dentist in Alberta, to have brought in the first springless buckboard buggies, and his herd of cattle branded "JM" was the beginning of Alberta's first cattle ranch. The "first" which gave him most personal pleasure was an ordinary chair that the ox-cart train freighted north from Fort Benton, in Montana. "I had spent more than fourteen years in the great North-West, but was now, for the first time, the happy possessor of a factory-made chair," McDougall said. "I found myself sitting in that chair, and, consciously and unconsciously, my hand would slip down over its smooth, varnished surface, and I felt the thrill of luxury tingle through my veins."

The Methodist's greatest ally was the chief of the Crees, *Maskepetoon* ("Broken Arm"). This "kingly" old man, as McDougall called him, had once scalped his own wife in a rage, been a prince among horse thieves, and a tiger in war. When Chief Broken Arm was converted to Christianity, he became known as "Peace Chief." The Rev. Steinhauer taught him how to read the Cree syllabic New Testament, and the convert had taken to heart the Biblical phrase, "Thou shalt love thy enemy." He carried his Bible on a cord strung around his neck, and preached non-violence to both his Cree people and the Blackfeet enemy. A raiding party of Crees once mistakenly fired a fusillade into the tents of a camp of converted Stoney Indians who were observing evening worship. Broken Arm pointed out that God had intervened to protect His children, because the Christianized Indians were on their knees praying and the shots passed over their heads. Another party of Crees caught the Blackfoot who had murdered Broken Arm's own father. The chieftain told the trembling captive:

"What makes you pale? At one time I would have glorified in drinking your blood, but that time is past. You must now be to me as a father. Wear my clothes, take my horse, and tell your people this is the way the Peace Chief now takes revenge."

When McDougall first met Broken Arm in 1861, the Peace Chief introduced the missionary to his tribe, and urged his people not to gamble or pound their drums during the Sabbath visit of the "God man." In turn, the Methodist built a special room at Victoria where Broken Arm could pray, and gave him spectacles to help him study the Bible. McDougall once saw Broken Arm shake hands and forgive the Blackfoot who had butchered the chieftain's son, and decided that the patriarch had been born with a spark of divinity.

In the spring of 1869, Yankee traders at Fort Benton brought smallpox to the Indians of Montana and the pestilence spread northward to Alberta. Before the epidemic was over, more than 3,500 pockmarked corpses lay rotting in the Canadian grasslands. The "Rider on the Pale Horse" visited every *tipi* and every mission station in Alberta. The disease wiped out almost half the Blackfoot confederacy, and decimated the Cree and Assiniboine tribes. It took 50 lives at McDougall's White Fish Lake mission, and killed 55 at Victoria. But the death toll was worst at Father Lacombe's missions: 150 dead at St. Paul des Crees and 320 at St. Albert, many of them Indian children in the Grey Nuns' orphanage. Lacombe and his fellow Oblates "multiplied themselves," as a bishop later phrased it, doctoring the sick, hearing the confessions of the dying, and burying the dead. Much of Lacombe's time was devoted to serving as a gravedigger, an axe or a knife being his only tools. Vaccine sold to the missionaries by corrupt traders at Fort Benton proved defective. Three of Lacombe's fellow priests were stricken with the disease, and Lacombe himself, while making the rounds of 30 Blackfoot encampments, reeled with nausea and told himself, "My hour has come. May God have pity on me." He took a painkiller, his fever subsided and, sucking on a camphor-filled quill, he continued to bury dead parishioners.

The McDougalls, father and son, also worked around the clock to quarantine and console the sick. John McDougall, who had swallowed a double dose of Dover's Powders, recorded, "In almost every fence corner around the mission, all along the banks of the river, were the dead and the dying." His 23-year-old Indian wife, Abigail, died. "Six years of companionship and mutual experience in life had been ours; many hardships had we shared, many pleasures as well, and now the faithful wife and mother had gone on," he wrote.

"I returned to my room and fought it out with my own sorrow. But oh, the suffering and misery of it all!" George McDougall confessed "my proud heart groans" when smallpox killed his three daughters, Flora, 11, Georgiana, 19, and Anna, an adopted Indian daughter of 14. The old evangelist wrote to the Wesleyan Society, describing how Georgiana was buried beside her sisters in the mission garden at Victoria:

"My kind neighbours brought the coffin and placed it at the gate, and my son and self carried her mortal remains to the grave. When we were filling in the earth, he uttered an expression which found an echo in my poor heart, 'Father, I find it hard to bury our own dead.' But just then the words of the Apostle were applied with such force to my mind that I could not restrain myself from shouting them aloud: 'O death, where is thy sting? O grave, where is thy victory? Thanks be to God who giveth us the victory through our Lord Jesus Christ!' "

As the toll mounted, the tribes turned against all whites. The *omikewin* – the loathsome scab – was a white man's disease. The Indians had believed in the false medicine of the white men, they decided, and now they must propitiate *Manitou* with acts of revenge. A war party of eleven Blackfeet attempted to raid one mission post, but ten of them died writhing and vomiting before they could even climb the stockade. At other posts, Indians tried to communicate their disease to the white men by throwing infected clothes into their gardens, spitting on windows, rubbing their gates with the sores of the dying. Seven hundred Blackfeet gathered to march on Fort Edmonton. The Chief Factor asked Lacombe to placate the avengers. The Oblate could not, this time, count on aid from Chief Crowfoot, because *Sapo-maxikaw* was sullen in his tent, mourning the death from the plague of his father, Chief Many Names, and his friend, Chief Natous. Lacombe picked up his crucifix and white flag and walked out the fort gates, calling out into the night: *"Ennastsisin*! Peace! It is I, The Man-of-the-Good-Heart, who calls you. I visited your sick. I tended your wounded. Do not attack the Big House. The white men are my brothers." Though they would not parley with him, the snipers ceased their firing. When daylight crept over the tense fort, the Blackfeet had left.

At the Methodist missions, as John McDougall phrased it, "We trusted in Providence, but kept our powder dry." Cree and Blackfeet alike shot the white men's cattle, stole 14 of their horses, and pillaged their gardens. McDougall beseeched Cree Chief Broken Arm to intercede with the rampaging Blackfeet on behalf of the white men. Aware that he might be slain by this enemy tribe, *Maskepetoon* agreed to try. "Who remembers a poplar leaf after it has fallen?" he asked. "Who will remember an Indian after he is dead?"

Accompanied by a peace embassy of six Crees, Broken Arm approached the Blackfoot camp of *Chief Nah-doos*, carrying an unfurled Union Jack flag in one hand and his Cree New Testament in the other. As the Crees drew near the enemy camp, a cavalry of Blackfeet charged toward them, and although his followers fled, Broken Arm stood like a statue. He opened his Bible, put on his green spectacles, and began to read aloud. When the Blackfeet saw what he was doing, they stopped their gallop, for the written word commanded their veneration. Broken Arm lifted his hand. "Listen to me, Blackfeet braves," he spoke. "We must forget old hates, your people and mine. The time has come to be brothers . . ." His words were cut short. A Blackfoot warrior named Swan fired a single shot, and the Peace Chief fell dead. His assassins hacked his body, and dragged the mutilated remains about by the tails of their horses, and because they feared the Cree Bible's black "medicine," they dispatched it to the nearest McDougall mission station. John McDougall mourned the Gandhi of the grasslands, and said, "I never felt more like going on the warpath." The older McDougall asked God to "forgive the demon-worshippers of death, for they know not their right hand from their left."

The missionaries all knew that the end of the pagan days on the Prairie were already in sight and during the 1870s and 1880s, both Lacombe and McDougall watched civilization wrap its coils around the redmen of the plains, squeezing them into reservations. The Methodist minister and Oblate priest were not passive witnesses, but participated in the subjugation of the Indian nation, though they did it with the best intentions. Unwittingly, they were the shock troops of the white man's conquest. They softened up the warlike Indians, making him malleable and defenceless. As McDougall phrased it, the missionary sought to convert the Indians into "a docile, reverent and teachable band of aboriginal men." Ultimately, both men came to hate civilization. They saw how it degraded a once-free race, and they felt guilty because they were partially responsible.

McDougall later wrote: "In the Long Knife country south of the 49th parallel, there was a distinct law for the white man as against the Indian. The white man could kill the Indian with drink, or take his wife, or defraud him in trade, or abuse him with insult. The Indian was not a man. He was a 'buck.' The Indian woman was not a woman. She was a 'bitch.' But let the Indian turn against the white man, and it was, 'Bring out the troops! Down with the Injuns! Wipe them out root and branch!' If these were the only products of modern progress, then for God's sake and humanity's also, give us barbarism."

Meanwhile, there was a more immediate threat to the plains Indians: the American *Moka-manus* – the "Long Knives." In the early 1870s, the tribes freely roamed after buffalo across the invisible "medicine line" separating present Alberta from Montana Territory, and whisky traders south of the border fed them bad liquor. Johnny Jerome Healy and his grogshops on the Whoop-Up Trail schooled the Blackfeet to murderous debauch. The raw *hootch* devastated the Indian economically. He depended on the buffalo, from horns to hocks, but his customary summer hunting season became one long drunk. During his orgy, the Indian would hand over his horse, his lodges, his rifle, his daughters, his remaining food, for more liquor. He would wake up with a hangover, flat broke, and find winter on hand, and his family starving. He had to beg for food or steal it from the whites. Lacombe heard of one Montana trader in Helena whose sugar was being stolen. The storekeeper strewed poison in his sugar barrel next night and left his door open. In the morning, six Indians were found dead, and the trader was congratulated with, "That was a cute notion, I guess."

"The disorders of all kinds which have taken place among the savages and these miserable traders of rum are frightful," Lacombe reported to his superiors. "We have done our best to inform the American Government of these unhappy infringements of its laws." The Government as represented by the military posts on the American frontier was, if anything, more rapacious than the whisky pedlars. The u.s. cavalry, aided by drunken vigilantes, often seemed to believe the only good Indian was a dead one. Indiscriminate slaughter of the buffalo, the meat and clothing staple of the Indians, became a crusade. Lacombe heard of a Yankee colonel who urged, "Kill every buffalo you see. Every buffalo dead is an Indian gone."

John McDougall was horrified at what he called the "sharpened-up barbarity" of the Yankees. He reported that the Americans had slaughtered 30 Blackfoot families and then put their chiefs in irons before burning them to death. Three cold-blooded murders had occurred within sight of his mission house door: "Kelly River desperadoes and Yankee whisky the cause." McDougall drew up a petition asking that the illicit whisky traffic be stopped, and had it signed by Samson, the Cree successor to the assassinated Chief Broken Arm. Lieutenant-Governor Adams G. Archibald of Manitoba issued a proclamation prohibiting the sale of intoxicants in the Canadian Northwest. The Methodist decided to visit the whisky forts on the Whoop-Up Trail to try to enforce prohibition – but the traders scoffed at him, and McDougall, like Lacombe, could only urge the Canadian authorities to send a mounted police force.

McDougall was smug when the Mounties arrived soon after and forced the whisky pedlars to pour their brew into the Belly River. But a few months later, in March 1875, he rode down to preach a sermon, "The Sword of Gideon," in the new Mounted Police barracks at Fort Macleod. "Quite a village had sprung up outside the fort, and here the frontier and wild West were typified in earnest," he observed. "Bull-whackers and mule-punchers and wolfers and former desperadoes and whisky smugglers were here in strong evidence, and gambling and drinking went on in modified form, even as before." He also noted that "the natives were being protected and crime was almost extinct."

Lacombe was equally disappointed with the reform regime. He built a 15-foot-square mission station beside Fort Macleod, with an earthen floor and spruce-log walls chinked with moss and mud, but the rowdies who gathered around the fort were hard to bear: "What poor Catholics! Dissolute life is common here." When the frontier village gave a reception to the visiting Governor-General of Canada, Lord Stanley, Lacombe was mortified: "Little enthusiasm – the good people of Macleod were occupied with drinking. Last night at nine was His Excellency's levee. Fiasco and failure! There were four ladies *deshabilées*. One of them, as we passed out with the Governor, commenced to leap about like a *danseuse* . . . What a *triste* affair! What a race of people! What rudeness!"

The two missionaries each hoped to attract a more civilized race of parishioners to the plains. Lacombe, of course, wanted to recruit Catholics. In 1875, he began touring Quebec and Massachusetts making colonization speeches. Thanks to his efforts, 600 French Canadians arrived in Manitoba in 1876, and in the following year 400 families travelled west. His recruitment speeches were larded with colourful Blackfoot phrases, and they usually ended with a clarion call: "Advance the work of colonization! Do not rest idle in the shade . . . The future is yours, if you will seize the present. Courage and tenacity – these form the secret of success!" McDougall decided to tour Ontario and the Maritimes to preach the gospel of what he called "The Great North-West." On the lecture circuit, he found that audiences were enchanted when he sang Wesleyan hymns in Cree. He was an accomplished story-teller. After reciting a few thrilling tales about his adventures in the West, the evangelical immigration agent had his audiences ready to pack. His challenging phrases rang out, "Brother Dominionites! This big country has room for millions. The whole land from Winnipeg to Victoria is one great ready-made farm . . . With manliness and pluck and Christian resolution, each one of you will feel as did Joshua and Caleb."

The flocks of new settlers drove both Lacombe and McDougall into a conflict of loyalties. The pioneers from Quebec and Ontario were hungry for land, but the land belonged to the Indians. Was it a Christian act to persuade the "original proprietors" – as McDougall called them – to cede their land to the white newcomers? The Dominion Government asked the Catholic and Methodist missionaries to be their official spokesmen in advising their Indian parishioners to sign the peace treaties, which would cede the Indian territories to the white men. Lacombe and McDougall agreed to do so, knowing the westward march of civilization along the new railroad was inevitable. Yet the missionaries had qualms about being the instruments which would push their friends into Indian reserves. When the Canadian Pacific Railway shipped its first locomotive down the Red River aboard a decorated barge pulled by the steamboat, *Selkirk*, Lacombe wrote: "Hah! I would look long in silence at that road coming on – like a band of wild geese in the sky – cutting its way through the Prairies; opening up the great country we thought would be ours for years. Like a vision I could see it driving my poor Indians before it."

McDougall's doubts are reflected in his memoirs, too. He describes how he negotiated peace treaties with Chiefs Sweet Grass, Samson and Pakan of the Crees. He would snatch a handful of grass and hold aloft the shortest blade. "This little, weak, lone grass represents the white man as he is now in this country," he would say. Then, exhibiting the handful of blades, he would say, "This bunch of many and strong grasses represents the multitude to come." Consequently, it would be wise to negotiate with the Queen Mother's Government for their rights while there was yet time. To himself, however, McDougall wondered whether he was doing the right thing. "There were in my audience many who had every reason to hate the white man. Wrong and injury and bestiality and crime had they suffered from his hands. Moreover, their idea of the white man's government was of a ruthless, despotic, absolute power, breaking treaties, hounding men hither and thither, building prisons and erecting gallows. Oh! these liberty-loving people hated the very mention of government." Despite misgivings, the tribal chieftains agreed to sign the treaties. After all, the Queen Mother's agents unequivocally guaranteed them "the right to pursue their vocation of hunting throughout the tract surrendered." Each Indian man, woman and child was to be paid $12, and each head chief was to get $25, a medal, a suit of clothes, a Union Jack, and a Winchester rifle. In the future, every member of a tribe would receive a yearly grant of $5 that would continue "forever." In addition, for every family of five persons, there would be a reservation of land consisting of 640 acres; and if the family agreed to farm, each band would get agricultural implements, barley and wheat seed, three cows and a bull.

McDougall was the chief Indian counsellor appointed by the Dominion Government when the Plains Crees signed Treaty No. 6 at Fort Pitt. Chief Sweet Grass asked the missionary, "Put yourself in our place; forget you are a white man; tell us what to do." McDougall wrote, "For a moment I felt somewhat embarrassed. Then I braced up and went to work to argue British justice and Canadian Government fair play . . . I strongly advised them to go before the Commissioners and signify their acceptance."

Lacombe was the official Indian advisor when the Wood Crees and Chipewyans signed Treaty No. 8 at Lesser Slave Lake. "Your forest and river life will not be changed by the treaty, and you will have your annuities as well, year by year, as long as the sun shines and the earth remains," the priest urged them. "Therefore I finish my speaking by saying: accept."

McDougall was present when the Blackfoot confederacy signed Treaty No. 7. Lacombe, ill at the time, heard about the grand ceremony from his associate Oblate, Father Constantine Scollen. On the morning of September 22, 1877, Chief Crowfoot gathered 4,000 of his painted tribesmen 60 miles east of present Calgary, at "Ridge Under The Water," later known as Blackfoot Crossing. On one side of the encampment, the Mounties in their scarlet coats and spiked white helmets guarded the treaty gifts piled in their bell-shaped tents. On the other side of the flat, seated under a huge council tent canopy, were the Treaty Commissioners, Lieutenant-Governor David Laird and Colonel James Farquharson Macleod.

Crowfoot passed his white-stone *calumet* to the commissioners for a peace puff, and then offered it to his fellow chieftains, seated on buffalo robes on the grass. He arose and addressed the dignitaries: "I hope you look upon the Blackfeet as your children now, and that you will be indulgent and charitable towards them." He looked upon his old friend, Colonel Macleod, whom he called *Stamixotokon* – meaning Buffalo Bull's Head, from the Mounties' uniform insignia. "The police have protected us," Crowfoot said, "as the feathers of the bird protect it from the frost of winter." He plucked a downy feather from his eagle's wing fan, and presented it to Lieutenant-Governor Laird, saying, "Keep us like this feather forever." He turned to his people, who were assembled around him in a semi-circular halfmoon. "I am satisfied; I will sign the treaty." As he made his mark on the parchment, cannons roared and bagpipes skirled and his cavalry braves mounted their painted ponies and fired their muzzle-loaders into the air.

Although Colonel Macleod pledged his word that the Queen Mother would keep her treaty agreements as long as water runs and the grass grows in spring, it was the beginning of the end for the roving lords of the Prairies. After those declarations of eternal brotherhood, the white man chopped away piecemeal at the peace treaties, and the red man was reduced to peonage and pauperdom. Within two years, Lacombe and McDougall reported that their Indian parishioners were subsisting on grass, devouring their horses, eating the carcasses of poisoned wolves. The buffalo herds disappeared, as, armed with rapid-firing Hotchkiss guns, white men slaughtered the buffalo by the thousands. American businessmen were eager to buy the hides for factory leather and the bones for manufacturing household articles. Starving Blackfeet lined up at the Mountie posts demanding the cattle promised them; Colonel Macleod was forced to admit the Queen Mother had broken her word.

By 1883, land-hungry immigrants from Europe were pouring into Winnipeg at the rate of a thousand a month, and the "Iron Horses" of the C.P.R. were cutting through the Indian reserves of Alberta. In May that year, 700 armed Blackfeet warriors staged a sit-down strike at Cluny, near the Bow River, and told the railroad gangs, "Your two long shining threads of steel run through our land. We will not permit your fiery wagons and iron road to go further."

Lacombe, then serving as chaplain for the railroad construction workers, rushed to the trouble spot on a C.P.R. hand-car. He pleaded with the navvies to stop working, or else the dispute might ignite a full-scale Indian war. "Let your Indians go to the devil," the railroaders replied. The Oblate sent wires to the C.P.R. directors who ordered the track-layers to pause until Lacombe negotiated a settlement with Crowfoot and his chieftains. In the tribal council, Lacombe handed out sugar, tobacco, tea and flour, and urged the Blackfeet to compromise. "If the railway is allowed to pass through your land up the Cluny Hills to Gleichen," he said, "we will give in return the same amount of land on the south side of the river as we take."

"The advice of the Chief of Prayer is good," Crowfoot declared. "We shall do what he asks." As a reward for his co-operation, the C.P.R. magnates granted Crowfoot a lifetime rail pass.

When the track reached Calgary, Sir George Stephen, president of the C.P.R., invited Lacombe to dine aboard his private railway car. The directors toasted the priest and proposed that he take the president's chair during the party. Lacombe told the *gros bonnets* ("big hats") he would gladly become president of the C.P.R. for one hour, on condition that Sir George take his place during that time as chaplain of his Calgary mission station. During his one-hour presidency, the Oblate granted himself a lifetime C.P.R. pass, which was inscribed for "Father Lacombe and an Assistant." The priest later loaned his pass freely to poor people who needed to travel by train. Father Paul Emile Breton, Lacombe's biographer, described how a train conductor one day found the pass in the hands of two nuns.

"Dear sisters," the conductor asked amiably, "which one of you is Father Lacombe?"

In 1885, the Catholic and the Methodist missionaries were confronted with their worst crisis. The messianic Louis Riel had set the whole Saskatchewan Valley aflame with his second revolt, and the Indians of the plains, as McDougall phrased it, were smoking "rebellion tobacco." The rebellion of that year was, in part, an expression of Indian protest against the restraints imposed on their way of life by the white man. Cree Chiefs Poundmaker and Big Bear had watched with grim foreboding the white man's "iron monster" invade their hunting grounds. Indians had been penned into reserves, and had heard the Dominion Government decree that henceforth rations were to be issued only to those warriors who agreed to farm. They felt they had been tricked by the missionaries, and were ripe for rebellion.

The Protestant white settlers of Alberta, vastly outnumbered by both Indians and *Métis*, turned to McDougall and Lacombe for help. Lacombe felt loyalty towards his Catholic *Métis* parishioners, pity for Louis Riel and sympathy toward the rebellious Crees. "If we are to be mastered by the whites, and to receive only crumbs from their tables," one reservation Cree had told him, "it is better for us to be killed by bullets than to starve ignominiously." However, Lacombe hoped to keep the Blackfeet in line, though he knew that Crowfoot had adopted the militant Chief Poundmaker as a tribal "son."

White officialdom held its breath when a special C.P.R. engine carried Lacombe to the Blackfoot camp, and Crowfoot was asked whether his tribe would join forces with Poundmaker. Parliamentarians applauded with relief when Prime Minister John A. Macdonald read the missionary's telegram in the House of Commons: "I have seen Crowfoot and all the Blackfeet. All quiet. Promised me to be loyal no matter how things may turn elsewhere."

John McDougall convinced Chief Samson and Chief Pakan to sign neutrality pacts, and to hold their warriors in leash, but the Methodist had qualms when Major-General T. Bland Strange of the Alberta Field Force asked him to help hunt down Chief Big Bear. Rev. John Maclean, McDougall's biographer and fellow missionary, wrote: "John McDougall was a great friend of Big Bear, but he was also a patriot . . . and as guide, chaplain and interpreter, he felt called upon to help the troops capture Big Bear dead or alive." After capture Big Bear and Poundmaker were sentenced to three years in prison for treason. Lacombe and McDougall pleaded for pardons and the two chiefs were released and returned to their reserves, only to die soon after – their spirits broken, their bodies withered by tuberculosis.

The two missionaries continued to perform their Christian duties until long into the twentieth century. The "Old Chief," as Father Lacombe called himself when his hair turned silver, championed the cause of Catholic separate schools in Western Canada; he presented his Blackfoot dictionary to Pope Pious X in a private audience in Rome; he was received in the Austrian Court of the Emperor Franz Joseph, where he pleaded for Ruthenian Catholic priests to help handle the immigrant "Sifton's Sheepskins" who were flooding the Prairies. He died at Midnapore, south of Calgary, aged 89, on December 11, 1916. The Indians wept as the Mounted Police led his funeral cortege through the streets of Calgary. A special C.P.R. train carried his body northward to St. Albert for burial but as he had willed, his heart was removed and buried in the Blackfoot country.

Less than five weeks later, on January 15, 1917, his 74-year-old friend, the Reverend John McDougall, died. The "Old Pioneer," as McDougall called himself when his beard turned snowy white, caught a chill after going to the Calgary railroad station to bid farewell to two of his sons, who were leaving to fight in the First World War. He had written six volumes of autobiography and two Indian romance novels; he had helped organize the Calgary Stampede in 1912; the Alberta Government had appointed him Temperance Commissioner; and in 1906 the Dominion Government named him Indian Commissioner. Once again, the Indians, the Mounted Police, and all Calgary turned out to mourn the death of an empire-builder of the Prairies.

In one sense, perhaps both missionaries had lived too long, for in their later years they looked with anguish at the way civilization had disrupted the lives of the Indians.

In 1884 Father Lacombe became principal of Alberta's first Industrial School for Blackfoot Children, a boarding school at Dunbow on the Highwood River. He pried 17 young Indians from their reluctant parents, but in the school they became wild as prairie ponies. They refused to bathe or have their hair combed; ripped the pillows in their dormitories; raced up and down the classrooms; and scoffed when the recess bell summoned them back to studies. At the end of that winter, all but two students had escaped. Lacombe tried to fill it by dragooning more docile Cree boys and half-breeds, but after the turn of the century he was forced to admit that the Indian school system was a failure.

In his disillusionment, he wrote: "We taught some boys and girls who were as bright as white children. That was only the beginning – the real problem came when they left school. To go back to their homes – not white, and not Indians any longer! Many were failures. Oh, it is very sad to think about all that – when you remember all the love and work and sacrifice we put into these schools. The poor Indians, how I pity them! My God, I offer you my sufferings."

Similarly, John McDougall realized the harm he had done by helping to subjugate the Indian race. As Indian Commissioner, he made a tour of inspection of the mangy reserves in British Columbia, Alberta and Saskatchewan, where he found his former parishioners squeezed into institutionalized slums, disenfranchised, and cheated of the title to their land. Before his death, the missionary wrote a report to the Department of Indian Affairs in Ottawa:

"They say: 'The Indian is dying, and he cannot die too soon for us.'

"They say: 'Damn the Siwash! Move him out of this country' – meaning, of course, contiguity to town, or railroad, or advancement in land prices, and quick speculation.

"The Indians are despotically made to conform to laws which they have no voice in creating. They are under the beck and nod of an Indian Agent, or Provincial Magistrate, or constable, in matters concerning which the white man beside them is given a free hand.

"They are in despair. They find themselves robbed of their manhood. They are placed far below the plane conceded to the basest and vilest and most degenerate of the white people.

"Such a condition these Indians cry out for deliverance from. In vain the long past, in vain his own life of toil on land and home – behold, this is not his.

"The Indian finds himself disinherited."

REVOLT ON THE PLAINS

Louis Riel: madman or martyr?

A PORTRAIT ALBUM

In the following pages are portrayed the leading characters in the most violent, and the most tragic, drama of the Canadian West. Gentlest among them was the mystic Louis Riel, whose quest to create a separate country for his half-breed buffalo hunters was twice crushed by an outraged Canada. Between his first insurrection at Red River, Manitoba, in 1869, and his defeat at Batoche, Saskatchewan, in 1885, he was twice in mental asylums and half forgotten in exile – yet, even today, he stands tall as a symbol of the racial and religious dichotomy that still plagues Canada.

`...VOICES IN THE PRAIRIE WIND'

He was only 41 when he died on the gallows at Regina in 1885 with the Lord's Prayer on his lips. Even in his boyhood, Riel showed signs of a deeply devout disposition. His mother (below, with Louis's son, Jean) arranged to send him away from St. Boniface to Montreal in 1858 to study for the priesthood, but Louis grew restless behind the walls of the Sulpician College. He was troubled by strange dreams and heard the same voices that whispered to him in the prairie wind. He felt that he was searching for a divine mission and, at college, he believed for a while that his mission was to redress the wrongs done to the Jews. When he returned to the Red River in 1868, however, he came to his true calling: to champion the cause of the mixed-blood Métis.

John C. Schultz led the forces who opposed the rebels at Red River. He became lieutenant-governor of Manitoba.

William McDougall was sent to rule Rupert's Land, but retreated in ridicule when Riel forbade his entry.

Picture of Louis Riel's Council in 1885. Taken beside Regina Court House at the time of their trial.

1. *Johnny Sansregret*
2. *P. Paranteau*
   (FAMOUS BUFFALO HUNTER)
3. *Pierre Gardiepui*
4. *Philip Garnot*
   (RIEL'S SECRETARY)

5. *Albert Monkman*
6. *Pierre Vandall*
7. *Babtiste Vandall*
8. *Touissant Lucier*
   (REPUTED STRONGEST MAN
   IN THE NORTHWEST)

9. *Maxime Dubois*
10. *Timmus Short*
11. ———— *Tourond*
12. *Emmanuel Champagne*

Ambroise Lépine, Riel's adjutant-general at Red River, was sentenced to death, but, in fact, spent two years in jail.

Gabriel Dumont, brilliant Métis field commander, was restrained by Riel. After defeat in 1885, he escaped.

~ THE VANQUISHED ~

Cree chiefs Big Bear (front, left) and Poundmaker (right) fought bravely but hopelessly for Riel's cause.

Despite his few isolated victories, Riel's rebellions were doomed from the beginning. At Red River, he did win better terms for his people in the new province of Manitoba – but he had to flee for his life from an angry army marching on Fort Garry. In Saskatchewan fifteen years later, his "army" of a few hundred half-breeds and Indians armed with antique weapons were pitted against 5,000 soldiers with Enfields, cannon and Gatling gun. Riel's inevitable defeat came on May 12, 1885.

Colonel Garnet Wolseley, a veteran of wars in the Crimea, China and India, led an expedition of British regulars and Canadian militia to quell the Red River rebellion.

~THE VICTORS~

While British Major-General Frederick Middleton dithered at the battle of Batoche, the raw Canadian volunteers he despised charged and won the day.

Paying a humiliating price for their aid to Riel, the great Cree chiefs Big Bear and Poundmaker were incarcerated in Stony Mountain Penitentiary, Manitoba. In this rare photograph, taken outside the penitentiary gates, can be seen: 1, Pioneer missionary Father Albert Lacombe; 2, Little Bear; 3, Warden Sam Bedson; 4, Father Clouthier, of Winnipeg; 5, Poundmaker; 6, an unknown priest. The clang of the gates behind the chiefs marked the official end of the 1885 rebellion. Broken in spirit, both died shortly after their release.

XIV

Messiah in Moccasins

A DOMINION GOVERNMENT surveyor named Colonel John Stoughton Dennis, an Orangeman from Protestant Toronto, appeared on the morning of October 11, 1869 in the outlying St. Vital grasslands of Red River Colony. Without asking permission, his crew began running a line across the farm of André Nault, a white-bearded *Métis*. Rake in hand, old Nault rushed over: "Get off my land." He spoke only French; the surveyor only English.

Dennis tried to explain that the half-breeds were squatting land the Hudson's Bay Company had just sold to the Dominion Government. On behalf of the new landlord, he was dividing the land into townships, as was the civilized custom of Anglo-Saxon Ontario.

The bewildered Nault argued that the *Métis*, as the sons of Indians, were the true owners of the plains. For decades the "New Nation" of *Bois-Brûlés* (those with skin the colour of burnt wood) had laid out its hay farms in two-mile ribbonlike strips fronting the river. That was the old tradition of French-Catholic Quebec. Nault ran off for help and returned with 17 mounted *Métis*. They were dressed in the fringed buckskin of buffalo hunters. All were armed with muzzle-loading rifles, except Nault's cousin.

This young man of 24, with compelling brown eyes and a commanding manner, leaped to the ground, planted his right moccasin, pink-stitched in a pattern of wild roses, on the survey chain, and said in English:

"You go no further."

With those four words Louis Riel touched off the first of his two rebellions, shocked two continents, and helped shape the map of North America. His first insurrection, as historians have called it, could more accurately be termed the "Resistance of the Half-breeds." Half Indian, half white, the *Métis* were resisting the H.B.C. counting-house merchants in London who had traded them to Ottawa for three hundred thousand pounds, as though they were so many beaver skins. The proud *Bois-Brûlés* were resisting the westward movement of immigrants from Ontario who ignored their racial, religious, lingual and political freedom as though the "breeds" were so many prairie dogs. Above all, the *Métis* resisted relinquishing their land. They were ready to die fighting for it, and some of them did.

The messiah in beaded moccasins who led them in their resistance was as full of contradictions as the people of his "Republic." During his 15 years of influence – a decade of it spent in exile – Louis Riel's name lit the Canadian West like a prairie grassfire. He incited passionate idolatry, and fanned fierce hatreds; few saw him objectively. He remains a baffling figure even today. He was obviously the sincere leader of a crusade; and yet he accepted a $1,600 bribe from Prime Minister Sir John A. Macdonald to stay out of Canada. He was a fervent advocate of responsible government; and yet he could not brook democratic opposition. He claimed to have feigned madness, Hamlet-like, when he was twice locked up into mental institutions, and yet the fact remains that he ran about stark naked proclaiming himself the new Jehovah. He abstained from drinking and smoking with monk-like austerity; and yet he wore purple silk vests and indulged in vulgar and bawdy humour.

His friends described him as a dark, handsome, strongly-built man, standing almost six feet tall in his moccasins. He had curly waves of brown hair parted on the right, a reddish-brown moustache arching over full lips, a restless man forever pacing vigorously. But an unfriendly British agent, Captain William F. Butler, saw him as "a short, stout man with a large head, a sallow, puffy face, walking up and down the room with theatrical attitudes and declamations . . . the little Napoleon, the Ogre. The picture of the black-coated *Métis* playing the part of Europe's great soldier in the garb of a priest and the shoes of a savage looked simply absurd."

Everyone agreed, however, that he was an orator. He could hold an audience transfixed for seven hours. His deep-set eyes became hypnotic, his bushy brows seemed to loom like promontories, his voice would throb like a cello or thunder like the legendary Jove. With a sympathetic listener, he was a brilliant conversationalist. In 1885, Dr. Michael Lavell, psychiatrist from Kingston Penitentiary, Ontario, interviewed the alleged madman for hours, and was deeply impressed by Riel's "rare charm. At times in conversation he maintained all the characteristics of his race, excitable and enthusiastic. At other times, his voice was soft, mellow and sweet." Lavell was attracted to Riel's "force of character, manly expression of countenance, intelligent and pleasing address." He was also, Lavell added, "shrewd, cunning, selfish, ambitious and vain."

In short, Riel was not all of a piece, neither a villain nor a saint. He was a mystic who heard voices in the wail of the prairie wind, saw his death in a flight of white geese. He was a poet, able, on the day that he died, to see a kind of classic inevitability about his fate, as though he were playing a role in a Greek tragedy.

The poet, statesman, orator and agitator was born in a mud-chinked, one-story poplar-log cabin where St. Vital now stands. The future champion of the half-breeds was only one-eighth Indian. He inherited his Montagnais blood and his radical temperament from his father, Louis Riel Sr., who in 1849 had led the *Métis* of Red River Colony in a free trade revolt against the H.B.C. monopoly. Young Riel's Canadienne mother, Julie, was a pious dedicated woman, daughter of Jean Baptiste Lagimonière, a celebrated Red River courier for Lord Selkirk. Young Louis admired his father (who would "permit no one to speak evil in my presence") and adored his mother (who was always praying, "her eyes constantly turned toward heaven"). The boy attended Mass at the twin-towered cathedral in St. Boniface and was an accomplished Latin scholar, at the school run by the Grey Nuns. Monsignor Alexander Taché, Bishop of St. Boniface, sent him at 13 to study for the priesthood at Montreal College.

Cooped up in the high stone walls of the college on top of Mount Royal, the young Louis felt lonely and homesick for the grasslands and red willow bluffs of Red River. His teachers regarded him as dreamy and introspective, proficient in Greek and philosophy, outstanding when declaiming the orations of Cicero. His fellow students considered him quick-witted and trigger-tempered, obsessively defensive of his mixed ancestry, always ready to defend minority groups in an argument. "To offer an opinion contrary to his was to irritate him," a schoolmate said.

When Louis was 19, his father died, and grief seems to have temporarily unhinged the youth's mind. He would skip classes to brood alone on a rock on Mount Royal. He wrote verses in the style of the French poet, Alphonse de Lamartine, that showed an intense preoccupation with his own singularity. He was now the absentee head of the Riel family, consisting of his mother and eight younger children. At this time he wrote a strange letter to the priest in St. Boniface that "I have no legitimate right to the property of the Riels." He was not Louis Riel, he said. The true Louis was drowned. He was now David Mordecai, a Jewish messiah, and pleaded with the *Métis* to help redress the wrongs done the Hebrews. Henceforth his divine mission was to save the Jews and the Gentiles.

Four months before graduating, he impulsively left the seminary. He spent a year learning politics and law in a Montreal law office, and then returned to Red River. When he stepped off the boat that mid-summer of 1868, he found the settlement disturbed. It was a motley collection of two stone forts, three saloons, log stores, mud shacks, and tents strung out along the wooded banks of the Red and Assiniboine rivers. The twelve thousand inhabitants were a *mélange* of races and colours, bound together by a sense of community; the six thousand *Métis* formed a majority. The attitude of Riel's friend, black-bearded Ambroise Lépine, was typical. Lépine was worried because the buffalo herds had vanished that season, and a grasshopper plague had ravaged the Red River crops. Furthermore, rumours that the Hudson's Bay Company was selling Rupert's Land to Ottawa left the buffalo hunter concerned that the *Métis* might be sold with it "like dumb, driven cattle."

About 4,000 of the colonists were English half-breeds. Many were as vacillating and unstable as their spokesman, James Ross. The son of Alexander Ross, late schoolmaster and Mountain Man, James Ross had been educated at the University of Toronto. On his return, he occasionally complained about the apathy of his people under "the incubus of the Company's monopoly—the peculiar government under which we *vegetate* – it cools our ardour – destroys our energies – annihilates our very *desires* for improvement." He complained and drank and vegetated.

Fifteen hundred of the settlers were white, and these were split into various factions. Ostensibly the Scottish and English retired fur traders had as their spokesman the 16 members on the Council of Assiniboia. But they were puppets appointed by the Bay directors in London. The Council Governor was 60-year-old Chief Factor William Mactavish. He was disgusted with the "greedy London directory" and the "arrogant" Dominion Government, neither of which had bothered to inform his Red River government, mere chattel that it was, about the impending sale of Rupert's Land. Anyway, Governor Mactavish was dying of tuberculosis.

Noisiest of the whites was a group of about 40 rowdies who called themselves the "Canadian Party." Their leader was Dr. John Christian Schultz, a politicking physician from Amherstburg, Ontario; he controlled the colony's sole newspaper, the four-page *Nor'wester*, and its only brick store, where he dealt in drugs, furs and real estate. Dr. Schultz had all the attributes of a successful frontier leader; he was handsome (finely-chiseled features with red-blond hair), tall (six feet, four inches), strong (he could wrench an oaken chair apart with his hands), and eloquent (in debates, they said, his beautifully-modulated voice could convince a skunk weed that it was a prairie rose). Regrettably, one diarist said, "Fate had manufactured a scoundrel out of material meant by Nature for a gentleman." He was an anti-*Métis* bigot, abusive and unscrupulous.

Schultz made a laughing stock of the colony's feeble government. He defied its constables to force him to pay money he owed to creditors. He beat up the bailiff and was dragged to jail, but a dozen of his cronies broke his cell bars and carried him off triumphantly on their shoulders. Schultz bragged openly that as soon as the Dominion Government took over he would appoint himself sheriff.

Some whites were Ontario Orangemen working with Colonel Dennis's surveys, and they soon allied themselves with Schultz. The survey paymaster was Charles Mair, part-time newspaper correspondent and author of a slender volume of poetry, *Dreamland*. In a dispatch to the Toronto *Globe*, Mair mocked Red River's "half-breed women who, having no coat of arms but a totem to look back to, make up for the deficiency by biting at the backs of their white sisters." Louis Riel retaliated with a witty riposte advising Mair to stick to poetry, "For in that way his writings would make up in rhyme what they lack in reason." The girls of Red River were more muscular in their literary criticism. One pulled the poet's nose, a second boxed his ears, and a third horse-whipped him in the post office.

Another man with a fateful role to play was Thomas Scott, a rabid Catholic-hater from North Ireland. Six feet two inches tall, with a pouting face and two glinting gold teeth, the 26-year-old Orangeman had won a reputation for pugnacity while serving with Hastings Battalion of Rifles in Ontario. En route to the Cariboo gold-fields, he had stopped off to work as a navvy, building the Dawson Road from Lake of the Woods to the colony. When a Red River court of half-breeds fined him four pounds for attempting to drown a man, Scott bawled obscenities at them and swore he would take vengeance.

The American mischief-makers were more devious. There was James Wickes Taylor, lawyer in St. Paul, Minnesota, novelist, and soon to be American consul in Red River Colony; he was actually an agent of the United States State Department who connived to buy Rupert's Land for $10 millions. There was Enos Stutsman, journalist, lawyer and customs agent at the North Dakota border town of Pembina; actually, though born legless, the 200-pound cripple was Taylor's courier, who subtly planted propaganda in the Red River Colony that the Canadian West was "the lawful and natural prey of the American eagle." And there was William B. O'Donoghue, a slim 25-year-old New York Irishman, a Catholic seminarian, mathematics professor at St. Boniface College, and organizer of the Yankee Fenian Brotherhood that was plotting freedom for Ireland by capturing the entire colony of Canada.

The last of the featured players in the Red River drama was the most pathetic. He was Henry Prince, Christianized son of Lord Selkirk's once great peace-maker, Chief Peguis. Prince ruled 600 Saulteaux Indians at the colony, but his tribesmen were easily debauched by the Schultz gang and the surveyors, and for a few bottles of *hootchenoo*, Prince's people sold all title to their land.

Louis Riel was quick to assume his own role as political revolutionary and *Métis* emancipator. From the steps of St. Boniface Cathedral, he began making impassioned speeches. The *Métis*, he said, needed safeguards to perpetuate their position. The newcomers were threatening to drive them out to the Saskatchewan country, keeping a few as menials to haul the baggage of the incoming Ontario immigrants. Prime Minister Macdonald had no right to survey their property before the official transfer of Rupert's Land and without consulting the Indians and the *Métis* – the rightful owners. Riel called upon the New Nation to take a stand. "If any one falls," he proclaimed, "a handkerchief shall be dipped in his blood and used in all future engagements as our national flag." The Catholics, including several priests, rallied to his call. A National Committee of *Métis* was organized, with Riel as secretary. The Fenian O'Donoghue, a gifted strategist, was named Treasurer, the Adjutant-General was Ambroise Lépine. Mustering 500 armed buffalo hunters, Lépine pulled up the surveyors' stakes. Though the Canadian Party sneered at the "Pemmican Government," the National Committee effectively turned back all trespassers.

The next move was up to Sir John A. Macdonald, and the usually astute Prime Minister bungled it. He regarded the inhabitants of the West as "miserable half-breeds" and he saw no need to guarantee the "squatters" legal title to their land, no need for a ceremony by which the reins of power would be handed over officially to the 150-member council already appointed by the Dominion Government. Rather, "to keep those wild people quiet," Macdonald named one of his cabinet ministers to be a "paternal despot" as Lieutenant-Governor of Rupert's Land. This man, William McDougall, was almost comically unsuited to his mission. He had a swollen ego, and an overbearing contempt for Catholics. "If not the most lovable statesman," a friend said, groping for a word of praise, he had "a strong, uncompromising intellect that chooses to force the enemy's citadel rather than stoop to the cunning arts of the tactician." The new ruler of two million square miles had been chosen for the job largely to get him out of Macdonald's hair.

McDougall left for Red River at the end of September, 1869. The Bay Committee in London had set December 1 as the date that Rupert's Land would be transferred to Canada. But McDougall was to take over what he called his "kingdom" one month later. On October 30, 60 carts creaked into the border town of Pembina. They carried McDougall, his ministers of state, relatives, equerries, maid servants and fox-hunting dogs. The mountain of baggage included 350 Enfield rifles (which Riel regarded as the illicit arms of a foreign invader) and an awesome gubernatorial throne of state (lampooned in a *Métis* ballad as the "monarch's toilet seat").

At Enos Stutsman's American customs house in Pembina, a *Métis* courier handed McDougall a note. Written in French and signed by Riel, it read: "The National Committee of the *Métis* of Red River orders Monsieur William McDougall not to enter the Territory of the Northwest without special permission . . ." It proclaimed the right of the New Nation, like that of any province, to parley for the terms by which it would enter Confederation. McDougall contemptuously brushed the messenger aside. "The time will come," he fumed, "when I will put my foot on their French necks."

While his caravan slowly creaked on, the Hon. McDougall sent forward his minister of militia to scout the road. This monocled English gentleman, Captain D. R. Cameron, was astounded to find a barricade across the trail, at St. Norbert. Cameron jumped from his carriage, lifted his monocle to his eye, and bellowed: "Remove that blawsted fence!" Ambroise Lépine gaped at him unbelievingly. Then he warned the "Donkey Captain of the Horse Marine," as the *Métis* called this phenomenon, that his caravan had until sundown to turn back to Pembina. McDougall obeyed, deciding that discretion, at this point, was wise. He moved his entourage into a crowded Pembina log cabin.

Riel's spies soon reported that McDougall's allies, Dennis and Schultz, were planning to move into Upper Fort Garry. Behind its 16-foot grey stone walls were barracks, *pemmican* storehouses, a jail and an executive mansion. More important, it had an arsenal of 390 rifles, with ample ammunition, and 13 six-pounder cannon. The fortress was garrisoned only by H.B.C. clerks and the ailing Governor Mactavish.

Riel decided on a bold move. "War must be met with war," he declared. "Just as we repel Indian war parties who approach the portals of the Colony with adverse intent, so must Monsieur McDougall be repulsed."

On November 2, at the head of 120 armed *Métis*, Riel rode through the open gates, and took possession of Fort Garry. The Republic of Red River would not surrender to Canada, Riel asserted, until the people were granted the right to elect their own legislature.

Sir John A. Macdonald, who at first had been amused at McDougall's predicament, now sent a frantic cable stopping payment of the three hundred thousand pounds to the Bay Company Committee. "Canada cannot accept North West until peaceable possession can be given," his wire dated November 26, read. "We have advised Colonial Office to delay issue of Proclamation."

To his would-be despot denned in a Pembina shack, the Prime Minister dispatched a cautionary letter. Since McDougall had no legal status – was, indeed, no more than an ordinary citizen – he had better sit tight until things quieted down. "Never forget that you are now approaching a foreign country," he advised McDougall. "You cannot force your way in."

But the Prime Minister had overlooked the ego of McDougall. He penned his own Royal Proclamation, by which the Queen's loyal Red River subjects were commanded to bow to the authority of "our trusty and well-beloved William McDougall." And with a flourish, he forged Queen Victoria's signature.

On December 1, in a 20-below-zero blizzard, McDougall, with six "ministers of state" and two pointer dogs, stumbled through the snow just across the border north of Pembina. While one courtier held a guttering lantern and another a small Union Jack, the Governor-elect read aloud his proclamation. Then he dashed for his sleigh and hurried back to Pembina.

News of the ceremony leaked out. Enos Stutsman wrote a satirical account for the St. Paul *Presse*. The Montreal comic paper, *Grinchuckle*, caricatured "Silly Wandering Willy." At Fort Garry, Riel immortalized the incident in a mock heroic ballad. McDougall now commissioned Dennis his "Lieutenant and Conservator of the Peace," with orders to post copies of his proclamation on the walls of Fort Garry. Dennis was further ordered to work with the Schultz gang in recruiting an army – of Saulteaux and Sioux Indians, if need be – to put down the insurgents. "I feel confident,"

McDougall wrote to Ottawa, "that this prompt display of vigour will inspire all inhabitants of the Territory with respect for your Representative, and compel the traitors to cry, 'God Save the Queen.' "

Riel recognized the Royal Proclamation as a counterfeit. (In his memoirs, he recalled how he flung the poster back at one of Dennis's men: "I says to him, 'Take that big *sheet*' – pronouncing the double 'e' very short'.") But Dennis's attempt to arouse the Indians alarmed Riel. He exerted all his persuasive powers to placate Chief Henry Prince's warriors and then turned his attention to his implacable enemy, Schultz.

Forty-eight members of the Canadian Party had barricaded Schultz's brick warehouse. It was the "loyalist headquarters" they said, calling it "Fort Schultz" and flying a Union Jack with "Canada" embroidered on it in white. The *Métis* called it "Fort Pork" because it was said to contain a consignment of government salt meat. Riel saw the "fort" as a threat. On December 7, he rode out of Fort Garry with 300 *Métis* marksmen, whooping and singing at the prospect of action. Behind them rumbled two field cannon with a cartload of ammunition.

Ignoring the rifles pointed at him from each window, Riel had his *Métis* encircle the warehouse and train the two loaded cannon on the door. "The Commandant" – as Riel sometimes signed his orders – then instructed Adjutant-General Lépine to deliver an ultimatum. "I will give Schultz and company exactly 15 minutes to surrender unconditionally. All their lives will be spared if they comply. In case the men refuse, we will wait an extra five minutes to allow the women and children, Indians and half-breeds to depart unmolested."

Ten minutes passed. Lepine was still inside, and the sound of argument could be heard. Riel looked at his watch in tight-lipped silence. The *Métis* at the cannon held the lanyard taut, tensely watching their Commandant. As Riel was about to give the order to fire, Schultz's door opened. A voice called out nervously, "Don't shoot, we give up."

Fifty people spilled out, including the wives of Charles Mair and Schultz. The two women insisted on accompanying the men being taken prisoner to Fort Garry. On the sleigh ride to jail, Riel gallantly gave his own coat to Mrs. Schultz. She was so astonished to find the hated Frenchman acting like a gentleman that, one witness said, she fainted away in a fit of hysterics. Among the Indians allowed to leave was a "squaw" heavily swathed in buffalo robes – Colonel Dennis, the Conservator of the Peace, was making his exit. He snowshoed down to Pembina to meet a crest-fallen McDougall. "The two together," Prime Minister Mac-

donald wrote bitterly, after recalling both and firing them, "have done their utmost to destroy our chance of an amicable settlement with these wild people."

McDougall's downfall was greeted with rejoicing at Fort Garry. On December 10, the flagpole flew the revolutionary banner of the *Métis* Republic: the *fleur de lis* and shamrock against a white background with a small buffalo in the fly. The fort cannon thundered a *feu de joie*. The boys' brass band from St. Boniface College played. Riel made a speech proclaiming his loyalty to the Queen, but demanding justice for the *Métis*. The crowd of eight hundred gave three cheers for Riel, three cheers for the Provisional Government, and three groans for the prisoners in the post.

It was easier to seize power than to keep it. Riel's authority was vested in his 500 buffalo hunters and guard duty made them restless. They preferred to race their horses on the Red River ice, or to enjoy a jollification at O'Lone's Red Saloon or Dutch George Emmerling's Hostelry. Although Riel banned the sale of liquor during the Christmas-New Year's holiday, 12 prisoners escaped their drunken jailers on January 9, 1870. Among them was the rambunctious Orangeman, Thomas Scott. The ringleader, Schultz, did not get away, though his wife did. A few were recaptured. One, W. F. Hyman from London, Ontario, froze his feet so severely he almost lost his toes. Riel found it hard to watch the doctor cut into the injured foot. "I pitied that young man," he said. "What a position mine is to have to bear all this. But I cannot help myself."

Riel was tougher when Schultz's newspaper, the *Nor'wester*, refused to publish one of the Republic's proclamations. He suppressed the paper and used its presses to publish his own sheet, *The New Nation*. Desperate for money to pay his *Métis* battalions, he approached Governor Mactavish with a demand for a loan of 1,000 pounds from the Hudson's Bay Company. Mactavish turned him down. Ignoring the bribe of $25,000 that the Yankee annexationists were waving at him, Riel arrested Mactavish and seized the Company's cash box. His hardest task lay in keeping his fellow colonists united under the banner of the Provisional Government. "I have spoken during the whole seven hours," he noted in his diary. "It is incredible what fears and misgivings I had to overcome in them. That which they feared most was the appearance of a rebellion against the Queen. It is only by force of saying to them that we remain faithful to the Queen that I convinced them."

The English half-breeds under James Ross were lukewarm. Riel had to fire them by reminding them they were all children of mixed blood, too long exploited as hewers of wood and drawers of water by a feudal Hudson's Bay Company. The pure-blooded Scottish and English Protestants were either neutral or resentful that French Catholics dominated the new political movement. Riel attempted to win their support with moderately-worded manifestos in *The New Nation*, (which some called "The New Damnation"). He signed his proclamations, "I am your humble, poor, fair, and confident public servant." He pleaded with them: "O my fellow countrymen, without distinction of language or creed, keep my words in your hearts." He harangued them: "Go. Return peacefully to your farms. Rest in the arms of your wives. Give that example to your children. But watch us act. We are going to work and obtain the guarantee of our rights and of yours. You will come to share them in the end!"

It was Sir John A. Macdonald who, unwittingly, helped Riel consolidate his government. The Dominion Prime Minister grew alarmed at reports that the American annexationists were offering $4 millions if Riel would allow the Stars and Stripes to fly over his Republic. Macdonald quickly appointed a special negotiator. This time he chose a diplomat: shaggy-browed, spade-bearded, canny Donald A. ("Labrador") Smith, a Scottish fur trader who later became Governor of the H.B.C., president of the Canadian Pacific Railroad, and a peer, Lord Strathcona. As an extra precaution, Macdonald gave Smith 500 pounds as a "golden bridge" across which malcontents in Riel's party might be lured.

Louis Riel out-manoeuvred him. He used the presence of Smith as a token that Ottawa recognized his Government. He assembled more than 1,000 colonists for a mass meeting in an open field outside Fort Garry. Interpreting Smith's words into French and Indian, he allowed Smith to drone on for ten hours in 20-below-zero cold. The weary, bored and numbed victims of Smith's oratory finally agreed to send 20 English-speaking representatives to the Provincial Government and join in drawing up a Bill of Rights for submission to Ottawa.

On February 10, the new regime was inaugurated with a grand fireworks display. Roman candles, originally stocked by Schultz to greet McDougall, flung fiery trails across the starlit sky. Riel, celebrating with "a good horn of brandy," watched the French and Scots shake hands and throw their caps in the air. He felt exalted. Without shedding a drop of blood, he had unified his countrymen. It was not for long. Using a jack-knife that his wife had smuggled inside a pudding, Schultz slashed a buffalo robe into strips and lowered himself from the jail window. In nearby Portage la Prairie, he and Thomas Scott began organizing an army

of Ontario settlers to liberate the rest of the prisoners and overthrow Riel.

About 100 "Portage Liberators," armed with clubs and a six-pound cannon hauled by four oxen, ran into the small village of Winnipeg. Thomas Scott broke into the home of Henri Coutu, a cousin of Riel's, smashed the furniture and threatened to kill Riel as soon as he found the blackguard. At Kildonan parish, cooler heads attempted to dissuade them from continuing. While they were arguing, a feeble-minded *Métis* boy, Norbert ("The Half-Wit") Parisien, happened to pass by. The crowd seized the youth and accused him of being a spy. In the morning Parisien snatched a rifle, and fled, hotly pursued.

A few minutes before, a respectable Scottish settler named John Sutherland had left Fort Garry with good news: at his urging, Riel had agreed to release the remaining prisoners on the pledge that they would not take up arms against the Provisional Government. The Scot had sent his young son, John Hugh Sutherland, to carry the news to Thomas Scott in Winnipeg. The fleeing Parisien heard the young courier's horse pounding toward him and thought it was one of his pursuers. He fired twice and shot Sutherland through lung and throat. The dying Sutherland is said to have pleaded for the life of his killer: "The poor simple fellow was too frightened to know what he was doing." But Thomas Scott rushed forward with a "big staff," according to a witness, and bludgeoned Parisien unconscious. He died six days later.

Riel bewailed the senseless mishap: "I understand that war, horrible civil war, is the destruction of this country." He dispatched a large party of his *Métis* who captured 48 of the "Liberators." Schultz slipped away but Scott was taken prisoner again.

"In prison, Thomas Scott began by insulting his guards, who were treating him well," Riel wrote in his memoirs. "A few days after, he proceeded to violence, resisting his guards by main strength and forcing the doors of the prison. On the last day of February, Scott was so violent that some of the *Métis*, in a fit of exasperation, seized him, dragged him out, and were preparing to sacrifice him. Then one of the French Councillors came by, snatched him away, and sent him back under guard to his cell."

On March 1, Riel visited the prisoner. "Be orderly and quiet," he beseeched Scott, "so I have the excuse of preventing you from being brought before the Council of the Attorney-General."

"They will never dare shoot me," Scott taunted.

"Ask me anything at all for a punishment you would prefer." Riel said he made this offer to placate him.

"I want nothing," retorted Scott. "You breeds are nothing but a pack of cowards." The slur so enraged the *Métis* guards that one told Riel, "If this insulter is not shot, the *Bois-Brûlés* will shoot you."

On March 3, Scott was brought before a seven-man tribune headed by Ambroise Lépine. He was charged with taking up arms against the Provisional Government and assaulting the captain of the guards. Scott sprang at Riel, the prosecutor, upsetting a table in trying to strike him.

One of the judges, Elzéar Lagimodière, offered to escort Scott across the border if he would promise not to return. "Take me there if you will," Scott said defiantly. "I will be back as soon as you. None of you breeds would dare condemn me to death."

Four of the seven judges did, and Scott was sentenced to be executed by a firing squad at noon the next day.

Later, André Nault, one of the court-martial judges, said of Scott, "He was a tall, rather slim man, very brave, but exceedingly violent. I am convinced he did not believe we would have the 'pluck,' as he called it, to go the whole length and shoot him. To the last instant, he thought we were only joking. We had no desire whatever to put him to death; he simply forced us to it."

All through the night, ministers, priests and Commissioner Donald A. Smith begged Riel not to blemish his six-month record of a bloodless insurrection with a pointless death. But Riel was immovable. "Scott has scorned everybody and persisted in his defiant conduct," Riel said. "The boldness of our enemies, encouraged by our patience, has become extreme. I must make an example to impress others. We must make Canada respect us. Scott must die . . ."

At noon on March 4, the Methodist pastor, the Rev. George Young, entered Scott's room carrying a Bible. After writing a letter to his mother, the doomed Orangeman was allowed to visit the cells of his fellow prisoners. At each door, he said, "Goodbye, boys." As he was marched out into the fort courtyard, his wrists manacled behind his back, he seemed suddenly to realize this was no adolescent joke. "This is horrible!" he groaned to Young. "This is cold-blooded murder!"

The pastor tried to comfort him with a prayer. Scott was blindfolded with a white cotton rag as he knelt in the snow. A firing squad of six *Métis* raised their rifles. None of them knew which three rifles held bullets or which only powder and wad. André Nault dropped a white handkerchief from one hand to the other, the firing signal. Two of the bullets struck Scott in the chest. He slumped forward, his blood gushing onto the fresh snow. He was still alive, moaning and writhing. Francois Guillmette, a member of the squad, drew out his Colt revolver and delivered the *coup de grâce*. The bullet entered through Scott's ear and blasted out through his mouth.

Riel stepped forward and asked the crowd to leave. The body was placed in a rough wooden coffin. That night Elzéar Goulet was ordered to weight it with chains and drop it secretly through a hole in the Red River ice. Scott's burial place was kept secret, it was afterward explained, "for fear the Orangemen would make a sort of pilgrimage ground of it."

It was a futile move. The ghost of Thomas Scott would haunt Riel for the rest of his life, as it haunts the Canadian nation to this day. In the east, Dr. Schultz was soon holding protest rallies, displaying a rope that he said had tied Scott's wrists, and a vial of the martyr's blood, which he sprinkled on the handkerchiefs of tearful women. Ontario cried "Murder!" and Scott's home county of Middlesex offered a $5,000 reward for the capture of what the Toronto *Globe* called the "desperate, depraved, devilish" Papists. Quebec, up to this time indifferent toward Confederation, now championed Louis Riel and the western *Métis*. The new-born Dominion Government, barely three years old, tried to placate both sides.

Five days after Scott's execution, Bishop Taché, Riel's old benefactor, was summoned to Ottawa from a papal conference in Rome. At St. Boniface Cathedral, the bishop told the *Métis* that Prime Minister Macdonald had promised them a general amnesty and a voice in dictating the terms of their entry into Confederation. The fireworks were over. Riel liberated his prisoners. He raised the Union Jack over Fort Garry. He sent three peace emissaries to Ottawa — a magistrate, a priest and a bartender — to negotiate provincial self-government.

On May 12, 1870, the Dominion Parliament passed the Manitoba Act. It gave Louis Riel everything he demanded in his Bill of Rights — except the promised amnesty, for Macdonald was wary of alienating the voters of Ontario. The act guaranteed the *Métis* 24 members in the legislature, four representatives in the House of Commons, separate schools, equality of language, and 1,400,000 acres of land.

The Manitoba Act was supposed to be an olive branch but to wave it firmly, Macdonald sent out a Red River Expeditionary Force of 1,200 men to restore "peace and order" in the new province. While 400 of the soldiers were British regulars, 800 were Ontario volunteers, all avid for Riel's blood. After 96 days of bedraggled marching and 47 portages, their commander, Colonel Garnet Wolseley, noted in his diary:

"Hope Riel will have bolted; for although I should like to hang him from the highest tree in the place, I have such a horror of rebels and vermin of his kidney that my treatment of him might not be approved by the civil powers."

On August 24, the "Jolly Boys," as the militiamen called themselves, approached Fort Garry, their green tunics black from the soaking rain. Riel was sitting down to a breakfast of cold meat when one of his scouts, James Stewart, burst into the room. "For the love of God, clear out! The troops are only two miles from the city, and you are going to be lynched."

Riel slipped out of one gate of the fort as Wolseley's troops entered by another.

Riel and O'Donoghue hurriedly lashed some fence posts together with their belts, cut the cable that held the ferry boat, and rafted across the Red River to St. Boniface. "You have left the fort?" Bishop Taché asked in surprise, as Riel came rushing into his quarters.

"Yes, Your Grace," Riel said bitterly. "We have fled because we have been deceived. Come and see the soldiers who approach the fort. We accepted Canada's friendship, and it laughed at us."

"What are you going to do?"

"The only thing for me to do is to get on horseback and bolt for the other side of the boundary."

Riel and O'Donoghue mounted horse, but before galloping for Dakota, they gazed for ten minutes across the river at the soldiers swarming into the stronghold that they had held for ten months. In the pelting rain, the former President of the Republic of the Red River turned to his former Treasurer: "No matter what happens now, the rights of the *Métis* are assured by the Manitoba Act. That is what I wanted. My mission is finished."

Wolseley's men swiftly made a mockery of their peace mission. The members of Riel's Provisional Government were hunted down. André Nault was pursued to Pembina, bayoneted, and left for dead. Elzéar Goulet was chased into the Assiniboine and stoned until he sank. Francois Guillmette was stalked, cornered, and killed with a bullet through his temple. A priest, Father Francis X. Kavanaugh, was wounded; a bartender, Bob O'Lone, was killed in his saloon; and the daughter of a Riel supporter, 17-year-old Laurette Goulet, died after being raped by four drunken soldiers. Riel's Adjutant-General, Ambroise Lépine, was seized in his home, tried and sentenced to be hanged. At the last moment his hanging was commuted to two years in prison, on condition that he stay out of politics.

Riel, with a warrant out for his arrest, flitted from one hiding place to another. At dusk one evening he emerged from a haystack in front of a friendly half-breed. "Tell them," he said, "that he who reigned over a fort is now a homeless wanderer with nothing to eat but two dried suckers."

The reign of terror slackened as the Lieutenant-Governor, Adams G. Archibald, assumed office. A humane Nova Scotian, he reported to Prime Minister Macdonald: "Many of the French half-breeds have been so beaten and outraged that they feel as if they were living in a state of slavery." The loyalty that Riel commanded impressed him. "Unless you expect to gather grapes of thorns or figs of thistles," he told Macdonald, "you can hardly hope to carry on responsible government here by inflicting death penalties on the leaders of the majority of the electors."

Riel's popularity worried Macdonald. Federal elections were imminent and he was certain that Riel would easily be elected in the Manitoba riding of Provencher. To obviate that embarrassment, Macdonald offered Riel – through Bishop Taché – $1,600 to stay out of Canada for a year. Almost incredibly, Riel accepted, rationalizing that his widowed mother and her children needed money; but his conscience was disturbed. "My lord," he said, when Taché handed him the bag of money, "if the one who wants me to go away was here, this little sack of gold ought to be flung at his head!" In the next election, in 1874, however, Riel would not be bought off. He won Provencher by a landslide and vowed he would take his seat in the House of Commons. With Orangemen eager to win the reward of $5,000 still on Riel's head, Macdonald was sure the *Métis* leader wouldn't dare show his face in Ottawa. "If we once get him here," he said, "he's a gone coon."

On March 31, that year, disguised with red whiskers, but wearing his moccasins, Riel glided into the House of Commons the day before Parliament opened. A former schoolmate, the member for Rimouski, Romuald Fiset, M.P., asked the Clerk of the House, Alfred Patrick, to swear in the new member. Only after Fiset and his protégé were about to leave the room did Patrick bother to read the new man's signature on the registry book. "To my astonishment," Patrick said, "I saw the name 'Louis Riel'. I looked up suddenly and saw them going out of the door. Riel was making a low bow to me."

Patrick dashed to summon the Minister of Justice, but it was too late. Riel's friends had him in hiding. His cloak-and-dagger gesture threw the House into an uproar. A motion was passed – seconded by the implacable Dr. Schultz, now also a member of Parliament, expelling Riel from the House. A year later, in the spring of 1875, Parliament banished Riel from Her Majesty's Dominions for five years.

CANADIAN ILLUSTRATED NEWS

Vol. 1.—No 25. MONTREAL, SATURDAY, APRIL 23, 1870. [SINGLE COPIES, TEN CE[NTS]
[$4 PER YEAR IN ADVAN[CE]

The Shot that Set the West Ablaze

The failure to avenge the execution of Ontario adventurer Thomas Scott – despite a $5,000 price on Louis Riel's head – rankled in eastern hearts for fifteen years. When Riel reappeared in the West in 1885, volunteers rushed to crush him.

The 65th Battalion crammed aboard the C.P.R. trains at Montreal. At the outset of the 1885 revolt, French and English rallied to defend the sovereignty of their still-new nation. Riel warned his *Métis* marksmen not to fire on these troops from Quebec, "nos amis Canadiens."

The War News in Montreal
Scene in front of "Star" Office
St James St.

Toronto's Farewell

These on-the-spot sketches show the 10th Royal Grenadiers and the Queen's Own boarding trains in Toronto on March 30, 1885. Scene 1 shows the thousands that thronged the depot platform to cheer the boys off to the war in the Northwest. Scene 2, a fond farewell, and just time for a hurried kiss; 3, a shower of bouquets at the Walker House (though the hotel flew the Stars and Stripes); 4, troops discussed the task and challenge ahead; 5, three colonels — Otter, Miller and Grasset; 6, loading the baggage and supplies; 7, the boys who stayed behind sang a rousing round of "Goodbye, Old Fellow"; 8, a time for tears; 9, the last glimpse, as the train is lost on the horizon. The Métis threat was the first test of the national will, and the people responded with a jamboree of patriotism that outshone by far the feeble celebrations that had greeted the birth of the nation just 18 years earlier.

The Long Wait

In a promised dozen days, railway builder William Van Horne had transported the fighting men to the West over rails partly laid on ice, in sleighs and open flatcars, with temperatures plunging to 50 below. The big rush ended in a long wait. At Qu'Appelle, the main base of operations, and again at Clark's Crossing, Major-General Frederick Middleton hedged and hesitated, uncertain how to deploy his force of citizen soldiers. The men whiled away the hours at camp with drill, or were left to lie around with their thoughts – there was time for a leisurely haircut, and someone even took the time to build a sentry hut out of straw.

On the Way to Join Riel

The Mounties might have taught Middleton much about the Métis method of warfare, but their offers to help were usually shrugged off. Major L. N. F. Crozier, figure 2, had already learned of the devastating effectiveness of Gabriel Dumont's ambush tactics, at Duck Lake, where the rebels fought his force of police and volunteers to a standstill. With Crozier is Samuel Steele, figure 3, who became the most famous Mountie of all, after taming the brawling Yukon during the gold rush. Figure 4 is Inspector Francis Dickens, son of Charles Dickens, the novelist.

It was a big country, the prairie that became a battleground in the spring of 1885. Indians and half-breeds had long ago learned the value of a pony in war, to cross the great distances and vast open spaces, but Major-General Middleton arrived in the West steeped in British tradition, convinced of the superiority of the foot-soldier. He did recruit two corps of mounted men at Qu'Appelle, to reinforce the North West Mounted Police scouting parties, but on the whole the obdurate British general had little use for the western horsemen or the eastern cavalry troops.

George Taylor Denison (seen seated in uniform) had distinguished himself leading his cavalry against the Fenians on the Niagara Peninsula in 1866, but he had little chance to prove the valour of his Ontario horsemen during the 1885 rebellion. Middleton ordered the cavalry corps well to the rear, to guard the communication lines, rather than to set them against Riel's riding rebels. This log cabin was at the present site of Humboldt, Saskatchewan. The mounted man was a courier; the civilian seated with Denison was Bill Scott, Humboldt's permanent population.

5

When Riel called for recruits, the Métis came riding to Batoche. Gabriel Dumont would mould them into a powerful guerrilla force.

Behind the Rebel Lines

No known war artists sketched the brief struggle from the Métis side in that snowy spring of 1885, but correspondents for eastern magazines sent back these conceptions of events behind the rebel lines. There is no record of Dumont using any cannons in the field, though they were used against him.

Riel had scant supplies, but no shortage of cart transport.
Almost indestructible, the Red River cart was built entirely
of wood, with hub of elm and axle of maple, the wheels bound
with rawhide. When the horse couldn't pull it, the passengers
helped. With the wheels removed, the cart became a raft.

THE ILLUSTRATED WAR NEWS

[Vol. 1, No. 1] TORONTO, APRIL 4th, 1885. [15c. per Copy.

The Skirmish that Stunned a Nation

On March 26, 1885, gunshots rang out over the ravines near Duck Lake – and the war for the West began. It was more a skirmish than a battle, this brief clash between the Métis, some Mounties and a group of volunteers, but when the news from Saskatchewan spread, it stunned the incredulous East: the half-breeds' distant grumbling had erupted into a shooting war. Even more unbelievable, and intolerable, Riel's rebels had won that first fight.

The cover of the first edition of the Illustrated War News (opposite) on April 4, 1885 portrayed the action at Duck Lake in a way that paled the glory of the Charge of the Light Brigade. The same journal, later in the year, offered the tamer but more accurate version shown below, depicting a cautious conflict, with the rebels sensibly sheltering behind the willows. Despite the sensation caused by the clash, the total death toll was 17, five of them Métis.

The main street of Battleford, N.W.T., in 1885. The province of Saskatchewan would not be created for another 20 years.

War Drums and War Paint

News of the Duck Lake fighting spread across the Cree camps like a prairie grass-fire. The myth of the Mounties had been shattered – white men were not invincible. Perhaps Louis Riel was a miracle-maker, the Indians said, and the white intruders could be pushed from the plains. The war drums throbbed as 200 Crees and a band of Assiniboines swooped down on the settlement of Battleford, looted the homes and stores, got drunk and danced to celebrate triumph over the white man.

During the looting orgy, 500 terrified settlers watched from behind the stockade of the N.W.M.P. barracks, on the opposite side of the North Saskatchewan River. For a month they were kept helpless and hungry behind the walls of the post, while the victory-crazed Crees continued their spree of destruction, burning buildings, axing furniture, tearing clothes. On April 24, a force of Mounties and militia under Colonel W. D. Otter marched into Battleford to lift the siege.

When Big Bear surrounded Fort Pitt with 250 Crees, the Mounties refused to surrender – but slipped away by river that night.

Attack and counter-attack marked the pursuit of Big Bear until, on July 2, the chief surrendered to N.W.M.P. Sergeant Smart at Fort Carlton, in present Saskatchewan.

Closing In

The victory Riel won at Duck Lake inevitably set in motion the machinery that would crush him. While the militia was being mustered in the East, two batteries of artillerymen – Batteries "A" and "B", Canada's only permanent force – were being rushed from Ottawa to Winnipeg. They arrived at the gateway to the West on April 5, just ten days after the first shot was fired. Gunners of "A" Battery (right) hauled their weapons over deep snowbanks, as the ring closed on the half-breeds and their Indian allies. But with over-cautious officers leading inexperienced troops, the Canadian victory did not come easily. At Cut Knife Creek (below), Cree chief Poundmaker outmanoeuvred Colonel W. D. Otter and his force of 325 militiamen and Mounties, and only the Canadians' two seven-pounder cannons and a Gatling gun saved them from a likely massacre. Poundmaker restrained his warriors from pursuing the retreating soldiers and police: even then, the chief knew that he might win a few battles, but he could never hope to win the war.

At Fish Creek, silhouetted against the sky on a grassy ridge, Middleton's troops made easy targets for the Métis sharpshooters.

The Canadian cannons at Fish Creek hit two log houses and bowled over three stacks of straw, a war correspondent reported.

Destination, Batoche

On the road to Batoche, Major-General Middleton led his Canadian troops through the Qu'Appelle Valley. At Clark's Crossing, Middleton inexplicably split this force in two, sending half his men across the South Saskatchewan River.

For three days, reduced to firing stones and nails in their muskets, the Métis fought the Canadians to a standstill at Batoche. On the fourth day, May 12, an impetuous Midlander gave the order to charge: Louis Riel's stronghold collapsed.

Once the Battle of Batoche had
been fought and won, and the West
secured for the new nation,
the veterans could return home to
a proud welcome. Back East,
a man could even buy a souvenir
album of his great adventure in the
West, published by the Canadian
Pictorial and Illustrated War News.
This sketch from that album
shows the Governor-General's Body
Guards capturing White Cap
and his band.

The war artist dramatizes
the capture of Louis Riel. After
hiding in the woods north of
Batoche, Riel set off to surrender
to General Middleton. On his
way, he met a group of Middleton's
scouts, led by a former Montana
buffalo hunter he knew. "God
has sent you here to arrest me," Riel
is reported to have said. "Had
some of these Canadians arrested me,
they might have shot me."

When Riel's captors reached
the Canadian lines, some soldiers
gathered around menacingly
to ask whether the prisoner was Riel.
The scout replied the man
was only Riel's cook — perhaps saving
the rebel leader's life —
for the time being.

Two Scenes, Two Sentiments. *The Canadian volunteers returned to garlands and kisses, but in Montreal's Victoria Square an angry French-Canadian mob later violently protested the execution of Riel. The old racial wound was reopened.*

XV

The War for the West

IN the decade of his exile, Louis Riel appeared to slip in and out of madness and those who had ridiculed the self-styled President of the Republic of the Red River seemed confirmed in their judgment. His career surely was at an end. In Washington, President Ulysses Grant refused to appoint him government agent to the Indians in the American West. Rejected and persecuted, he took refuge in the rectory of Father Fabien Barnabé, in Keeseville, New York, and his mind retreated into a shadow world of religious hallucination. He laughed hysterically in the middle of church services; he wept for hours at night; he bellowed like a bull: "I am a prophet." He declared he was part of a divine trilogy, the other members being, Count de Chambord of France and Don Carlos of Spain. In his visions they were all bulls: Chambord a white bull, Carlos a black bull, Riel a red bull. One of Riel's many biographers, Joseph Kinsey Howard, defined his emotional state: "The compulsions which had plagued the *Métis* for generations, which had made potential schizophrenics of a whole race, ripped his mind apart."

In March, 1876, friends had Riel admitted to Longue Pointe Asylum near Montreal. Psychiatrists today would probably say he was temporarily manic-depressive: he oscillated between fits of frenzied weeping and periods of rationality. He smashed all the candles in the choir to show the Mother Superior he must be treated as a gentleman. He stood for hours with his arms stretched against his cell wall to prove he was Christ crucified. But the hospital superintendent, Dr. F. X. Perrault, later testified: "I perceived that with him insanity was being simulated. Upon making the observation to him that I was not to be taken for his dupe, he confessed to me that, in effect, he was shamming the insanity."

Three months later, he was transferred to Beauport Asylum, near Quebec. There he scribbled poetry, memorized a dictionary and proclaimed himself "Louis David Riel, Prophet, Infallible Pontiff, and Priest King." In January, 1878, he was released from Beauport, certified by the superintendent, Dr. Francois Roy, as cured "more or less."

In the Keeseville rectory of Father Barnabé he again found sanctuary and love. The curé's sister, Evelina, a blue-eyed blonde in her late twenties, was intrigued by Riel's magnetic personality, his haunted eyes, his heroic past. He promised to marry her as soon as he found a steady job in the American West. When he drifted across Montana, a roving Indian trader, Evelina's longing letters followed him: "Pray that God will put into my heart the virtues that I must have to be a perfect Christian and worthy helpmate, dear Louis . . . Your little sweetheart, who loves you and desires your happiness."

One March day in 1882, Evelina picked up a Montana newspaper and read of the marriage between Louis Riel and Marguerite Monet Bellehumeur. He had married a timid, dark-skinned *Métis* girl of 18 who could neither read nor write, and who spoke with her husband only in Cree. The angry Evelina now wrote him, saying that God would curse him for "having destroyed forever the future of one who has only one regret . . . of having known and loved you."

Riel settled down to the humdrum life of school-teacher at the little Jesuit mission of St. Peter's, Montana, on the Sun River. He fathered two children, took out American citizenship, worked from six in the morning until eight at night teaching half-breed and Blackfeet boys. He was quiet, sober and religiously devout.

Some people thought that Riel had lost his crusading zeal. Others noted that it flared whenever he talked of "the *Métis*, those poor tragic people . . . the brave hunters who are treated like savages, who are of my blood, of my religion, who have chosen me as their leader, who love me, and whom I love as brothers." His messianic dream had not, in fact, been extinguished. It was destined to be reignited, to be fanned to a full and frightening blaze by events then occurring 700 miles north in the Saskatchewan Valley. Four horsemen were already riding south to plead with him to lead them in what was to become the bloodiest battle of the Canadian West.

When the delegation of saddle-weary half-breeds galloped into St. Peter's that Sunday, June 4, 1884, Riel was at the mission church kneeling in prayer. At 40, he continued to wear a black coat and beaded moccasins; but his eyes had a faraway look and his chestnut-coloured beard was as long as a prophet's.

The man who strode into the church at the head of the other three delegates embraced Riel with an affectionate bear hug. "Uncle Gabriel," Riel called him. Gabriel Dumont was a legendary figure, a sort of Robin Hood in fringed buckskin. The *Métis* called him the "Prince of the Braves." A scarlet sash woven by the Indians in L'Assomption, Quebec, was flung over his buckskin. A white feather cockade was tucked jauntily into his black Stetson. He was only five foot, seven inches but his shoulders and chest were bull-like. He had a large head, a scraggly grey beard and the hips of a plains rider. At 46, he could still outride, outdrink and outshoot all comers; at 800 yards they said, he never missed with his Winchester carbine, nicknamed *"La Petite."* On the buffalo hunts his word was law. Any captain (captains were elected for each battalion of ten hunters) who challenged his command was publicly flogged. Yet, for all his toughness, Dumont always prayed each morning and night ("Lord, strengthen my courage, my faith, and my honour"), and always donated a dozen buffalo to the poorer families in his camp.

When the white settlers began crowding into the new province of Manitoba, Dumont had led his buffalo hunters further west to the Saskatchewan Valley. Other Red River nomads had followed. Saskatchewan and Alberta – then known as the North West Territory – was then dotted with hundreds of whitewashed, mud-chinked *Métis* log cabins. It was the last prairie frontier. The Saskatchewan River, coloured like coffee frothing with cream, cut a rich gash through the valley. The buffalo found shelter in the thick aspen, wolf willow, and jackpine, and a man had no trouble filling his wife's stew pot. To be sure, white Anglo-Saxons had begun to settle near the Mounted Police posts of Prince Albert, Fort Carlton and Fort Pitt and even at Pile O' Bones, which they had grandly renamed Regina, but they did not interfere with the *Métis*.

But by 1884 the buffalo herds had vanished. The C.P.R. was still building further westward and the main herds had been slaughtered south of the border. The *Métis* now looked to their strip farms for sustenance, but these were threatened, too. Ontario surveyors were once again sub-dividing their two-mile ribbons of land. Eastern land speculators, anticipating the success of the railway, were claiming title to *Métis* farms. The half-breeds' petitions to Ottawa had been answered with silence or evasion. Three of Riel's old enemies in the Red River Rising were now in the Department of Interior. The agent who investigated *Métis* grievances was Charles Mair, who had been horsewhipped by the half-breed women for his insults. The Deputy Minister was Colonel John Stoughton Dennis. Prime Minister Sir John A. Macdonald was himself Minister of the Department.

The *Métis* had needed a dynamic spokesman to champion their rights. Dumont was eloquent with his rifle, but he couldn't read or write. So a committee calling itself the "People of Saskatchewan" had elected four delegates, headed by Dumont, to ride to Montana and bring back Louis Riel.

"God has given me a cause to defend," said Riel. He appointed Dumont his Adjutant-General.

A musketry volley greeted Riel's arrival with his wife and infant son and daughter at Batoche on July 1, 1884. Thirty miles southwest of the English community of Prince Albert, the village of *Métis* cabins straggled for about three miles along the poplar and aspen bluffs of the South Saskatchewan River. At one end was the gabled trading store of Xavier Batoche; at the other was Gabriel's Crossing, where Dumont maintained a free ferry, a full-sized billiard table and, for his wife, a foot-treadle sewing machine. The centre of the colony was the whipsawn Catholic church, where Oblate Father Alexis André greeted Riel warmly: "You are the most popular man in the country."

All summer and fall, Riel addressed meetings, advising moderation. He ended each speech to the English half-breeds with a toast to the Queen. Legend suggests that he won over the Indians by predicting an eclipse which he read in an almanac. Actually, all he did was listen sympathetically to the grievances of the two leading chiefs of the Cree reserves.

Chief Poundmaker was handsome, intelligent and dignified. He wore a cinnamon bear warcap tufted with eagle feathers and a leather jacket studded with brass nails. His reserve near the English town of Battleford, 100 miles west of Batoche, held 200 warriors. Chief Big Bear was a wizened old man in his sixties, an orator and a peace-maker, concerned with the education of the young. His reserve, surrounding the English hamlet of Frog Lake, 200 miles west of Batoche, had 12 lodges. Both chiefs told Riel that Ottawa had betrayed their "sweet promises" of cattle and farm implements, reneged on their treaties, cut their rations, and sent them corrupt Indian agents. "They take our lands," said Big Bear. "They sell them, and they buy themselves fine clothes. Then they clap their hands on their hips and call themselves men. They are not men. They are an unsightly beast. Their faces are twisted from the appearance of honest men."

Riel promised to incorporate the Indian complaints in a petition to Ottawa. His December Bill of Rights asked for more liberal treatment of the Indians; free title to the land occupied by the *Métis*; provincial status for the territorial districts of Saskatchewan and Alberta; vote by ballot; local responsible government; and representation in the Dominion Parliament.

Sir John A. Macdonald brushed these requests aside. The people in the West were always complaining. "If you wait for a half-breed or an Indian to become contented," joked Sir John, "you may wait till the millenium." If he gave them scrip money in exchange for title to their land, "they will either drink it, or waste it, or sell it." When the Mountie outposts warned him of Indian war drums in the Northwest, "Old Tomorrow" wired back that the "present effervescence" would subside. But just in case, Macdonald secretly ordered the Mounted Police to increase their Saskatchewan force.

The "secret" came out in the worst possible manner. At the Hudson's Bay Company post of Fort Carlton, 20 miles west of Batoche, a group of *Métis* asked the factor, Lawrence Clarke, "Have you heard whether the government is going to answer our petition?"

Clarke disliked the *Métis*. "Yes," he said, exaggerating a small kernel of truth. "Five hundred Mounties are on their way to Fort Carlton to answer you with bullets."

Louis Riel assembled his men and announced: "It has commenced. Justice commands us to take up arms. *Marchons, mes braves!*"

On March 18, 1885, he marched his men to the Catholic church in Batoche to commandeer it as a military headquarters. One of Father André's Oblates (Father Julien Moulin) protested strongly. "Listen to him!" Riel said. "He protests – he is a protestant!" The priest continued to block their entry. No Oblate would serve as their chaplain, he warned. None of them would receive the holy sacrament.

Riel pushed him aside, shouting, "Rome has fallen! I will administer the sacraments myself." Next, he arbitrarily picked his own "Provincial Government." He called its 12 members the *Exovidate*, from the Latin *ex* and *ovede*, indicating that they were chosen "from the flock." They unanimously named Riel their "prophet in the service of Jesus Christ" and the flag they hoisted over the church was a coloured print of the Holy Virgin sewn on a white banner. Then, with Adjutant-General Gabriel Dumont seated on a syrup box and Secretary Philippe Garnot scribbling on brown wrapping paper, Louis Riel dictated his orders.

Riel probably intended to merely stir up a demonstration to bring pressure on Ottawa but, when the Dominion leaders appeared to ignore him, his dormant megalomania – as well as the more militant Dumont – pushed him toward increasingly extreme measures. On March 21, he wrote to the neutral English half-breeds of Prince Albert urging the "Dear Brothers in Jesus Christ" to "try and defend our existence, rather than to see it crushed . . ." When they rejected his plea, he resorted to threat: either they join him and enjoy a peaceful celebration of the Queen's birthday or he would summon his *Métis* allies from Montana, "and perhaps our difficulties will end in an American fourth of July."

In a rousing speech to his *Métis*, Riel exhorted:

"For the love of God help us to save Saskatchewan! . . . To arms! Or will you crouch and submit? . . . Murmur, growl, and threaten. Stir up the Indians . . . Render to God glory, honour and adoration. But to the tyrants of the world render that which is due them. Fling back into their teeth the authority they have usurped. Tumble them down from power. That is what God orders!"

Riel's naiveté was also evident when he demanded that Major L. N. F. Crozier, in charge of the Mounted Police at Fort Carlton, surrender his government supplies and arms. "Major, we respect you," Riel wrote. "Let the cause of humanity be a consolation to you for the reverses which governmental misconduct has brought upon you." Crozier was asked to sign a pledge of honour that: "Because I love my neighbour as myself, for the sake of God, to prevent bloodshed, and principally the war of extermination which threatens the country, I agree to the above conditions of surrender."

Of course, Crozier refused. Dumont then felt justified in seizing ammunition from nearby trading posts. Unco-operative *Englise* were imprisoned, their arms roped behind their back, in the nine-foot-deep sand cellar underneath Xavier Batoche's store. A platoon of agile buffalo hunters shinnied up the poles and slashed the telegraph wires connecting Batoche with Prince Albert. The telegraph line leading east was left intact. Until the last minute, Riel hoped that Ottawa would telegraph peace terms.

On March 26, Crozier marched out of the fort with 56 Mounted Police, pulling a seven-pounder cannon in a sleigh, and 41 English volunteers from Prince Albert, wielding muskets and stove-top shields. Crozier, a hot-tempered Irishman, was determined to teach Riel a lesson. The *Métis* met them at Duck Lake, midway between Fort Carlton and Batoche.

It was a hollow, ringed on three sides by thick clumps of poplar and wolf willow. Two horsemen – Dumont's young brother, Isidore, and a half-blind Cree chief named Falling Sand – came riding down the far hillside waving a white blanket of truce. Crozier ordered his men to barricade themselves behind their sleighs. Then he and an English half-breed interpreter, Gentleman Joe McKay, galloped forward to parley with the two rebels. Crozier thrust out his hand to the unarmed Indian. Apparently mistaking his gesture, the Indian grabbed for McKay's rifle. Gentleman Joe pulled his pistol and fired. Isidore Dumont fell dead from his saddle.

Crozier spurred back to his horse sleighs and shouted, "Fire away, boys!" And they shot Falling Sand.

From the poplar and willow bluffs, 200 buffalo muzzle-loaders fired. The government force was surrounded on three sides by *Métis* sharpshooters. On a white stallion, Louis Riel rode up the crest of the hill, holding aloft a foot-and-a-half-long crucifix. "In the name of God the Father Almighty I command you to fire! In the name of the Father, Son and Holy Ghost, I command you to fire!"

Major Crozier, blood trickling down his cheek from a wound, looked around with dismay. Twelve of his men were dead and eleven lay wounded in the snow. He had led them into an ambush, like buffalo boxed in a half-breed compound. On the *Métis* side, five had died and Gabriel Dumont wounded while recklessly seeking vengeance for his brother's death. In his dictated memoirs, the Adjutant-General revealed that as he fired he laughed aloud, "not because I took any pleasure in killing, but to give courage to my men." When a bullet furrowed his scalp, a comrade, seeing him fall, cried out, "Gabriel is dead!" Dumont staunched the blood from his forehead with handfuls of snow, staggered up on his knees, and shouted, "Courage! As long as I haven't lost my head, I'm not dead!" His men rallied and began shooting again.

Outmanoeuvred and outnumbered, Crozier ordered a retreat. Dumont, tied onto a horse by his comrades, shouted, "Follow and destroy them," but Riel counter-manded the order: "In the name of God, don't kill any more. There has been too much bloodshed already!" Dumont bowed to the will of his leader.

The next day, after prayers for the dead, Riel, assembled his troops and ordered three rousing cheers for Dumont. "Thank God," Riel chanted, "who gave you so valiant a leader."

Now Dumont was able to announce the news brought by courier that Crozier had abandoned and burned Fort Carlton. He was marching to Prince Albert, 50 miles away. Dumont knew Crozier's force would have to pass through a narrow spruce grove perfect for ambush. "We could have killed a lot of them," he said in his diary. "But Riel, who was always restraining us, formally opposed the idea."

It was too late now for restraint. Up and down the North Saskatchewan River, Indian war drums throbbed with the news: "The Red Coats have been beaten. The palefaces are weak. Take up your scalping knives."

At Battleford, 200 Crees, led by war chiefs Little Pine and Strike-Him-On-The-Back, joined a party of Assiniboines, butchered a government Indian agent and then swooped into the white settlement. Five hundred of the English settlers – 300 of them women and children – huddled behind the stockade of the Battleford Mountie post and watched the yelling warriors looting their homes, burning their stores, hacking pianos, and strutting about in stolen gowns. The whites remained besieged and hungry for a month.

At Fort Pitt, 28 civilians and 20 Mounties under Inspector Francis ("Chicken-stalker") Dickens, laconic and red-whiskered son of the famous novelist, were surrounded by 250 ragged but armed warriors led by Big Bear. They demanded that Dickens give them ammunition, clothing, tea and tobacco, as well as a blanket for Big Bear who complained "he was very cold." Dickens haughtily refused, then quickly evacuated the isolated fort at midnight. The heavily outnumbered Mounties escaped in a leaky scow, and for six days fought ice, gale and sniping Indians on the Saskatchewan, until half frozen, they reached the besieged fort at Battleford. Dickens made a single entry in his journal: "Very cold weather. Travelled."

At Frog Lake, Big Bear's war chief, Wandering Spirit, streaked yellow paint on his cheeks, put on his lynx-skin bonnet, assembled 30 braves for a thirst dance, and then led them to the reservation church where nine whites had gathered. Wandering Spirit jabbed his rifle at Thomas Quinn, the Indian agent, and ordered him to march as prisoner with the other settlers to Big Bear's lodge. Three times Quinn refused. On his fourth refusal, Wandering Spirit shrilled, "You have a thick head!" and fired point-blank in Quinn's face. The agent dropped dead, and the Crees chanted: *"Nipuhao!* Kill!"

John Delaney, the farm instructor, whom the Indians hated almost as much as they hated Quinn, fell dying with two bullets in his body. His wife flung herself on his body and asked Oblate Father Francois Fafard to administer the last rites. "My poor brother," said Fafard, making the sign of the cross over him, "I think you are safe with God." An Indian fired, and the priest fell, shot through the neck. His assistant, Father Félix Marchand, rushed toward the dying priest, and then plunged face down in the dirt fatally wounded. John Gowanlock, grist mill operator, clutched at his wife's arm as a bullet pierced his chest. "My dear wife," he moaned, "be brave to the end." Mrs. Gowanlock never forgot how he swayed, "reaching out his arms towards me as he sank. I caught him, and we fell together. I lay upon him, resting my face upon his, and his breath was scarcely gone when I was forced away by an Indian."

The widow Gowanlock and Delaney were saved from what they called "a fate worse than death" by two *Métis* who bought them from the Crees for two horses and $30. But the remaining settlers were being murdered and mutilated; their heads were hacked off and their hearts sliced out. The Indians broke open two kegs of sacrificial wine, donned the priests' black robes, set fire to Frog Lake, and danced in front of the flames. (Wandering Spirit, Miserable Man, Bad Arrow, Iron Body, Little Bear, and Round the Sky were later tried and hanged.)

The Frog Lake massacre outraged eastern Canada. It moved Sir John A. Macdonald, where Riel's posturing and petitions had failed. The Department of the Interior increased the Indians' rations and handed out money scrip for the *Métis* land claims. Then Macdonald mobilized the Dominion's first truly national army and fought a civil war that cost $5 millions, killed 105 (70 whites, 35 rebels), wounded 141 and left racial scars that have not completely healed to this day.

The Northwest Field Force of 5,000 soldiers was raised within a few weeks. From the east came 3,000 volunteers: shoe clerks, piano tuners, factory labourers, marching with Enfields under such names as the Royal Grenadiers from Toronto, and the Halifax Battalion from Nova Scotia, and the Voltigeurs from Quebec City. From the west came 2,000 men, ranchers, Cariboo miners, English remittance men, drilling with Martini-Henry rifles under the name of the Rocky Mountain Rangers and the Winnipeg Light Infantry and the Moose Mountain Scouts. There were 3,000 non-fighting volunteers, including kitchen-wagon teamsters, the medical corps, and Canada's first Red Cross unit. There were nine cannons and a deadly new weapon: the Gatling gun. Invented during the American Civil War, by Dr. R. J. Gatling, a doctor from North Carolina, it was said to crank out 1,200 bullets a minute.

In contrast, Adjutant-General Dumont commanded 350 half-breeds and Indians, and 250 of them had rifles, mostly muzzle-loaders or shotguns that had to be loaded with powder horns and wadding. When his scouts reported the forces gathering at Qu'Appelle, near Regina, Dumont knew his only hope lay in guerrilla attacks. He told Riel, who was asking the Almighty to smite the "giant Goliath," that he proposed to "Harry them by night. Prevent them from sleeping. By the end of three nights they'll be at each others' throats."

Riel demurred. "Uncle Gabriel, that is too much like the Indians. Besides, if we do as you say, we may be in danger of firing on our French-Canadian friends among the troops."

"I wouldn't consider as our friends those who joined the English to kill and plunder us!"

"If you knew them," Riel insisted, "you wouldn't try to treat them in that way."

Dumont pounded his forehead in frustration, but as he said in his memoirs, "I had confidence in his faith and his prayers, and that God would listen to him." God was kind to the *Métis* in the commander of the Canadian army, a 60-year-old retired British soldier, Major-General Frederick Dobson Middleton. He had graduated from Royal Military College at Sandhurst, fought the Maoris in New Zealand, marched to the relief of Lucknow, served in Burma, and almost won a Victoria Cross in the Sepoy Mutiny. He was also a Colonel Blimp, walrus-moustached with a long cavalry sword.

Middleton was condescending toward the "squalid and dirty" Indians. He did not conceal his contempt for his own colonial "citizen soldiers." As they sloshed through saline swamps waist-deep in muck, his main concern was that the salty water made very sour tea. He was horrified when his men, in below-zero cold, desecrated Her Majesty's uniform with "hideous red comforters they wore round their necks." When he announced that his headquarters would be in the saddle, aback his black gelding, the privates joked that his headquarters were where his hindquarters ought to be. He alienated his Canadian officers, especially the Westerners, who knew the terrain and understood the *Métis*. He refused advice except from ex-Imperial regulars "of good birth." His strategy was a compound of blunders. He made no use of the 500 Mounted Police, the best cavalry in the land. He weakened his force, sending one division to lift the siege of Battleford, another on a wild-goose chase after Big Bear. He believed Riel's sharpshooters to be "much over-rated" and thought he would take Batoche with 800 men. He then proceeded to split them, marching 400 men down each bank of the wide, bridgeless South Saskatchewan River. He thus isolated half his force on the bank of a river they could not cross, listening for bugle signals they could not hear, and watching for code guidance from signal flags they could not see.

As his scouts reported Middleton's floundering advance, Dumont chafed to head them off. He finally told Riel, "I can no longer follow your humanitarian counsel. I've decided to fire on the invaders."

"All right," said Riel. "Do as you wish."

"I wish to treat them as we would buffalo," said Dumont, and that is exactly what he did.

On April 24, a sleety morning, at a gully called Fish Creek, 22 miles south of Batoche, Dumont led the enemy into a classical buffalo pound. The tea-coloured creek dribbled through a 40-foot ravine into the east side of the Saskatchewan, and the hillsides were studded with poplar bluffs and dappled with purple pasque flowers. It was Duck Lake again, with two extra advantages. Deeply-grooved buffalo wallows, camouflaged by the brush, made natural pits and, as each soldier appeared on the lip of the ravine, he was silhouetted against the sky – a perfect target for Dumont's 150 marksmen.

A murderous musket fire greeted Major C. A. Boulton's Mounted Scouts. Boulton, an ex-surveyor jailed in Riel's Red River Revolt, yelled, "Halt and dismount! Extend in skirmishing order and lie down." The rebels kept popping up, shooting then dropping back. Boulton could only guess where they were from the white puffs of smoke that hung over their pits. "Fire away, boys, and lie close," Boulton shouted.

The scouts were cut down like weeds. Captain Gardiner, who was crouched beside Boulton, groaned, "Major, I'm hit! Oh, I'm hit again!" Trooper D'Arcy Baker murmured, "Oh, Major, I'm hit!" as a bullet struck his chest. Captain H. G. Wise, who was sent back to hurry the main force, had his horse shot from under him. Boulton took sour satisfaction out of noting, "One Indian in full war paint leaped forward, dancing and shouting his war cry, apparently out of sheer bravado. He was immediately shot and fell in the open, where his body remained all day."

The elderly and brave General Middleton, waving his cavalry sword, himself led an infantry charge to "dislodge these troublesome 'Pitties.' " He was turned back by bullets that grazed his black charger Sam and ripped through his tall fur hat. Then he brought his cannon to bear.

Down in the ravine, Dumont soon grew desperate. Eighty-eight of his Indians had deserted as soon as the cannons started shelling them, and his half-breed marksmen were running low of cartridges. He told his men to concentrate their shot on bull's-eyes. "I don't know if I killed many men, because I took cover immediately after each shot," he recalled later. "But I couldn't have missed often. I saw an officer who was aiming at us. I hastened to finish him off, and our young men began to laugh derisively when they heard him crying like a child. They shouted for joy, and the cannon continued to roar all the time."

With only seven cartridges left, Dumont took a gamble. "I decided to set fire to the prairie grass to make the enemy withdraw. I figured on going under cover of the smoke, to pick up the ammunition and arms which they would abandon in their flight. I instructed my men to shout and sing during this operation."

Choking with smoke, the troops did withdraw.

The *Métis*, with light casualties of four dead and two wounded, counted it a victory and celebrated with two bottles of brandy left by a fleeing medical officer. Dumont toasted the Queen and then Louis Riel. Their prophet had been standing all day in Batoche, fervently praying with his arms uplifted to form a cross; when he tired, two *Métis* took turns at holding up his arms. "I attribute our success to Riel's prayers," said Dumont.

General Middleton, tallying ten dead and 40 wounded, was forced to reappraise the *Métis*. "I could not help having a feeling of admiration and respect for their stubborn defence," he wrote, generously saluting Dumont's strategy. Two weeks later, on May 9, he began the Battle of Batoche with a stratagem of his own; he launched the first – and last – warship to sail the Prairies.

This was the paddlewheeler *Northcote*, a wheezy old tub, whose two decks exposed an arthritic engine, a decrepit smokestack, and a wart of a pilothouse. It was "armoured" with two-inch planks ripped from Gabriel Dumont's barn; and its decks were buttressed with sacks of oats, mattresses, even Dumont's billiard table and his wife's sewing machine. Middleton put 50 soldiers aboard and ordered the captain to meet him on the South Saskatchewan loop just above Batoche. At a prearranged signal they would strike the rebel stronghold together, the amphibian force tooting its whistle, the land force blowing its bugle.

When the sternwheeler splashed down the shallow Saskatchewan toward Gabriel's Crossing, Dumont galloped along the south bank and signalled his *Métis* to drop the overhanging ferry cable that spanned the river. The man-o-war was skinned like a rabbit, its smokestack and pilothouse shorn off, and its lower deck was raked with musket fire. The crippled tub drifted until it stuck on a sandbar below Batoche, where its captain whistled plaintively for rescue.

Middleton was too busy to come. "Much to my

annoyance," he wrote in his memoirs, "as we got near the river, we heard a rattling fire and the steamer's whistle, showing that the latter was already engaged. We fired a gun to let them know we were on hand and pushed on." He was even more annoyed when his 850 invaders reached the outskirts of Batoche and were repulsed by "a galling fire kept up by a totally invisible enemy." Dumont's 250 *Métis*, taking advantage of every slough and hollow and poplar copse, had dug an elaborate network of trenches and foxholes. Each musket pit had a parapet of loopholed logs and was camouflaged with earth and wolf willow branches. Only one half-breed could be seen: Louis Riel, as if seeking martyrdom, walked from pit to pit, holding his crucifix, exhorting his men with prayers.

Middleton, true to his traditional training, could not adapt to the bush terrain. He set up his headquarters on a fully exposed position on a ploughed field and launched a futile offensive. The fixed carriages of his cannons could not be wheeled low enough to bombard the musket pits on the hillslope; the nine-pound shells spat harmlessly into tree tops. The machine-gunner cranked his Gatling gun, but the *Métis* held up wood dummies that caused him to doubt the Gatling's effectiveness. The gun was obviously scoring hits but the pesky enemy didn't fall!

Outnumbered four to one, reduced to firing horse-shoe nails and stones in their muskets, Dumont's buffalo hunters, without suffering a casualty, held the Canadian army at bay for three days. Their wives, including Riel's pregnant wife, Marguerite, took refuge by day in riverside caves. At night they crept out to collect spent bullets on the battlefield and melt them into balls for their husbands' muskets. At dawn their Adjutant-General practised sniping. "Seated on one heel with a knee on the prairie ground," as Dumont described it, he once shattered a mirror General Middleton was using for his morning shave.

At noon on the fourth day, May 12, the *Métis* met their inevitable defeat. Colonel Arthur T. Williams, a federal M.P. and son of a British officer, told his Fort Hope Midlanders that he'd had his bellyful of Middleton's dillydallying. He pulled out his revolver and gave the order, "Charge, boys, charge!" The General, who had been lunching at his headquarters, rushed out cursing. Rank insubordination! His bugler blew the retreat until both he and the General had purple faces. But the Midlanders, joined by the equally impetuous Royal Grenadiers of Toronto, didn't give a damn what the English General was bugling. The red-and-black tunics kept swarming forward toward the rebels' log trenches. Middleton eventually accepted the situation and called up the rear echelons to support the attack.

At least 12 *Métis* were bayoneted to death and three wounded that afternoon. Some rebels fled to the woods and some in the pits raised white handkerchiefs. Robert A. Allan, of Allan's Mills, Ontario, a trooper in the 90th Battalion, jotted in his diary: "The rebels coming in and giving themselves up. It is surprising to see so many old men, some with grey hair, and a lot of these were killed." One white-bearded man would not give up: José Ouellet, aged 93. He was in a log pit with Dumont, firing gleefully at the enemy with a fowling piece almost as ancient as himself.

"Father," Dumont pleaded with him. "We must retreat." He repeated it several times but Ouellet grinned and put him off. "Wait a minute. I want to kill another Englishman."

"All right," said Dumont. "Let us die here."

A bullet struck Ouellet, reddening his white beard with blood. "Goodbye, Father," Dumont said softly. "I thank you for your courage."

Dumont himself retreated to the woods where he met Riel, who was urging a band of *Métis* to go on resisting. "We are beaten," said Riel, when he saw his Adjutant-General. "What are we going to do?"

"We must die," said Dumont. "You should have known that in taking up arms, Louis, we should be defeated. Very well – they must destroy us." Dumont said he was going to slip through the enemy lines and bring some meat and flour to the women, who had been forced to eat dog flesh in the mud caves. "If any of the Orangemen try to stop me," he said, "I will knock over a few of them."

"Uncle Gabriel, you mustn't expose yourself too much," Riel cautioned him.

Dumont slapped his Winchester butt. "The enemy cannot kill me," he said.

It was the last time that Dumont saw Riel. The two leaders spent the next three days in the hills surrounding Batoche, separately trying to rally their forces. But the *Métis* were demoralized. Dumont swore he would stage a one-man guerrilla war, but, on the fourth day, his brother-in-law, Moise Ouellet, informed him that Riel had signed a note of surrender. Dumont refused to believe it. "Go to the devil!" he shouted. Ouellet showed him the declaration and Dumont knew that the end had come. Yet the Prince of the Prairies could not resist a few last defiant words. "You tell Middleton," he said to Ouellet, "that I'm in the woods and I still have 90 cartridges left to use on his men!"

Mounted on his famed stallion, Dumont rode across the border to become a legend of the frontier. Buffalo Bill Cody's Wild West Show hired him to shoot coloured glass balls while he galloped around the circus arena with Annie Oakley. In a re-enactment of the Battle of Batoche, he was billed as: "The peerless Gabriel Dumont, the hero of the Half-breed Rebellion."

Louis Riel disdained escape and he walked into General Middleton's tent to surrender. "How do you do, Mr. Riel?" said the General. "Pray be seated."

Middleton, who was to be knighted and rewarded with $20,000, described Riel as "a mild-spoken and mild-looking man, with a short, brown beard and an uneasy, frightened look about his eyes, which gradually disappeared as I talked to him. He had no coat on, and looked cold and forlorn, and as it was still chilly out of the sun, I commenced proceedings by giving him a military great coat of my own."

In a tent next to his own, Middleton put Riel under personal guard of Captain George Holmes Young. By ironic coincidence, Captain Young was the son of the Methodist chaplain who had comforted Thomas Scott in the Red River Rising.

"What changes time makes," Riel joked sadly. "Fifteen years ago you and your father were my prisoners. Now I am your prisoner." Young kept a day-and-night watch on Riel, even sleeping under the same blankets with him. Middleton conversed constantly with Riel for two days and classed him "sane enough in general, every-day-subjects, but he was imbued with a strong, morbid, religious feeling mingled with intense personal vanity."

Riel's trial for high treason was news on two continents in July, 1885. Spectators packed the little rented courtroom in Regina. At a special table, a dozen newspaper correspondents scribbled notes. Women in their Sunday best vied for seats. Riel sat in the wooden prisoner's box, sometimes kneeling to pray. It was thought Gabriel Dumont might try a last-minute rescue, and the prisoner was taken to and from his police barracks cell every day disguised in a Mountie's uniform.

It was perhaps as fair a trial as violently-biased men could give. The judge, Hugh Richardson, was a part-time magistrate from Ontario. The six-man jury was all white, all English, all Protestant. The indictment smacked of medieval retribution for witchcraft, charging Riel with not "having the fear of God in his heart, but being moved and seduced by the instigation of the Devil." Riel's three Quebec defence attorneys tried to save their client from the gallows by pleading he was insane and not accountable for his actions. As evidence, the minutes of the *Exovidate* were presented as the incoherent outpourings of a warped mind.

Today, despite some absurdities and the omni-present vanity, much of Riel's writings seem lucid, some

of it far-sighted. He prophesied the decline of the British Empire as a world power and predicted that its place would be taken by the United States. He foresaw an ecumenical movement which would obliterate "division between Catholics and Protestants. It might take a hundred years," he said, but "a century is but a spoke in the wheel of eternity," and the time would come when "my children's children will shake hands with the Protestants of the new world in a friendly manner."

"Alienists," as psychiatrists were called in those days, differed sharply on whether Riel was mad. As the seven-day trial neared its end, Riel was permitted to address the jury. He rose calmly, and for an hour delivered the most moving and impassioned oration ever heard in the Canadian West.

"The Northwest is my mother," he said, "and I am sure my mother country will not kill me." Vividly he pictured the way of life on the plains, of the buffalo hunt that his people had fought to preserve: "the coursers rearing, neighing, dancing, digging at the ground with eager hooves." He accused the white "pioneers of civilization" – curling his lip – of feeding rotten Hudson's Bay pork to the kennelled Indians, of forcing the *Métis* to pay for the tranquility of the Northwest at the price of their blood. "The one who has the courage to speak out against those evil men," he said, "instead of being an outrageous man becomes, in fact, a benefactor to society." Was he an egotist? "Perhaps I am. A man cannot have individuality without paying attention to himself." Had he delusions of being persecuted? "I have been hunted as an elk for 15 years." Was he a false prophet? "I am the founder of Manitoba." Was he a mad visionary? "We all see into the future more or less. I believe I have a mission, and if I have been astray, it is not as an imposter, but according to my conscience."

Riel said he would prefer to die, rather than have his cause impugned as the vision of a madman. "If you decide to execute me, gentlemen of the jury, I shall have the satisfaction of not being reputed by all men as insane, as a fool, as a lunatic." So, having woven his own noose, he sat down.

The jury pronounced him guilty – with a recommendation of mercy. Judge Richardson sentenced him to be hanged.

Petitions for pardon rained upon Ottawa from all over the world – from France, England, Ireland, the United States. There were three stays of execution while an appeal was heard before the Privy Council in London. Queen Victoria had her Governor-General in Canada ask for executive clemency. Prime Minister Macdonald could not be moved. He seemed to believe he had to pull this political thorn out of his flesh, though it meant ripping French and English Canada asunder. Orange Ontario cried that the murderer of Thomas Scott ought to be strangled in his traitorous rag, the French flag. Sir Wilfrid Laurier spoke for Quebec when he exclaimed on the floor of the House of Commons: "Had I been born on the banks of the Saskatchewan, I would myself have shouldered a musket." His speech helped Laurier gain the leadership of the Liberal Party and when he became prime minister eleven years later, his Immigration Minister, Clifford Sifton, peopled the plains with minority groups. Sir John A. remained obdurate. "Riel shall hang," he declared, "though every dog in Quebec bark in his favour."

Riel had spent the weeks of waiting scratching down his memoirs on 50 cents' worth of foolscap, passed through the grated window of his cell by his jailer, Mounted Police Superintendent R. Burton Deane. When Deane had informed him that his sentence had been suspended for another month, Riel had managed a felicitous pun: "It is more pleasant to have the sentence suspended than the man." In gratitude for the reprieve, Riel composed a poem which began with a tribute to the "merry noble Captain Deane" and which ended:

O God's Providence
Look down on me,
A small existence
Smiling tears to thee.

On the night of November 15, Riel prepared to die in the morning. He knelt in his cell in the barracks at Regina and he prayed with a small statue of St. Joseph, the patron saint of the *Métis*, clenched in his fingers. He had confessed his sins, forgiven his enemies, and now he felt exalted, almost light-hearted. "I accept death with joy and gratitude," he said to Father Alexis André, who knelt beside him. "Other men live unaware of the hour of their death. I know the hour of my death."

The priest asked Riel if he was ready to meet his Maker. "Do not fear," Riel said. "I will not shame my friends or gladden my enemies by dying like a coward."

During the long hours of the night he wrote a farewell letter to his aged mother, Julie, in St. Vital. He wanted her to read it aloud to his illiterate wife, Marguerite, whose newly-born child had lived for only two hours, and who was herself to die within a year, of tuberculosis.

Dawn was breaking through the barred window, pink and dove-grey, when Deputy Sheriff Gibson came to get him. The police officer hesitated at the cell door. "Mr. Gibson, you want me," said Riel. "I am ready." In a black frock coat and beaded moccasins he mounted the scaffold. He held a candle in one hand and an ivory crucifix in the other. Father André was weeping.

For the last time, Riel looked out over the plains. It was a beautiful crisp morning. A flock of fall geese bugled overhead and the bunch grass glittered with hoar-frost. His nostrils were filled with the sweet scent of wolf willow. He bade a silent farewell to the plains that were the lost heritage of his people. Then the hangman dropped a white cotton hood over his eyes. Riel began to say the Lord's Prayer. He was half-way through it, about to intone "deliver us from evil," when the trapdoor opened. His body plunged nine feet and quivered, like an Indian medicine bundle dangling from the lodge pole of one of his ancestors. His body was placed in a black-painted coffin of rough oak boards. The following night his *Métis* followers spirited away the body and buried it in the shadow of St. Boniface Cathedral with a granite tombstone, marked simply; "Riel, 16 Novembre, 1885."

A contemporary sketch of the hanging of Louis Riel.
Even a plea for clemency by Queen Victoria was
turned down by the implacable Sir John A. Macdonald.

XVI

The Whipcracker

ONE blustery midnight in 1899, William Cornelius Van Horne, the Yankee Dutchman who was president of the Canadian Pacific Railroad, was playing poker with some of his cronies in the mahogany-lined warmth of his private railway car, the *Saskatchewan*. He had just devoured two roast chickens with whisky, now he was gobbling English biscuits stacked with black caviar, washing them down with a magnum of champagne while he dealt out the cards.

"Van, I don't know how you do it," said one of his friends, W. L. Elkins of Philadelphia. "You've already built the world's biggest transportation system . . . But still you won't rest. I declare you must be fired with coal and powered by steam."

"How do I do it?" Van Horne patted the girth of his 200 pounds and reached for a perfecto cigar. "Oh, I eat all I can. I drink all I can. I smoke all I can. And I don't give a damn for anything."

It was a fair summation of the philosophy of the master-builder who linked the Canadian nation with almost 3,000 miles of steel. He was 56 when he made the remark, still a dynamite blast of energy. He had thick knotted fingers, a black prow of a beard, a head as bald as a bullet, heavy-lidded blue eyes, and a square Dutch face. His speech was like pistol-fire, fast, decisive, smoky with oaths. He was the last of those railway magnates who used to be called rugged individualists and today are known as robber barons. He was often tyrannical. "The people of this country, especially of the West, like the sound of the whipcracker," he said. He was sometimes ruthless. "A railway," he said when breaking a strike with non-union labour, "is not a reform school." He had the acquisitive itch. He became a millionaire many times over, dominating 30 major Canadian corporations.

Yet he was no primitive money-grubber. He was blessed with the gifts of laughter and imagination and there was even some poetry in his soul. He cared deeply about painting, and a dozen of his own oils hang at the Montreal Museum of Fine Arts. He was a dedicated palaeontologist, and nine rare fossils which he discovered are displayed at Chicago University bearing the name *van hornei*. He was an avid botanist, experimenting with tulips and hyacinths, and is credited with having developed a triple-trumpet *datura cornucopia* of great beauty. Museum curators on four continents recognized him as an expert on Oriental pottery and porcelain, and he could identify almost any ceramic while blindfolded, naming the kiln where it had been fired. He believed that money talked, but he did not "give a damn" for wealth as an end in itself. "A half million dollars?" he used to say scornfully. "Hell, that's good only for buying five Rembrandt paintings." He was a slave-driver, but he had no use for the tycoons of the nineteenth century who piously urged their underpaid hirelings to worship work next to God. "I had to chop wood when I was an orphan boy – the only real work I ever did in my life – and I hated it," he said. "But building the C.P.R., that was fun – absolute enjoyment."

Nor did Van Horne "give a damn" for Ottawa's politicians and Montreal's financiers. He regaled them with feasts cooked by his own hands in rude bunkhouses. He beat them at all-night poker and billiards. He played the violin for them or played practical jokes on them. Then he drank them under the table.

The one antagonist this American turned Canadian did respect was James Jerome Hill, a Canadian turned American. Ironically, Hill was the railroad mogul who discovered Van Horne for the C.P.R. Yet the two engaged in a life-long duel, battling for passengers and freight with the *élan* once shown by the Nor'westers and the Gentlemen Adventurers when grappling for the monopoly of the fur trade. Perhaps Van Horne feuded with Hill because they were so much alike. Hill was a portly, bald-headed, black-bearded pirate of the same age and temperament as Van Horne. "I believe in the survival of the fittest," Hill once said when detonating explosives under the right-of-way of Edward H. Harriman's rival Union Pacific railway. He was a scrapper whose credo was: "There is a good deal in having nerve."

In a fight with bows and arrows as a boy in Guelph, Ontario, he lost one eye. At 18, he left home and was soon setting up a freight line of paddlewheelers on the Red River. This led him to the St. Paul, Minneapolis & Manitoba Railroad which he expanded across the West by gaining control of the Great Northern Railway. He collected railroads the way J. P. Morgan collected silver snuff boxes, amassing holdings worth $54 millions in a day when $10 was a worker's weekly pay.

Like Van Horne, Jim Hill had a temper that blew hot or cold depending on whim. He once tore out a telephone and heaved it through a window. He fired a Great Northern clerk because he had said his name was Spittles; it *was* Spittles, too, but he got fired anyway. And, when Hill once came along in his private coach after a blizzard and found a Great Northern crew trying to clear six feet of snow off the tracks, he sent them inside for coffee, and took pleasure in showing them how to shovel. Hill and Van Horne were both railroad buccaneers of the brass-knuckles school, but there was a difference. Hill liked reading biographies of Napoleon and other adventurers, and learned from them: "You have to keep your eyes open and catch hold of things, or they'll catch hold of you." Van Horne favoured books about explorers and scientists, and his governing passion was: "To make things grow and put new places on the map." Van Horne rejected analysis of himself, just as he spurned analytical novels. "I don't care *why* people do things in novels or in real life," he said. "I don't care a rap for the moral processes that make a character. I want something doing. Working out motives and lines of thought is about as useful as a signboard on Niagara Falls. Nothing is left to your imagination."

Van Horne was born in 1843 in a log cabin in Chelsea, Illinois, near the Old Oregon Trail. His father, an impoverished Dutch lawyer who had argued cases with Abraham Lincoln, died when the boy was eleven. Young Van Horne was expelled from school three years later for drawing irreverent caricatures of his teachers. He helped support his mother and two sisters by delivering telegraph messages at $15 a month. When not studying Morse code, collecting fossils, and memorizing books on geology, he was playing poker – which he later defined as "not a game, but an education." On his fifteenth birthday, he became a full-fledged railway telegrapher. At Joliet, he developed his memory by trying to recall car numbers on passing Michigan Central Railway freight trains, and gave rein to his high spirits by running a live ground wire from the superintendent's office to a steel plate in the railway yard for the fun of seeing men jump at a mild electric shock. When the superintendent got the hot foot, Van Horne was fired amid steaming oaths.

Despite his penchant for horseplay, Van Horne was driven by a merciless ambition. When his widowed mother was reduced to feeding her children three meals of hominy grits a day, he resolved to get away and make some money. And when he saw the chief executive of the Michigan Central pull into the yards in his private coach . . . "I found myself wondering if even I might not somehow become a general superintendent and travel in a private car. The glories of it, the pride of it, the salary pertaining to it – all that moved me deeply. I made up my mind then and there that I would reach it." He did, ten years later, at the age of 28. Working days, nights, Sundays and holidays he progressed from ticket agent to train dispatcher to president of the debt-ridden Southern Minnesota Railroad. He pulled it out of bankruptcy virtually singlehandedly. He replaced the striking Brotherhood of Engineers with his own office staff, declaring: "From the union's standpoint the scab may be a mean man, but sometimes he is an heroic one." Sleeping only four hours a day he aggressively fired incompetents, and energized the others with free lunches, "grub to take the wrinkles out of your bellies."

Van Horne was the first railroad man who subsidized immigrant farmers to settle along the tracks, thus fashioning the key to the settlement of the Canadian West . . . and creating traffic. When a grasshopper epidemic threatened to devastate the crops of the Minnesota pioneers, Van Horne invented a horse-drawn contraption smeared with tar to kill the pests.

Inevitably, Jim Hill heard of this hustler from the West and arranged to meet him. Hill was then running the St. Paul, Minneapolis & Manitoba in partnership with two Canadian Scots. One was Donald ("Labrador") Smith, the ex-Hudson's Bay factor with the craggy eyebrows and shaggy red whiskers who had negotiated with Riel. The other was Smith's cousin, George Stephen, another red-whiskered wheeler-dealer who had risen from a draper's apprentice in Aberdeen, Scotland, to president of the Bank of Montreal. By a canny financial manipulation, Stephen, Smith and Hill had gained control of the St. Paul railroad for a profit of some $100 millions.

Now Hill told Van Horne of the gigantic railroad he and his two fellow Scots had contracted to build across Canada. When British Columbia confederated with Canada in 1871, it was on the condition that a railway was to link the Pacific province with Ontario and the Maritimes within ten years. Now, in February, 1881, millions of dollars had been spent, and fewer than 200 miles of trans-continental track had been laid. British Columbia, cut off from the east by the Rocky Mountains, was threatening to join the United States unless Prime Minister Sir John A. Macdonald made good his promise. So Hill, Donald Smith and George Stephen had just incorporated the Canadian Pacific Railway Company. They were to get $25 millions in cash from the Canadian Government and twenty-five million acres of land to lay 2,900 miles of track within ten years. The U.S. had had forty million people when it built its first trans-continental railroad, Canada now had no more than four million. Its west was an empty wilderness, peopled according to the 1881 census, by fewer than 170,000 settlers, who had travelled by Red River wagon, horse and canoe; most of these were in Manitoba. Winnipeg, the principal Hudson's Bay post on the Prairies, was a tent-and-shanty town of barely 350 people.

The job, said Hill, required "a pioneer of great mental and physical power." Hill sent Van Horne to Smith and Stephen, who agreed: "He's the man. Let him shoot the works." They gave him the highest salary ever paid to the general manager of a railroad.

It was 40-below zero when Van Horne arrived in Winnipeg on the last December day of 1881. He set up headquarters over the wooden shack that was the Bank of Montreal. One of his cigar butts tossed in the waste basket burned it down and he had to move, cursing, into the vestry of Knox church. From these new quarters he announced, "We're going to bust every record. We're laying 500 miles of track in *one season*. And from now on, if I give an order and a damn fool uses the expression 'can't' or 'fail,' that man must go."

"We did not like him when he first came up to Winnipeg as 'General Boss of Everybody and Everything,'" J. H. E. Secretan, chief locating engineer, recalled in his memoirs, *Canada's Great Highway*. "His ways were not our ways . . . And he told me once, 'If I could only teach a sectionman to run a transit, I wouldn't have a single damn engineer about the place.'" Later, Secretan came to regard Van Horne as "the great magician – the most versatile man I have ever encountered. He was a born artist and often when he was talking to me, made sketches on his blotting pad, well worth framing, but which he tore up as fast as he drew them . . . He detested all sycophants and people who were afraid of him: he rather admired the man who had an opinion of his own and the courage to give his reasons for daring to have it."

Van Horne immediately imported 3,000 Swedes from Minnesota. He brought steel rails from the Krupp plant in Germany and spruce lumber by ox train from Rat Portage. Heavy snow blanketed the Prairie as ten thousand pick-and-shovel navvies, spikers, fish-platers, bolters, pile-drivers – plus 1,700 teams of horses – began pushing the rails westward toward Calgary. Overnight, cities of white tents blossomed beside the prairie gopher holes; but the men had little time for sleep, or the gambling casinos, or the hurdy-gurdy girls who followed their camps to fleece them of their special two-dollars-a-day pay. Night gangs of construction workers, known as "Van Horne's flying wing," followed right behind the contractors. They laid as much as 20 miles of track in three days. Van Horne worked around the clock with them, jumping off a flat car of rails at the end of steel to organize target-shoots among them, swapping cuss words and yarns with them, joining them in singing:

For some of us are bums, for whom work has no charms,
And some of us are farmers, a-working for our farms,
But all are jolly fellows, who come from near and far.
To work up in the Rockies on the C.P.R.

"Van Horne *looks harmless*," commented a Winnipeg newspaper. "So does a she mule. And so does a buzz saw. To see Van Horne get out of the car and go softly about, you'd think he was an evangelist on his way west to preach temperance to the Mounted Police. But you are soon undeceived. If you are within hearing distance, you will have more fun than you've ever had in your life." He bullied, coaxed and teased to get his surveyors moving faster. Some were won by his art expertise and his love of nature. In his memoirs, *When the Steel Went Through*, P. Turner Bone tells how his fellow easterners were enraptured when they caught their first glimpse of the Rockies. "There were, however, no kodaks with which to take snapshots," he wrote, "So we developed a taste for sketching: and it was our custom when we paid a visit to a neighbouring engineer's camp on a Sunday, to take our portfolio of sketches and water colours with us to submit them for inspection and criticism." Van Horne was soon recognized as the most knowledgeable critic of them all.

Some Cree tribes were troublesome. In Saskatchewan, Chief Piapot pulled out 40 miles of survey stakes and his braves staged a sit-down strike on the rails. Van Horne bribed them away with tobacco and free railroad passes.

By late fall of 1882, despite a Red River flood, Van Horne had 480 miles of main track on the plains. Next, he had to thread the steel over the bogs north of Lake Superior and across the western mountains which, scoffed the Liberal Opposition leader in Parliament, Edward Blake, "will never pay for the grease on the axles." Van Horne climbed the mountains to see for himself. He travelled by stagecoach, scow, packpony. At Yellowhead Pass he walked on two loose cottonwood planks over the Mountain Creek trestle and gazed at the torrent 160 feet down, where his scouts, a few days before, had crashed to their death. He looked at his engineer, Sam Reed, an old friend from Illinois, who was clinging to the trestle on hands and knees, and said: "Those preliminary surveys will no doubt prove of great value to future alpinists. But I'm building a *railroad*, Sam." He had decided to scrap the Yellowhead surveys. The C.P.R. was going through Kicking Horse Pass to the south.

One midnight, Secretan found Van Horne at his church desk surrounded by blueprints. He threw one over at Secretan. "Look at that," he fumed. "Some infernal idiot has put a tunnel in there. I want you to go up and take it out."

"But this is on the Bow River – a rather difficult section. There may be no other way."

"Make another way! That's a mud tunnel. How long would it take us to build it?"

"A year or eighteen months."

The general manager slammed his first on the desk. "Hell's bells, are we going to hold up this railway for a year and a half while they build their damned tunnel? Take it out!"

At the door, Secretan turned, "Mr. Van Horne. Those mountains are also in the way. And the rivers don't run right for us, either. While we're at it, should we knock *them* down, too?" As he left he glimpsed his chief lying back in his chair, his belly quivering with laughter.

Van Horne was able to laugh at everything, even himself. When he fell in a creek he put on the largest pair of pants in the camp, split them up the back, laced them with clothesline, and joined in the laughter. When rations ran out and he had to go two days on "blasted bannock," he said, "I don't mind the fact it's made of flour that leaked into the cook's saddle-bag. But I *do* mind that the flour lay in that damn saddle-bag beside a curry brush, old boots, and a pair of stockings that haven't been washed in weeks."

He loved to show off his dare-deviltry. When an engine-driver refused to take his locomotive over a teetering trestle, Van Horne climbed into the cab. "Get down," he said, "and I'll take her over myself."

"Well, if you ain't afraid of getting killed, with all your money," said the engineer, "I ain't afraid, either."

"We'll have a double funeral," yelled Van Horne. "At my expense, of course!"

Van Horne admired his advance surveyors who crept crablike along the rock shelves of the Fraser River canyon walls, seeking toeholds for themselves and a path for the C.P.R. Secretan records the comment of a Yankee pilot on first seeing Hell's Gate Canyon:

"Wal, Capting, I was *pre*-pared for it to be *per*-pendicular, but my God, sir, I never thought it would *lean back*!" Secretan wrote that "many a time I was slung up with a line under my armpits laboriously trying to find room for the tripod of a transit on a narrow ledge of projecting rock . . . 1,300 feet above the rushing, roaring white waters of the Fraser river." As a tribute to his courage, Van Horne sent him the latest copies of the London *Illustrated News*, two boxes of prime cigars, and a keg of Hudson's Bay rum.

But the true heroes of the Rockies were the Chinese navvies. Andrew Onkerdonk, the luxuriantly-bearded Dutch American engineer in charge of the C.P.R.'s British Columbia sector, imported 2,000 of them from China. Two hundred died of scurvy while kept below hatches en route, and the pigtailed survivors were greeted on arrival with a proposed law stipulating "that no man wearing his hair more than five and one-half inches in length be deemed eligible for employment in construction of the C.P.R."

Van Horne backed Onkerdonk as his fellow Yankee declared that it was unseemly for British Columbians to show prejudice against immigrants from the British colony of Hong Kong. "You must have this labour," he said, "or you cannot have the railway." It was truly said that the steel track along and across the mountain gorges was greased with the blood of the Chinese coolies. They gave their lives to blast 15 tunnels through the 69 miles of precipices extending from Yale to Lytton. With a steam winch and a capstan, they pulled the supply sternwheeler *Skuzzy*, 120 tons, through the murderous Black Canyon of the Fraser. In their honour, the rapids at one point are named China Riffle.

Van Horne now turned his attention to the Lake Superior link. But in trying to carve a railroad through this jungle of swamp and spruce, he collided headlong with James Jerome Hill. When the C.P.R. contract was signed, Hill declared it would be too expensive to lay track around the north shore of Lake Superior's quicksand. He wanted the C.P.R. to dip south into U.S. territory – his own territory. Hill planned a spur line from Sault Ste. Marie to his St. Paul, Minneapolis railway, which would give him a tidy profit freighting Canadian traffic on U.S. soil.

Van Horne refused. "It's my idea to build straight through – as near Lake Superior as possible," he told the directors. "That way, supplies for the construction workers can be transported by water. Besides, using Mr. Hill's branch line plainly puts the mighty C.P.R. at Mr. Hill's tender mercies." Sir John A. Macdonald sided with Van Horne and so did Smith and Stephen. Hill resigned from the C.P.R. board, sold his shares, and threatened, "I'll get even with Van Horne, if I have to go to hell for it and shovel coal."

To see what he was up against, Van Horne paddled a canoe from Jack Fish Bay to Red Rock in Lake Superior, floundering through mosquito-infested swamps. "It's 200 miles of engineering impossibility," he said. "But we'll bridge it." To help his men lay track through the bogs, he imported from Chicago the first track-laying machines used in Canada. To avoid cutting through the rock hills, he employed high timber trestles. To eliminate the cost of hauling in explosives, he built three dynamite factories. Even then, the expense was appalling: $700,000 to blast one mile; half a million to drain a lake. One quagmire alone sucked down seven tiers of track and three locomotives.

By the spring of 1884, Van Horne had 9,000 men laying track on the muskeg, and he had no cash for the payroll. Hill, bent on revenge, had launched a smear campaign in the newspapers and C.P.R. stock had tumbled from $60 to $34. Van Horne, an adroit poker player, had managed to bluff the creditors. ("Go, my friend. Sell your boots and buy C.P.R. stock.") But, cornering the Prime Minister in a corridor of the House of Commons, he confided that the C.P.R. was broke. "Sir John, you must ask Parliament for another loan for the C.P.R.," the railwayman urged. "We and you are dangling over the brink of hell."

"Well, Van Horne," replied Macdonald. "I hope it will be delayed a while. I don't want to go just yet."

Sir John was reluctant to go to Parliament because of the opposition of the Liberals. "They're already crying," he said, "that the Government is pouring a lake of money down the C.P.R. sink holes."

"It's to the Government, or to the penitentiary," he was warned. "The day the C.P.R. busts, the Conservative Party busts the day after." "Old Tomorrow," for once, moved fast. He pushed through Parliament an additional C.P.R. loan of $22,500,000.

Van Horne raced to his company's office to telegraph the good news. The operator was slow. Van Horne shoved him aside and sent it himself. Then he raced to the construction site and pressed his men on. To earn extra cash, Van Horne shipped buffalo bones east and sold them; he put steamers on the Great Lakes, grossing a few millions.

The Lake Superior country was, however, sucking up more millions still. Hill renewed his campaign to depreciate C.P.R. stock. Sir John A. Macdonald fought two more loans through Ottawa: first one of $5 millions, then one for a last million. The Prime Minister called a halt.

"It is clear as noonday, Sir John," wrote Van Horne, "that the C.P.R. is against the wall. Unless you yourself say what is to be done, nothing but disaster will result." The Prime Minister turned a deaf ear to what he called "the sharp Yankee."

"Have no means of paying wages," Van Horne telegraphed. "Pay car can't be sent out. Unless we get relief, we must stop." Again the Prime Minister did not answer. Smith and Stephen, who had invested their own fortunes in C.P.R. stock, believed they had reached the end of the road. "It may be that we must succumb," said Stephen, looking sadly around the board table. "But that must not be as long as we individually have a single dollar in our pockets."

In the winter of 1885, the Prime Minister told the promoters that the Liberal Opposition refused to feed another nickel to the C.P.R. "White Elephant." A miracle was needed and one arrived. It came with news that Louis Riel was arousing the Indians and the *Métis* to take up arms in the Northwest. Van Horne felt like enshrining the messianic Riel. Riel had given him one last chance. Van Horne reminded Sir John it had taken 96 days for Colonel Garnet Wolseley to march troops from Ontario to Red River to quell Riel's first insurrection. "Put two batteries of General Middleton's soldiers in our hands," Van Horne said, "and I guarantee we'll transport them to Winnipeg within a dozen days."

The Prime Minister was sceptical. The C.P.R. had four trackless gaps totalling 105 miles on the north shore of Lake Superior. The snow was reportedly "piled mountains high," it was 30-below zero, and many volunteers had as yet no uniforms. Still, he had no alternative. If he waited until spring, the twenty thousand Indians in the West might go on the warpath. "Go ahead," he told Van Horne, "and that may put a new face on the question of the loan."

Van Horne was confident: he had moved Yankee troops on the Chicago & Alton during the Civil War and knew how to manoeuvre under primitive conditions. Forty-eight hours after Maconald had given him the green light his trains were loading troops in eastern stations. While the bands played *The Girl I Left Behind Me*, volunteers, many wearing civilian shoes and carrying a lunch, kissed their sweethearts and got aboard for the "ride" west.

Thousands of Chinese labourers from the United States threw down temporary tracks on top of the Lake Superior ice; and Van Horne ran roofless flat cars over frozen rivers. When no track was laid, the men sat back to back in open bobsleighs. Where no sleighs were available, they waded through snow drifts on foot, their thinly-soled shoes icicled, their eyes partially protected with makeshift goggles against snowblindness. When they staggered into the waiting trains, Van Horne fed them hot steak dinners and strong coffee, but many had to be carried aboard. His first troop trains chugged into Winnipeg only four days after departing from Ontario. The British War Office compared Van Horne's achievement favourably with Napoleon's feat in taking his army across the Alps. By April 10, the entire Expeditionary Force was in the Northwest and, on April 30, the C.P.R. got its new loan.

With the Liberal Opposition chastened, Macdonald was able to push through a bill, allowing the C.P.R. to sell $15 millions' worth of first mortgage bonds. But who would buy them? Hill had stepped up his smear campaign and in New York and London it was rumoured that the C.P.R. was bankrupt.

Van Horne and the directors waited tensely while Stephen sailed to London to find a buyer for the bond issue. He cabled back the battle cry of his Scottish clan: "Stand fast, Craigellachie!" His cousin, Donald Smith, knew what it meant: he had the money. Lord Revelstoke, head of the banking house of Barings, had bought the entire issue.

Van Horne shook hands with Smith, with the other directors in the board room. They kicked the furniture, tossed chairs, and joined arms for a Highland fling, while Van Horne leaped on top of the table and did a Dutch clog dance.

At Eagle Pass in British Columbia, on November 7, 1885, Donald Smith hammered in the last spike. At his right elbow was Van Horne. He had vetoed the use of a diamond spike. "The last spike," he said, "will be just as good an iron spike as there is between Montreal and Vancouver." The assembled work gang and the half-dozen railway magnates, their top hats incongruous in the wilderness, asked Van Horne to solemnize the occasion with a speech. Van Horne cleared his throat.

"All I can say," he said, "is that the work has been well done in every way." He had finished the world's longest railroad five years before its contract specified. The board now appointed Van Horne president. He faced two major problems: the need for freight and traffic, and the challenge of Jim Hill, now threatening to thrust his Great Northern Railroad into Manitoba and British Columbia to take cross-Canada traffic through the States.

Van Horne set himself up as the C.P.R.'s one-man press agent. Soon after the last spike was rammed home, he offered a free railway ride to eastern and European newspaper editors. "I bet I can run you the 840 miles from Winnipeg to the Rocky foothills," he wagered, "between dawn and dusk." He made it, too. But to shorten the odds Van Horne arranged the press junket for June 21 which was the longest day of the year.

His next task was to find farmers for 300 million acres of prairie land. He looked with scorn at the colonizing methods of the Hudson's Bay Company. "One of the most hidebound concerns in existence," he snorted. "The London board is a collection of pernickety and narrow-minded men, who don't know enough to manage a peanut stand." He appointed as colonizing agents priests who induced French Canadians in New England to leave their factories for the West. He dispatched platoons of lecturers to Europe to lure immigrants. He offered free western homesteads to doctors and teachers, a cheap cent-a-mile rate to farmers, one hundred free pure-bred shorthorn bulls to cattle ranchers. He stocked railroad cars with goods and left them on side-tracks for three days so that settlers' wives in the bush could do their shopping. He went into the wheat business, built a streamlined million-bushel elevator at Fort William, Ontario. Hill sneered that the prairie farmers could never raise enough wheat to fill it. Van Horne persuaded them to grow high-quality Red Fife wheat by offering free shipment to any farmer buying it for seed. His agents outbid other grain buyers and thousands of bushels were stacked outside C.P.R. stations. When Hill photographed the congestion to show the C.P.R.'s inadequate equipment, Van Horne himself circulated the photos to show the West's overflowing bounty.

As the Prairies filled, Van Horne turned to the Rockies. "Since we can't export the scenery," he announced, "we'll import the tourists." He sketched designs for C.P.R.'s modern string of hotels, from baronial Banff Springs to the log cabins on the Divide. He composed the advertising slogan "Wise Men of the East, Go West by C.P.R." and, when Montreal's new Windsor Station was opened, he wrote: "Beats all Creation, that C.P.R. Station!"

The "Mogul of Monopoly," Jim Hill called Van Horne, who blocked Hill's plans for a north-south line in Manitoba and British Columbia. In retaliation, Hill wouldn't sell tickets on his Great Northern Railway to passengers travelling C.P.R. to the Orient.

In 1895, Van Horne, now more Canadian than any Canadian, accepted a title – the first non-British subject to wear the Knight's Cross of the Order of St. Michael and St. George. But he hadn't really changed. On the morning his knighthood was listed the doorman at his C.P.R. presidential office on the fifth floor of Montreal's Windsor Station, bowed low. "Good morning, Sir William," he said.

"Oh hell!" muttered Van Horne, and locked himself up in his office.

When the *Times* of London respectfully asked what Sir William's family coat-of-arms was, the big eater from Illinois replied: "A Dinner Horne, Pendant, upon a Kitchen Door." He preferred the company of men like Hill, with whom he later became friends. They would play poker and billiards in Van Horne's private car, the *Saskatchewan*, and Hill would visit in Montreal at Van Horne's 52-room mansion on Sherbrooke Street West, bringing a Rubens or an El Greco to add to Van Horne's art collection. "Van," Hill said once, taking his rival's arm affectionately, "We disagree about business matters. But our personal relations are so pleasant we would do anything for each other."

In June, 1899, at the age of 56, Van Horne resigned as C.P.R. president. Then, restless, he became president of the giant salt mines at Windsor, Ontario. He threw his energy into streamlining the Toronto and Winnipeg streetcar systems, and just for fun (and profit), he touched off a battle between the Dominion Coal Co. and the Dominion Iron and Steel Co., though he was a director of both. The two companies amalgamated and Van Horne became vice-president.

"It's wonderful to have the world by the tail," he said. He went to Cuba to electrify the mule-pulled streetcars of Havana, decided to built a railroad, and financed it in New York on a week-end. "Van Horne," said Mario Menocal, President of Cuba, "did more for us in one year than Spain did in four centuries."

In the 1900s Van Horne spent his spare time breeding prize cattle at his 4,000 acre ranch near Selkirk, Manitoba, and raising peaches at his private 1,000-acre island in the Maritimes' Passamaquoddy Bay.

He scoured the art galleries of Europe bidding for Rembrandts, Titians and Murillos. When reporters asked him, after an illness, if he was tired, he ran up and down St. James Street, Montreal, to show them how well he was.

When he died on September 11, 1915, Cuba declared a day of national mourning. The C.P.R. system, now a network of 17,000 miles of track and a fleet of Pacific Ocean liners, was halted in silent homage for five minutes. His body was conveyed to Joliet, Illinois, in his old private car, the *Saskatchewan*; and as the funeral train crossed the country, railroaders and farmers thronged the stations. The train crossed the border and slowly chugged south over Jim Hill's railway tracks, and Hill, who was to die a year later, watched them lay Van Horne in the ground.

His monument is the C.P.R. and his feat is commemorated by the faded photograph taken at Craigellachie in Eagle Pass, entitled in Canadian school history books: "The Driving of the Last Spike." It seems as striking in its way as any of the figurines painted on the Oriental vases that Van Horne treasured. In the forefront are the railroad workers – French Canadians, immigrant Swedes, what looks to be a *Métis* on the far left, a white-moustached Englishman on the far right – dressed in labouring clothes. One looks at these long-dead immigrants and their faces seem indistinguishable from those of the pioneers that preceded them westwards.

In the centre are the two bearded Scotsmen – Donald Smith, who used to count muskrat skins for the Hudson's Bay Company in Labrador, and George Stephen, once a draper's assistant at Pratt and Keith's store in Aberdeen – and their faces seem reminiscent of those other hard-driving pioneering Scots, Alexander Mackenzie, Simon Fraser, James Douglas and George Simpson.

Finally, one sees Van Horne: hands thrust deep into the pockets of his wrinkled black coat, vested puncheon belly unbuttoned, eyes closed. He does not look happy. It is as if he were sorry to see the job finished. He had no more mountains to shear, no more lakes to drain, no more canyons to span. Yet he had fulfilled the dream that had fevered the imagination of every explorer in Canada from Pierre Radisson to David Thompson. They had all known strangeness, beauty, wonder and violence on their travels, but where they had failed, he had triumphed. He had discovered the Northwest Passage – a usable one that led to the riches of Cathay. And in doing so he had forged the steel bonds of Canada's nationhood.

THE STEEL GOES WEST

Makers of the nation boldly spoke of a land "from sea to sea," but it was an empty motto until West was linked to East by 3,000 miles of railroad steel. Scoffers said it was a fantastic scheme, and it certainly was. But the railroad builders did succeed, and this album of contemporary photographs shows how it happened.

Four Miles a Day

The surveying teams raced ahead across the plains, often just one hop in front of the construction gangs. Their orders were to keep as close to the American border as possible.

Working day and night, the tracklayers didn't always have time for permanent camps. With little leisure, tired and hungry, they slept and ate in two-story boarding cars that moved west with them.

C.P.R.
CONSTRUCTION
TRAIN
ON C. AND E.
ARRIVED
STRATHCONA.
EDMONTON 60.Y
1891.

Even the prairie sometimes had to be flattened. It took
10,000 men and 1,700 teams of horses to push C.P.R. track westward up to four miles a day; once, 20 miles in three days.

Track-laying machinery used the assembly-line technique,
and could quickly put down 2,640 heavy ties per mile. The work
was hard but the pay good. A man could earn two dollars a day.

The Fraser Canyon was too much for this engine, which blew its stack near Yale, B.C., 1897. Isolated maintenance depots set up along the new C.P.R. western lines sometimes developed into important towns.

Hazards of the High Country

A snowshed under construction in the Selkirk Mountains, 1885. When the avalanches of ice and rock came roaring down in Kicking Horse Pass in the spring, the early sheds often had to be extended or rebuilt.

Lumber was cheap and handy, and engineers threw long flimsy looking trestles – like this one over Five-Mile-Creek – across entire valleys. These bridges swayed under a heavy locomotive, to the consternation of the early passengers.

Blasting Through the Barrier

The C.P.R. didn't expect their men to move mountains . . . just to blast their way through them. In the early stages of the mountain work, before rails were laid to bring machines to the tunnel sites, men had to drill by hand; three men were expected to chisel through 18 feet of rockwall a day.

Dynamite was dangerous to haul and so it was manufactured in the West at Emory and Yale, 1,300 pounds a day, enough to move millions of tons of granite, and cut a path through the Rockies.

Pushed by the dynamic will of William Van Horne, the track-layers worked at breakneck speed, though many of them had to be taught how to handle a pick and shovel. The gangs came from everywhere: unemployed bricklayers, bartenders and clerks, disheartened farmers and even coolies from China (who stayed on to establish the West's restaurants and laundries).

The C.P.R. funds were often desperately low, and the payroll cars were slow in coming along the completed lines. Once, at Beavermouth, B.C., 300 angry workers — some armed with pistols — marched and shouted for their pay. Eight determined Mounties stopped them from tearing down the camp. But the pay came through, and the steel rolled on, until Pacific was linked to the plains.

The Word 'Can't' Didn't Exist

A supply column of sleds comes in over the deep snow to feed the work gangs, 1884. If the winter halted track laying, the men simply turned to the forest and cut ties for new track.

In 1885, C.P.R. President George Stephen boasted that "not one train has been delayed a minute on all our lines in the Northwest by snow or cold weather." The rotary snow-plough was his trump card.

◁ *The skinned poles of the telegraph, still regarded with awe by most Canadians, headed into the highlands alongside the new track.*

The First Cross-Country Train Reaches Vancouver

On May 23, 1887, Engine 374 slowly and proudly chugged into Vancouver. The arrival of that first cross-country passenger train heralded a new era for Canada. The promise had been kept – the nation was linked "from sea to sea." More than that, Vancouver was established as a Pacific port and Canada had a direct gateway to Japan and China. In real terms, this was the "Northwest Passage" that the early explorers had dreamed of . . . a highway of steel, spanning a continent and opening the way to the rich trade of the Orient.

In 1884 William Van Horne chose Vancouver as the C.P.R.'s western terminus, in preference to Port Moody, because of the superior harbour facilities. At Coal Harbour, a 1,000 foot wharf was built, three freight sheds, a passenger station. The official completion of the C.P.R. had been marked at Craigellachie, on November 7, 1885, where the rails building from each end met. It had cost a considerable number of lives, millions of dollars, and caused the fall of a government (in 1873), but when the sound of a hammer hitting the final spike echoed through Eagle Pass, it signalled the final act in the taming of the Canadian West.

First Train in Vancouver

Photo by DEVINE

The railroad was finished, the West was tamed — but Canada was still the emptiest country on earth. This advertisement helped light the fuse of the population explosion — and sell the millions of acres owned by the C.P.R. Teachers and doctors were lured by free homes; would-be ranchers got free cattle.

Epilogue

W HAT did they achieve, these far-Westerners? In a country where history has been so telescoped – Alberta and Saskatchewan were made provinces as recently as 1905 – it is hard to measure the true scope of their attainment. And it is impossible, in any one book, to even mention all the men and women who played important parts in the drama. Yet one can glance back and marvel at the stubbornness of the trail blazers. There they were flung into a "great lone land" of empty spaces where everything seemed to be conspiring against them.

Their compatriots in the Old World were indifferent to them. When New France was ceded to England in 1763, Voltaire dismissed it as "a few acres of snow." When President James K. Polk was clamouring for the Oregon country in 1845 with his sabre-rattling cry of "Fifty-four forty or fight!", the British Colonial Office's emissary, Captain John Gordon, commander of *H.M.S. America*, reported that it wasn't worth fighting for. Because the salmon in Oregon waters did not rise to his angler's fly, that gentleman did "not think the country worth five straws."

The Yankees with their "awful swallow for territory" were perpetually poised to gulp them. In the phrase of one politician proclaiming America's Manifest Destiny, the whole Saskatchewan Valley was "like a ripe plum waiting to fall into our laps." It was no thanks to Benjamin Disraeli that the Canadian West did *not* slip into the American grasp; in 1853, that British prime minister was quite ready to cut asunder the Hudson's Bay Company territory which had become "a millstone around our necks."

The land itself was cruellest of all to them. To withstand the bitter cold of the Canadian frost kingdom, as one fur trader put it, "one ought to have his Blood compos'd of Brandy, his Body of Brass, and his Eyes of Glass." And no explorer expressed the hardships of vagabondage away from home as eloquently as did Pierre Esprit Radisson: "What fairer bastion than a good tongue, especially when one sees his owne chimney smoak, or when we can kisse our owne wife or kisse our neighbour's wife with ease and delight? It is a different thing when victuals are wanting, worke whole nights & days, lye down on the bare ground, & not always that hap, the breech in the water, the feare in the buttocks, to have the belly empty, the weariness in the bones, the drowsinesse in the body by the bad weather you are to suffer, having nothing to keep you from such calamity."

Yet, in spite of inimicable geography, climate and politics, the firstcomers to the Canadian West forged ever forward. It was a triumph of the will, of courage, of human tenacity. Whether they were driven by curiosity to follow the next bend in the river (Mackenzie, Fraser, Thompson), or the hell-raising spirit of adventure (Ross, Cox, Ruxton), or dreams of wealth (Henry, Simpson, Douglas), or the desire to civilize the barbaric (McDougall, Lacombe, Riel), each of these pioneers performed, firstly, a memorable feat by the simple act of surviving.

Individually, these dedicated men penetrated the mists of an unmapped jungle; they shot hundreds of rapids in flimsy birchbark canoes; they tramped thousands of miles in moccasins and snowshoes; they endured blizzards and grizzly bears and starvation; they corrupted and duelled with cannibalistic Indians, and sometimes they murdered one another. Yet, collectively, they did no less than tame half a continent.

An Acknowledgement

THE author received nothing but kindness from the academic historians. My greatest debt is to the staff of the Public Archives of Canada in Ottawa. I wish especially to thank Dr. W. Kaye Lamb, Dominion Archivist, and also his associates, William G. Ormsby, Wilfred Smith, Pierre Brunet and George Delisle. In Montreal, Mrs. I. M. B. Dobell, archivist at the McCord Museum, McGill University, was an unfailingly cheerful source of aid, and Dr. G. R. Lowther, curator of anthropology at McGill University, instructed me on complicated Indian lore.

In Claresholm, Alberta, Canon S. H. Middleton, better known as Chief Mountain, helped me to separate the fact from the myth relating to his beloved Blackfoot parishioners, and Norman Grier, president of the Fort Macleod Historical Association, taught me to be cautious with the memoirs of retired whisky traders.

I wish to thank: – Miss Edith Firth, head of the Canadian history and manuscript section of the Toronto Public Library; Miss Jean Gibson, librarian at the University of Toronto; Mrs. Shirlee A. Smith, librarian for the Hudson's Bay Company; Hartwell Bowsfield, provincial archivist for Manitoba; Hugh A. Dempsey, archivist for the Glenbow Foundation, Calgary; Allan R. Turner, provincial archivist for Saskatchewan; George Shepherd, curator of the Western Development Museum, Saskatoon; Willard E. Ireland, provincial archivist for British Columbia; Richard R. Hanson, librarian for the Washington State Historical Society; Mrs. Nancy A. Hacker, librarian for the Oregon Historical Society; Frederick P. Todd, director of the West Point Museum, New York; and J. Russell Harper, chief curator of the McCord Museum.

One half of these chapters appeared, in condensed form, in *True*, *Argosy* and *Liberty* magazines. I owe a debt to various specialists who made helpful suggestions: – Harold Pfeiffer, of the Human History Branch, Department of Indian Affairs and Northern Development, Ottawa; Dr. W. Stewart Wallace, the dean of North West Company scholars; Marjorie Wilkins Campbell, that champion of William McGillivray.

I thank also these non-professional collaborators who provided ancestral diaries, pioneer memoirs and regional histories: – Emma Abrahamse, Coronation, Alta.; Frank W. Anderson, Calgary, Alta.; Raymond Andrew, Ladner, B.C.; Syd Allen, North Vancouver, B.C.; Mrs. John Armstrong, Hamilton, Ont.; Sister Augustina, Vibank, Sask.; Mrs. May Ballingall, London, Ont.; Glen Bannerman, Ottawa; Everett Baker, Shaunavon, Sask.; O. E. Baril, Bonnyville, Alta.; Alan Bean, Maymont, Sask.; Eileen Bean, Maymont, Sask.; Carl E. Beech, Winnipeg; J. S. Bell, Vancouver; Mrs. Minnie R. Bell, Portreeve, Sask.; W. A. Bell, Leduc, Alta.; Mrs. H. J. Bennett, Waverley, N.S.; J. M. Bennett, Willow Bunch, Sask.; E. E. Bent, Landis, Sask.; L. Bergersen, Regina; Mrs. M. Gergren, Lake Cowichan, B.C.; W. G. Bock, Sr., Eastend, Sask.; F. R. Bolton, Newcomerstown, Ohio; E. J. Bonfoy, Victoria, B.C.; Paul Bonneau, Gravelbourg, Sask.; Mrs. Ellen Bowden, Lacombe, Alta.; Mrs. Jessie R. Bothwell, Regina; Don C. Brestler, Calgary; Mrs. Fred Brandly, Three Hills, Alta.; Mrs. Maude Bridgman, Weyburn, Sask.; Mrs. Olvetta Brigham, Clinton, Ont.; Mrs. Elsie K. Brown, Royal Oak, B.C.; Peter William Brown, Three Hills, Alta.; Mrs. R. E. Brown, Chilliwack, B.C.; Hilda Browne, West Vancouver, B.C.; Ina Bruns, Lacombe, Alta.; Dorothea Bublitz, Whalley, B.C.; Catherine M. Buckaway, Jansen, Sask.; J. Bueckhert, Main Centre, Sask.; William R. Burrell, Aneroid, Sask.; H. S. Burton, New Westminster, B.C.; Jack Cahill, Vancouver; Mrs. Bertha Caldwell, Port Alberni, B.C.; Edith Campbell, Oxbow, Sask.; Mrs. E. Campbell, Victoria, B.C.; Gray Campbell, Sidney, B.C.; Mrs. J. E. Campbell, Regina; Mrs. J. R. Campbell, North Vancouver, B.C.; Milton Neil Campbell, Hamilton, Ont.; William O. Carlson, St. Paul, Minn.; Knox Carmichael, Victoria, B.C.; Mrs. W. B. Carmichael, Wynot, Sask.; E. L. Carter, New Denver, B.C.; Bill Cameron, CJDV, Drumheller, Alta.; Mrs. Donald Cameron, Hinton, Alta.; Arthur Carlisle, Medicine Hat, Alta.; Mrs. R. Cassell, Red Lake, B.C.; Mary E. Checketts, Farmington, Mich.; N. Chevelday, Elaine Lake, Sask.; Rabbi

Arthur A. Chiel, Tuckahoe, N.Y.; Sheila Chrestensen, Loreburn, Sask.; Sister Clare Marie, Allan, Sask.; Mr. and Mrs. Gordon Clark, Ottawa; Mrs. Joseph Y. Clark, Costa Mesa, Calif.; Mrs. L. Clarke, Conquest, Sask.; Mrs. Wilbert Clarke, Mantario, Sask.; W. A. Cohoon, Saskatoon; Dabney Otis Collins, Denver, Colo.; W. A. Collins, Sudbury, Ont.; Goldia V. Cook, Enderby, B.C.; Maisie Emery Cook, Edmonton; Grace W. Cousins, Medicine Hat, Alta.; W. J. Cousins, Lethbridge, Alta.; Andrew Cowan, Ottawa; Jack Cowell, Saskatoon; Catherine Cox, Grenfell, Sask.; Alma Criddle, Winnipeg; Herbert Cumming, Blenheim, Ontario; Mrs. Mary Cumming, Evansburg, Alta.; Frank Currie, Mawer, Sask.; Mrs. Betty Dains, North Burnaby, B.C.; August Dahlman, Readlyn, Sask.; Ellen Daniels, Saskatoon, Sask.; Hjalmur F. Danielson, Winnipeg; Dora Davies, Edmonton; Betty Davis, North Burnaby, B.C.; Mrs. George E. Devins, Hamilton; Roy Devore, Edmonton; Mrs. R. E. Desmet, Lethbridge, Alta.; E. C. Dirks, Welwyn, Sask.; Mrs. Ella Dixon, Hamilton; Mrs. Margaret Dobbie, Victoria, B.C.; F. Douglas, London, Ont.; William Douglas, Winnipeg; Dorothy Dumbrille, Alexandria, Ont.; C. O. Dumouchel, Marshall, Sask.; Mrs. Isabel Eaglesham, Weyburn, Sask.; Mary Earle, Cornwall, Ont.; George Eddlestone, Victoria, B.C.; George E. Eddy, Wilkic, Sask.; O. V. Edgington, Wilkie, Sask.; Victor Fairweather, Oliver, B.C.; Mrs. Julie Fidler, Winnipeg; Mrs. Martha Fidler, CKRM, Regina; Mrs. L. M. Finigan, Halifax; Mrs. Nancy E. Fisher, Valemount, B.C.; Mrs. Bruce Fleming, Swift Current, Sask.; H. J. Fleuty, Niagara Falls, Ont.; Mrs. Steenie Fisher, Alberni, B.C.; John B. Fraser, Fort Langley, B.C.; A. L. Freebairn, Pincher Creek, Alta.; Mary E. Froehlich, Swift Current, Sask.; W. H. Fribance, Hamilton, Ont.; H. S. Ferris, Wawanesa, Man.; Vern Gabriel, Quill Lake, Sask.; A. W. Garratt, Milestone, Sask.; Mrs. J. Garrison, Victoria, B.C.; Mrs. Alex Gartenburg, Woodham, Ont.; C. T. Garvin, Cobourg, Ont.; Ernest S. George, Edmonton; Abraham Gitson, Cleveland, Ohio; John H. Gibbard, Mission City, B.C.; W. R. Gillespie, Vancouver; Mrs. M. H. Gladwin, Middle Musquobodoit, N.S.; Joseph Golden, Windsor, Ont.; Geoffrey B. Golding, Wainwright, Alta.; Mrs. Nellie Gorrill, Lister, B.C.; E. W. Gosnell, Winnipeg; Ellen E. Gould, Vermilion, Alta.; Bernard Goulet, Ottawa; Nicholas de Grandmaison, Calgary; Mrs. Elizabeth Green, Winnipeg; Ed Green, Sechelt, B.C.; Wilson F. Green, Winnipeg; Francis L. Greenlay, Vancouver; Mrs. P. M. Greenwood, Adanac, Sask.; A. E. Gregory, Campbell River, B.C.; Norm Grier, Fort Macleod, Alta.; Harry Griffin, Haney, B.C.; Bernice Grymaloski, Semans, Sask.; Karl E. Gustafson, Lansford, Pa.; William Haddow, Toronto; J. V. Hall, Orillia, Ont.; H. T. Halliwell, Fort Macleod, Alta.; R. M. Hanson, Vancouver, B.C.; W. Hanner, Winnipeg; Mrs. K. T. Hamm, Wilkie, Sask.; Mrs. George A. Harris, Vancouver; H. F. Harris, Vancouver; H. R. Harrison, Duncan, B.C.; Charlotte I. Hazle, Dartmouth, N.S.; Mrs. A. Hegel, Roche Percee, Sask.; Mrs. Fred Heidt, Fruitvale, B.C.; Donald Herd, Fanny Bay, B.C.; Bruce Hicks, East Saint John, N.B.; Phyllis Higinbotham, Guelph, Ont.; Thomas H. Hilliar, Hamilton, Ont.; G. H. Hoehn, San Gabriel, Calif.; Hazel A. E. Hill, Trail, B.C.; Mrs. R. T. Hollies, Calgary; Mrs. Ira L. Holmes, Saskatoon; Mrs. W. Horner, Winnipeg; Morris Holota, Hafford, Sask.; Mrs. Inez B. Hosie, Regina; C. J. Hipkiss, Delisle, Sask.; Mrs. Esther Holmes, Saskatoon; Peter Hultgren, Midale, Sask.; Mrs. J. G. Humphrey, Nokomis, Sask.; F. C. Humphries, Vancouver; Rev. E. M. Hubicz, Gimli, Man.; Mrs. Marjorie Hunter, Beechy, Sask.; E. Hurst, Shoal Lake, Man.; G. Hurton, Carman, Man.; Mrs. M. Hustad, Penticton, B.C.; A. Hartwell Illsey, Calgary; Mrs. Roy Jackson, Neepawa, Man.; Gilbert Johnson, Marchwell, Sask.; Mrs. Veronica Johnston, Lethbridge, Alta.; W. A. Johnston, White Rock, B.C.; Cliff Juyn, Viscount, Sask.; Leonard L. Joubert, Williamstown, Ont.; Louis Karpan, Maymount, Sask.; Arthur G. Kelly, Spy Hill, Sask.; Dan Kennedy, Montmartre, Sask.; Mrs. S. C. Kennedy, Peace River, Alta.; Corey Kilvert, Winnipeg; Eddie Klymochko, Mundare, Alta.; Faris Kneeshaw, Bradford, Ont.; Mrs. Gordon Konantz, Winnipeg; Fred Kossman, Edmonton; W. Kristjanson, Winnipeg; H. M. Kyle, Victoria, B.C.; Mrs. Louise M. Laas, Salmon Arm, B.C.; U. B. Lassiter, Bassano, Alta.; Eric Lamb, Hudson Bay, Sask.; Mrs. Harry Landa, Saskatoon; Mrs. John E. Layne, Cardston, Alta.; Mrs. Lloyd Leachman, Maidstone, Sask.; F. W. Lindsay, Quesnel, B.C.; Mrs. Lorne Linklater, Burnham, Sask.; Mrs. Ruth Linnell, Summerberry, Sask.; Charles Landell, Bayview Village, Ont.; H. Stanley Loten, Dundas, Ont.; Phil S. Long, Moose Jaw, Sask.; Mrs. J. Longbottom, Victoria, B.C.; A. J. Loveridge, Grenfell, Sask.; William Lyon, Perdue, Sask.; Loretta Mangan, Fernie, B.C.; R. Malone, CJME, Regina; Alex B. Manson, Stratford, Ont.; Henry Matkin, Calgary; G. W. K. Macdonald, Toronto; Rev. E. J. Macdonald, Alexandria, Ont.; Mrs. L. MacDonald, Edmonton; John S. MacDonald, Alberni, B.C.; Judge Ian Macdonell, Toronto; I. U. MacLennan, Smallwell, Alta.; Hugh P. MacMillan, Alexandria, Ont.; Harry Martin, Dawson Creek, B.C.; Ralph L. McCall, Acme, Alta.; Doris McCoy, Shannon Park, N.S.; Robert McCulloch, Killarney, Man.; Mrs. K. McDermott, Banff, Alta.; Mrs. Hazel S. McCardell, Edmonton; M. McFall, Saltcoats, Sask.; J. L. McIntosh,

Dimsdale, Alta.; V. I. McKenzie, Chemainus, B.C.; David McKenzie, London, Ont.; Minnie E. McHolm, Port Hope, Ont.; Mrs. Alice M. McLachlan, Calgary; Mrs. John McLane, Spirit River, Alta.; Roy McLaughlin, Beaver, Man.; James McNamee, North Surrey, B.C.; Mrs. Ed McPhee, Springside, Sask.; Jim McRae, Toronto; Marjorie McRae, Talmage, Sask.; Eugene Anton Materi, Melville, Sask.; Mrs. B. A. Matthews, Hardisty, Alta.; William J. Mathieson, Moose Jaw, Sask.; Mrs. C. T. Meggs, Vancouver; George A. Moderly, Prince Albert, Sask.; Dorothy F. Morrison, Carberry, Man.; Mrs. Jack Muxlow, Meadow Lake, Sask.; Canon S. H. Middleton, Claresholm, Alta.; Mrs. Tom Nisbet, Wiseton, Sask.; Lula Nielson, Lethbridge, Alta.; Mrs. R. J. Norman, Saskatoon; W. J. O'Neill, Smithers, B.C.; George A. Park, Yarbo, Sask.; Edwin Parkin, Vancouver; Mrs. E. Parsons, Fort Langley, B.C.; Mrs. Grace M. Parsons, St. Thomas, Ont.; Mrs. Irene Paproski, Scarboro, Ont.; Mrs. W. John Patton, Winnipeg; Mrs. Lillian Pease, Prince Albert, Sask.; Mrs. F. F. Perlett, Tugaske, Sask.; Mrs. E. Perry, Vineland, Ont.; John Peters, Delburne, Alta.; Mrs. Clara Petersen, Crammond, Alta.; Mrs. J. E. Peterson, Bashaw, Alta.; A. Phelps, Yorkton, Sask.; Mrs. Olive L. Phelps, Toronto; John Pinckey, Rosetown, Sask.; Mrs. A. A. Pioer, Clavet, Sask.; Jean Pisak, Esterhazy, Sask.; Mrs. Clifton Plamondon, Plamondon, Alta.; George Ploss, Welland, Ont.; J. O. Plummer, Scarboro, Ont.; S. D. H. Pope, Saanichton, B.C.; Lita R. Porter, Czar, Alta.; Hazel Powell, Calgary; Clarence S. Preston, Carnduff, Sask.; H. A. Purdy, Regina; Stuart Raydon, Orton, Ont.; Stanley Redick, Collingwood, Ont.; Arthur J. Reynolds, Toronto; J. M. Reid, Brandon, Man.; Mrs. D. Ridehalgh, Pointe Claire, Que.; Margaret Riel, Peterborough, Ont.; R. Robinson, Delisle, Sask.; George R. Ronald, London, Ont.; Mrs. L. A. Roper, Victoria, B.C.; T. G. Ross, Assiniboia, Sask.; Winifred E. Ross, Worthing, England; Walter H. Ruehlin, Toledo, Ohio; Ada Ryan, Salt Spring Island, B.C.; Mrs. H. E. Sanders, Nelson, B.C.; Kathleen Samuel, Cold Lake, Alta.; Mrs. Lily G. Sather, Wanham, Alta.; Marjorie Schendel, Oxbow, Sask.; P. E. Scrivner, Wolseley, Sask.; Charles Setter, Winnipeg; Mrs. M. Shannon, Peterborough, Ont.; Harry Shave, Winnipeg; Mrs. G. E. R. Shaw, Edmonton; John Shaw, Victoria; P. C. Shaw, Penticton, B.C.; R. L. Shaw, Herbert, Sask.; Mrs. Marion Shore, Prince Albert, Sask.; W. C. Shovar, McBride, B.C.; J. G. Simpson, Belwood, Ont.; Mary Louise Simpson, Vancouver; H. R. Skelton, Vancouver; Norma Sluman, Toronto; Rupert Shriar, Winnipeg; C. G. I. Smith, Minden, Ont.; Mrs. Cormack Smith, Winnipeg; Mrs. Olga Smith, Fairview, Alta.; Mrs. Rose Smith, Winnipeg; Wilfred G. Smith, Oak Lake, Man.; Stanley A. Sneesby, Armstrong, B.C.; James Solar, Smuts, Sask.; Fred N. Spackman, Cardston, Alta.; Frank E. Spinden, Banhead, Alta.; Cyril Stackhouse, Saskatoon; Mrs. Arthur Stanger, Winnipeg; Mrs. Albert Stephenson, Darwell, Alta.; Mrs. Edith G. Stewart, Regina; S. J. Stewart, New Westminster, B.C.; Emil Stock, Leader, Sask.; Mrs. John E. Stone, Neepawa, Man.; Maud Strike, Shellbrook, Sask.; Roy St. George Stubbs, Winnipeg; J. H. Summers, South Burnaby, B.C.; Olaf Sveen, Steelman, Sask.; Doris Swallow, Yorkton, Sask.; Vic Swanston, Calgary; Mrs. Marjorie Talbot, North Surrey, B.C.; Mrs. Mary K. Tennis, Austin, Man.; Mrs. Gertrude M. Thompson, Pleasantside, B.C.; William Thomson, Regina; H. G. Thunell, Viking, Alta.; Rev. H. Treffry, Florence, Ont.; Mrs. Agnes Turner, Vancouver, B.C.; T. A. C. Tyrrell, Toronto; Helen E. L. Upper, Port Hope, Ont.; W. J. Vipond, North Surrey, B.C.; J. J. Waite, Prince Albert, Sask.; Janet Ware, Vulcan, Alta.; R. L. Ware, Calgary; Nathan E. Watts, Sidney, B.C.; David Weir, Winnipeg; Roy C. Weir, Rhippen, Sask.; Mrs. J. Weir, Vancouver; Myrtle Weldon, Elkhorn, Man.; Mrs. Fred Wenzel, Regina; Mrs. Carman Whiteford, Virden, Man.; Arthur D. Williams, Balmoral, Man.; Mr. and Mrs. Rex Williams, Regina; Mrs. Z. Williams, Regina; Mrs. Bob Williscraft, High Prairie, Alta.; Mrs. Margaret Woods, Golden, B.C.; Mrs. Mae Worth, Duncan, B.C.; Arthur W. Wright, Aneroid, Sask.; Dallas B. Wright, Miami, Fla.; M. Yeo, Assiniboia, Sask.; J. E. Ziebart, Trenton, Ont.; Charlotte Zurbregg, Stratford, Ont.

F.R.

A Bibliography

Books

ADAM, MERCER G. *The Canadian North-West* (Rose Publishing, Toronto, 1885)

ADAMS, BARBARA ANN. *Early Days at Red River Settlement* (Minnesota Historical Society, 1894)

BALLANTYNE, ROBERT M. *Hudson's Bay; or Everyday Life in the Wilds of North America* (Blackwood, Edinburgh, 1848)

BARBEAU, MARIUS. *Pathfinders in the North Pacific* (Ryerson, Toronto, 1958)

BEGG, ALEXANDER. *History of the North-West* 3 vols. (Hunter, Rose, Toronto, 1894)

~ *Red River Journal* Edited by W. L. Morton (Champlain Society, Toronto, 1956)

BELL, CHARLES N. *The Selkirk Settlement* (The Commercial, Winnipeg, 1887)

BENEDICT, RUTH. *Patterns of Culture* (Houghton, Mifflin, Boston, 1934)

BERRY, DON. *A Majority of Scoundrels: History of the Rocky Mountain Fur Company* (Harper & Brothers, New York, 1961)

BERTRAND, J. P. *Highway of Destiny* (Vantage, New York, 1959)

BLACK, NORMAN F. *History of Saskatchewan and the Old North West* (North West Historical Co., Regina, 1913)

BOON, T. C. B. *The Anglican Church* (Ryerson, Toronto, 1962)

BOWES, GORDON E. *Peace River Chronicles* (Prescott Publishing Co., Vancouver, B.C., 1963)

BREBNER, J. BARTLET. *Canada: A Modern History* (University of Michigan Press, Ann Arbor, 1960)

BRETON, REV. PAUL E. *Big Chief of the Prairies: Life of Father Lacombe* (Palm Press, Edmonton, 1955)

BRYCE, REV. GEORGE. *Romantic Settlement of Lord Selkirk's Colonists* (Musson, Toronto, 1909)

~ *Selkirk, Simpson, Mackenzie, Douglas: Makers of Canada Series* (Morang & Co., Toronto, 1910)

BURPEE, LAWRENCE J. *The Discovery of Canada* (Macmillan, Toronto, 1948)

BUTLER, WILLIAM F. *The Great Lone Land* (Sampson, Low, Marston & Co., London, 1891)

~ *The Wild Northland* (A. S. Barnes, New York, 1904)

CAESAR, GENE. *King of the Mountain Men: Life of Jim Bridger* (E. P. Dutton, New York, 1961)

CAMPBELL, MARJORIE W. *The Saskatchewan* (Rinehart, New York, 1950)

~ *The North West Company* (Macmillan, Toronto, 1957)

~ *McGillivray, Lord of the Northwest* (Clarke, Irwin, Toronto, 1962)

CARELESS, J. M. S. *Brown of the Globe* (Macmillan, Toronto, 1959)

CHALMERS, J. W. *Red River Adventure* (Macmillan, Toronto, 1959)

~ *Fur Trade Governor: George Simpson* (Institute of Applied Art, Edmonton, 1960)

CHEADLE, WALTER *Cheadle's Journal of a Trip Across Canada* Annotated by A. G. Doughty and Gustave Lanctot (Graphic Publishers, Ottawa, 1931)

CLELAND, R. G. *This Reckless Breed of Men* (Knopf, New York, 1950)

COOKE, DAVID C. *Fighting Indians of the West* (Dodd, Mead, Toronto, 1954)

COX, ROSS. *The Columbia River* Edited by Edgar I. Stewart and Jane R. Stewart (University of Oklahoma Press, Norman, 1957)

COWIE, ISAAC. *The Company of Adventurers* (William Briggs, Toronto, 1913)

CREIGHTON, DONALD. *John A. Macdonald* 2 vols. (Macmillan, Toronto, 1952 and 1955)

CRONIN, KAY. *Cross in the Wilderness* (Mitchell Press, Vancouver, B.C., 1959)

DAVIDSON, G. C. *The North West Company* (University of California Press, Berkeley, 1918)

DAVIDSON, WILLIAM M. *Louis Riel 1844-1855* (Albertan Publishing Co., Calgary, 1955)

DENNY, SIR CECIL E. *The Law Marches West* Edited by W. B. Cameron (J. M. Dent, Toronto, 1939)

~ *Riders of the Plains* (Calgary Herald, Calgary, 1905)

DE VOTO, BERNARD. *Across the Wide Missouri* (Houghton Mifflin, Boston, 1947)

~ *The Course of Empire* (Houghton Mifflin, Boston, 1952)

DICK, EVERETT. *Vanguards of the Frontier* (Appleton-Century, New York, 1941)

DICKIE, D. J. *The Canadian West* (J. M. Dent, Toronto, 1926)

DOWNS, ART. *Wagon Road North: Story of the Cariboo Gold Rush in Historical Photos* (Northwest Digest Ltd., Quesnel, 1960)

ELLIOTT, GORDON R. *Quesnel, Commercial Centre of the Cariboo Gold Rush* (Cariboo Historical Society, Quesnel, 1958)

GALBRAITH, JOHN S. *The Hudson's Bay Company as an Imperial Factor* (University of Toronto Press, Toronto, 1957)

GARD, WAYNE. *The Great Buffalo Hunt* (Knopf, New York, 1959)

GIBBON, JOHN MURRAY. *The Romantic History of the Canadian Pacific Railway* (Tudor Publishing Co., New York, 1937)

GRAY, JOHN MORGAN. *Lord Selkirk of Red River* (Macmillan, Toronto, 1963)

GUNN, DONALD. *History of Manitoba* In collaboration with Charles R. Tuttle (MacLean, Roger & Co., Ottawa, 1880)

HANKS, LUCIEN M. *Tribe Under Trust: A Study of the Blackfoot Reserve* In collaboration with Jane Richardson (University of Toronto Press, Toronto, 1950)

HARDY, W. G. *From Sea Unto Sea* (Doubleday, Garden City 1960)

HARGRAVE, JAMES. *The Hargrave Correspondence 1821-1843* Annotated by G. P. De T. Glazebrook (Champlain Society, Toronto, 1938)

HARGRAVE, LETITIA. *The Letters of Letitia Hargrave* Annotated by Margaret Arnett MacLeod (Champlain Society, Toronto, 1947)

HARMON, DANIEL WILLIAMS. *Sixteen Years in the Indian Country* Annotated by W. Kaye Lamb (Macmillan, Toronto, 1957)

HEALY, WILLIAM J. *Women of Red River* (Russell Lang & Co., Winnipeg, 1923)

HEARNE, SAMUEL. *A Journey from Prince of Wales' Fort in Hudson's Bay to the Northern Ocean* Annotated by Samuel Glover (Macmillan, Toronto, 1958)

~ *Coppermine Journey* Edited by Farley Mowat (McClelland & Stewart, Toronto, 1958)

HENDAY, ANTHONY. *Journal of Anthony Henday* Annotated by L. J. Burpee (Royal Society of Canada, Ottawa, 1907)

HENRY, ALEXANDER (THE ELDER). *Travels and Adventures in Canada and the Indian Territories* Annotated by James Bain (George N. Morang, Toronto, 1901)

HENRY, ALEXANDER (THE YOUNGER). *New Light on the Early History of the Greater Northwest, Journals of Alexander Henry* Annotated by Elliott Cues (Francis P. Harper, New York, 1897)

HILL, ROBERT H. *Manitoba: History of its Early Settlement* (William Briggs, Toronto, 1890)

HOLBROOK, STEWART H. *The Age of the Moguls* (Doubleday, Garden City, 1953)

HOLMAN, F. V. *Dr. John McLoughlin, Father of Oregon* (Clark Co., Cleveland, 1907)

HOWARD, JOSEPH KINSEY. *Strange Empire* (William Morrow & Co., New York, 1952)

HOWAY, F. W. *British Columbia: The Making of a Province* (Ryerson, Toronto, 1928)

~ *British Columbia and the United States* In collaboration with W. N. Sage and H. F. Angus (Ryerson, Toronto, 1942)

HUGHES, KATHERINE. *Father Lacombe, Black-Robe Voyageur* (McClelland & Stewart, Toronto, 1920)

HUTCHISON, BRUCE. *The Fraser* (Clarke, Irwin, Toronto, 1950)

~ *The Struggle for the Border* (Longmans, Toronto, 1955)

INNIS, HAROLD A. *The Fur Trade in Canada* (Yale University Press, New Haven, Conn., 1930)

~ *Peter Pond, Fur Trader and Adventurer* (Irwin & Gordon, Toronto, 1930)

IRVING, WASHINGTON. *Astoria* (Putnam's, New York, 1859)

JEWITT, JOHN R. *Narrative of the Adventures and Sufferings of John R. Jewitt* (Privately published, New York 1815)

JENNESS, DIAMOND. *The Indians of Canada* (National Museum of Canada, Ottawa, 1932)

JOHNSON, R. BYRON. *Very Far West Indeed* (Low, Marston, Low & Searle, London, 1872)

JOSEPHY, ALVIN M. *The American Heritage Book of Indians* (American Heritage Publishing Co., New York, 1961)

KANE, PAUL. *Wanderings of an Artist Among the Indians of North America* (Radisson Society of Canada, Toronto, 1925)

KELSEY, HENRY. *Journal of Henry Kelsey* Annotated by Charles N. Bell (Dawson Richardson Publications, Winnipeg, 1928)

KENNEDY, H. A. *Book of the West: Story of Western Canada* (Ryerson, Toronto, 1925)

KIDD, KENNETH E. *Canadians of Long Ago: Story of the Canadian Indians* (Longmans, Toronto, 1956)

LAMB, W. KAYE. *The Letters and Journals of Simon Fraser 1806-1808* (Macmillan, Toronto, 1960)

LAUT, AGNES. *The Adventurers of England on Hudson Bay* (Glasgow, Brook & Co., Toronto, 1914)

~ *The Cariboo Trail* (University of Toronto Press, Toronto, 1964)

LAVENDER, DAVID. *Land of Giants* (Doubleday, Garden City, 1958)

LONGSTRETH, T. M. *The Silent Force* (Century, New York, 1928)

MACBETH, R. G. *The Romance of Western Canada* (William Briggs, Toronto, 1918)

MACKAY, DOUGLAS. *The Honourable Company* (Tudor Publishing Co., New York, 1938)

MACKENZIE, ALEXANDER. *Voyages to the Frozen and Pacific Oceans* Annotated by Charles W. Colby (Radisson Society of Canada, Toronto, 1927)

MACKENZIE, CECIL W. *Donald Mackenzie, King of the Northwest* (I. Deach, Jr., Los Angeles, 1937)

MACLEAN, JOHN *McDougall of Alberta: A Life of Rev. John McDougall* (Ryerson, Toronto, 1927)

MACLENNAN, HUGH. *Seven Rivers of Canada* (Macmillan, Toronto, 1961)

MACLEOD, MARGARET A. *Cuthbert Grant of Grantown* In collaboration with W. L. Morton and Alice R. Brown (McClelland & Stewart, Toronto, 1963)

MARTIN, CHESTER B. *Lord Selkirk's Work in Canada* (Humphrey Milford, Toronto, 1916)

MASSON, LOUIS F.R. *Les Bourgeois de la Compagnie du Nord-Ouest* 2 vols. (A. Coté & Co., Quebec, 1889)

MCCOURT, EDWARD. *Revolt in the West: Story of the Riel Rebellion* (Macmillan, Toronto, 1958)

MCDONALD, ARCHIBALD. *Peace River: George Simpson's Canoe Voyage to the Pacific in 1828* (J. Durie & Son, Ottawa, 1872)

MCDOUGALL, REV. JOHN. *George Millward McDougall: Pioneer, Patriot, Missionary* (William Briggs, Toronto, 1880)

~ *Forest, Lake and Prairie* (William Briggs, Toronto, 1895)

~ *Saddle, Sled and Snowshoe* (William Briggs, Toronto, 1896)

MCDOUGALL, REV. JOHN.
    (*continued*)
~ *Pathfinding on Plain and Prairie* (William Briggs, Toronto, 1898)
~ *In the Days of the Red River Rebellion* (William Briggs, Toronto, 1903)
~ *On Western Trails in the Early Seventies* (William Briggs, Toronto, 1911)

MCILWRAITH, T. F. *The Bella Coola Indians* 2 vols. (University of Toronto Press, Toronto, 1948)

MCINNES, C. M. *In the Shadow of the Rockies* (Rivingtons, London, 1930)

MCLEAN, JOHN. *James Evans: Inventor of the Syllabic System of Cree Language* (William Briggs, Toronto, 1890)

MCLEAN, JOHN. *Notes on a Twenty-five Year's Service in Hudson's Bay Territory* Annotated by W. S. Wallace (Champlain Society, Toronto, 1932)

MCLOUGHLIN, JOHN. *Letters of John McLoughlin from Fort Vancouver to the Governor and Committee* Edited by E. E. Rich, introduction by W. Kaye Lamb, in 3 vols. (Champlain Society, Toronto, 1941, 1943, 1944)

MIDDLETON, F. D. *Suppression of the Rebellion in the Northwest, 1885* Annotated by G. H. Needler (University of Toronto Press, Toronto, 1948)

MIDDLETON, REV. S. H. *Indian Chiefs* (Lethbridge Herald Printing, Lethbridge, 1951)

MOBERLY, HENRY JOHN. *When Fur Was King* In collaboration with W. B. Cameron (Dutton, New York, 1929)

MONTGOMERY, R. G. *The White-Headed Eagle: John McLoughlin* (Macmillan, New York, 1935)

MORICE, REV. A. G. *History of the Northern Interior of British Columbia* (John Lane, London, 1904)

MORTON, ARTHUR SILVER *Under Western Skies* (Thomas Nelson & Sons, Toronto, 1937)
~ *A History of the Canadian West to 1870-71* (Thomas Nelson & Sons, London, 1939)
~ *Sir George Simpson: A Pen Picture of a Man of Action* (J. M. Dent, Toronto, 1944).

MORTON, W. L. *Manitoba: A History* (University of Toronto Press, Toronto, 1957)

NEEDLER, G. H. *Louis Riel* (Burns & MacEachern, Toronto, 1957)

NIX, JAMES E. *Mission Among the Buffalo* (Ryerson, Toronto, 1960)

NUTE, GRACE LEE. *The Voyageur* (Appleton, New York, 1931)

OGDEN, PETER SKENE. *Snake Country Journals* Annotated by E. E. Rich and K. G. Davies, in 2 vols. (Hudson's Bay Record Society, London, 1950 and 1961)

O'MEARA, WALTER. *The Savage Country* (Houghton Mifflin, Boston, 1960)

ORMSBY, MARGARET A. *British Columbia: A History* (Macmillan, Toronto, 1958)

PINKERTON, R. E. *The Gentlemen Adventurers* (McClelland & Stewart, Toronto, 1931)

PRITCHETT, JOHN P. *The Red River Valley 1811-1849* (Yale University Press, New Haven, 1942)

PYLE, JOSEPH G. *Life of James J. Hill* 2 vols. (McClelland, Goodchild & Stewart, Toronto, 1917)

REID, J. H. S. *Mountains, Men & Rivers* (Ryerson, Toronto, 1954)

RIEL, LOUIS. *L'Amnistie: Mémoire sur le Causes des Troubles du Nord-ouest* (Bureau du Nouveau Monde, Montreal, 1874)

ROBERTSON, COLIN. *Correspondence Book, 1817 to 1822* Annotated by E. E. Rich (Champlain Society, Toronto, 1939)

RICH, E. E. *Hudson's Bay Company 1670-1870* 3 vols. (McClelland & Stewart, Toronto, 1960)

ROSS, ALEXANDER. *The Red River Settlement* (Smith, Elder & Co., London, 1856)
~ *Fur Hunters of the Far West* Annotated by Kenneth A. Spaulding (University of Oklahoma Press, Norman, 1956)

RUXTON, GEORGE FREDERICK. *Life in the Far West* Annotated by Leroy R. Hafen (University of Oklahoma Press, Norman, 1951)
~ *Ruxton of the Rockies* Edited by Leroy R. Hafen, compiled by Clyde and Mae Reed Porter (University of Oklahoma Press, Norman, 1950)

SECRETAN, J. H. E. *Canada's Great Highway: From the First Stake to the Last Spike* (Longmans, Toronto, 1924)

SELKIRK, EARL OF. *Lord Selkirk's Diary 1803-1804* Annotated by Patrick C. T. White (Champlain Society, Toronto, 1958)

SHARP, PAUL F. *Whoop-Up Country: The Canadian-American West 1865-1885* (University of Minnesota Press, Minneapolis, 1955)

SHEEPSHANKS, REV. J. *A Bishop in the Rough* Edited by Rev. D. Wallace (Smith, Elder, London, 1909)

SIMPSON, ALEXANDER. *Life and Travels of Thomas Simpson, the Arctic Discoverer* (Richard Bentley, London, 1845)

SIMPSON, GEORGE. *Simpson's Athabasca Journal 1820-1821* Annotated by E. E. Rich (Champlain Society, Toronto, 1935)
~ *Fur Trade and Empire: Simpson's Columbia Journal 1824-1825* Annotated by Frederick Merk (Harvard University Press, Cambridge, 1931)
~ *Simpson's Columbia Journal 1828* Annotated by E. E. Rich (Champlain Society, Toronto, 1947)
~ *Narrative of a Journey Round the World 1841-1842* (Henry Colburn, London, 1847)

SIMPSON, THOMAS. *Narrative of Discoveries on the North Coast of America* (R. Bentley, London, 1843)

SOMERSET, DUCHESS OF. *Impressions of a Tenderfoot in the Far West* (John Murray, London, 1890)

SOUTHESK, EARL OF. *Saskatchewan and the Rocky Mountains: Diary of Travel, Sport, Adventure in 1859 and 1860* (James Campbell & Son, Toronto, 1875)

STANLEY, GEORGE F. G. *Birth of Western Canada: A History of the Riel Rebellion* (Longmans, Green, London, 1936)
~ *Louis Riel* (Ryerson, Toronto, 1963)

THOMPSON, DAVID. *Narrative of Explorations in Western America 1784-1812* Annotated by J. B. Tyrrell (Champlain Society, Toronto, 1916)
~ *David Thompson's Narrative* Annotated by Richard Glover (Champlain Society, Toronto, 1962)

VAUGHAN, WALTER. *The Life and Work of Sir William Van Horne* (Century Co., New York, 1920)

WADE, MASON. *The French-Canadians 1760-1945* (Macmillan, Toronto, 1955)

WALLACE, W. STEWART. *Documents Relating to the North West Company* (Champlain Society, Toronto, 1934)

~ *The Pedlars from Quebec* (Ryerson, Toronto, 1954)

WEST, REV. JOHN. *Substance of a Journal at Red River Colony 1820-1823* (L. B. Seeley & Son, London, 1824)

WILLSON, HENRY B. *The Great Company* (Smith, Elder & Co., London, 1900)

WOOD, LOUIS A. *Red River Colony* (Glasgow, Brook & Co., Toronto, 1915)

YOUNG, REV. EGERTON R. *Apostle of the North: Rev. James Evans* (Fleming H. Revell Co., Toronto, 1899)

YOUNG, REV. GEORGE. *Manitoba Memories* (William Briggs, Toronto, 1897)

Publications

Alberta Historical Review
The Beaver
Canadian Historical Review
The British Columbia Historical Quarterly

Manitoba Historical Society Reports
Okanagan Historical Society Reports
Royal Society of Canada Transactions
Saskatchewan History

Index

Picture Credits

Order of appearance in the text of pictures listed here is left to right, top to bottom. After the first recording, principal sources are credited under these abbreviations:

EB   Alberta Government Photograph, from the Ernest Brown Collection

AMNH   American Museum of Natural History

CIN   Canadian Illustrated News

CIWN   Canadian Illustrated War News

GF   Glenbow Foundation

JRRC   John Ross Robertson Collection

MA   Manitoba Archives

OHS   Oregon Historical Society

BCA   Provincial Archives, Victoria, British Columbia

PA   Public Archives of Canada

ROM   Royal Ontario Museum

SSC   Sigmund Samuel Collection

SHSW   The State Historical Society of Wisconsin

TPL   Toronto Public Library

WAG   Walters Art Gallery

WPMAM   West Point Military Academy Museum

COVER   "Indian Horse Race" by Paul Kane, Royal Ontario Museum, Sigmund Samuel Collection.

2-3   "Half Breeds Running Buffalo" by Paul Kane, ROM Ethnology.

4   Toronto Public Library.

5   "Blackfoot Indian on Horseback" by Karl Bodmer, American Museum of Natural History.

6-7   "The Launch of the North West America at Nootka Sound" John Ross Robertson Collection, TPL.

8   TPL West Point Military Academy Museum; JRRC, TPL; TPL; TPL; Manitoba Archives.

9   New York Historical Society; Public Archives of Canada; New York Public Library; MA; MA; JRRC, TPL; Glenbow Foundation.

10-11   MA.

12   GF; GF.

14-15   GF.

16   Canadian Illustrated News, TPL.

19   GF.

22   GF.

25   "The Blackfeet" by A. J. Miller, Walters Art Gallery.

26   "Assiniboin Indians" by Karl Bodmer, SHSW; "Mehskeme-Sukahs, Blackfoot Chief and Talsickinstomick, Piekann Chief" by Karl Bodmer, SHSW.

27   Painting by Karl Bodmer, SHSW; ROM; GF; AMNH.

28   "Cun-ne-wa-Bum" by Paul Kane, ROM Ethnology.

29   Alberta Government photograph from the Ernest Brown Collection; MA.

30   "Indian Women in Tent" by Peter Rindisbacher, WPMAM.

31   "Indian War Dance" by Seth Eastman, Kennedy Galleries; SHSW.

32-33   EB.

34-35   "Trappers on Snowshoes" by Peter Rindisbacher, SHSW; SHSW.

36   SHSW; GF.

37   "Clal-lum Women Weaving a Blanket" by Paul Kane, ROM Ethnology; National Museum of Canada.

38-39   "Indian Camp—Colvile," by Paul Kane, ROM Ethnology.

40   "Murderer of Dr. Whitman" by Paul Kane, ROM Ethnology.

42   PA.

46   TPL.

47   TPL.

49   "The Bison Attacked by Dog Trains" by Peter Rindisbacher, WPMAM; "Yell of Triumph" by A. J. Miller, WAG.

50   GF.

51   "Indian Hunting Buffalo" by Peter Rindisbacher, SHSW; "Buffalo Hunt, Chasing Back" by George Catlin, ROM Ethnology.

52-53   "Buffalo Driven over Cliff" by A. J. Miller, WAG.

54   "Hunting Moose in Winter" by George Catlin, ROM Ethnology.

55   "Death of a Moose" by John Reade, ROM, Sigmund Samuel Collection; "Indian Hunting Duck" by Peter Rindisbacher, SHSW.

56   "Buffalo Herd Grazing" by George Catlin, ROM Ethnology.

58   "Indian Taking Scalp" by Peter Rindisbacher, WPMAM.

64   "Working a Canoe up a Rapid on St. Lawrence" by W. H. Bartlett, JRRC, TPL.

66   Provincial Archives, Victoria, B.C.

70   "Fort Garry, 1857" by J. Fleming, JRRC, TPL; JRRC, TPL.

71   Painting by E. Brisebois, GF; painting by William Armstrong, JRRC, TPL.

72   Geological Survey of Canada.

73   ROM, SSC.

74-75   "Old Fort Edmonton" by L. P. Hurd, ROM, SSC.

76   JRRC, TPL; ROM, SSC.

77   BCA; BCA; GF.

78   JRRC, TPL; BCA.

82   "Source of the Columbia River" by Henry James Warre, GF.

88   PA.

89   BCA.

93   MA; "Prairie Landscape" by A. Neison, ROM, SSC.

94   GF; GF.

95   GF; GF.

96   MA; MA.

97   "Osborne Brown's First Home" by Miss Brown, GF.

98-99   "A Home in the Great West" by A. Garde, GF.

100   GF.

101   GF; MA.

102-103   MA.

108-109   Denver Public Library Western Collection, TPL.

110   Oregon Historical Society.

114   Picturesque Canada, TPL.

117   WAG.

118-119   "Bourgeois—W-r and his Squaw" by A. J. Miller, WAG.

120   "Setting Traps for Beaver" by A. J. Miller, Northern Natural Gas Company Collection, Joslyn Art Museum; WAG.

121   OHS.

122   OHS.

123   GF; BCA; TPL; OHS; MA; GF; PA; PA; Chateau de Ramezay.

124   McCord Museum of McGill University; MA.

125   Joslyn Art Museum.

126   JRRC, TPL.

127   "Bivouac of a Canoe Party" by F. A. Hopkins, PA; "York Boat Ascending the Mackenzie River" by F. A. Hopkins, ROM, SSC.

128-129   GF.

130   Hudson's Bay Company; "The Fur Trader" by Cornelius Kreighoff, GF.

131   Paintings by Day after H. Jones, ROM, SSC.

132   "Fort Prince of Wales" by Samuel Hearne, JRRC, TPL.

133   Harper's Weekly, N.Y. Public Library.

134-135   Bettmann Archive.

136   "Fur Trader in Council Teepee" by Frederic Remington, Harper's Weekly, N.Y. Public Library.

140-141	TPL.
146	MA.
148-149	"Sir George Simpson's Canoe" by William Armstrong, ROM, Mrs. P. C. Band Collection, SSC.
152	BCA; BCA.
153	MA; BCA.
154-155	BCA.
156	BCA; GF.
157	BCA.
158	BCA.
159	BCA.
160	BCA.
164-165	BCA.
169	"Drunken Frolic Among the Chippewas and Assiniboins" by Peter Rindisbacher, WPMAM; RCMP.
170	GF; N.Y. Public Library.
171	Geological Survey of Canada; RCMP.
172	CIN, MA.
173	PA; PA.
174	CIN, MA.
175	CIN, MA; CIN, MA; CIN, PA.
176	CIN, MA; CIN, GF.
179	New York Historical Society.
186	"The Missionary" by Frederic Remington, SHSW.
193	GF.
194	RCMP.
195	MA.
196	MA; MA.
197	RCMP.
198	MA.
199	Hudson's Bay Company; RCMP.
200	JRRC, TPL.
209	Canadian Illustrated War News, GF.
210-211	CIWN, MA.
212-213	CIWN, MA.
214	RCMP.
215	GF.
216	RCMP; RCMP; PA.
217	GF.
218	GF.
219	GF.
220	CIWN, GF.
221	ROM, SSC
222	CIWN, GF.
223	ROM, SSC; CIWN, GF.
224	CIWN, GF.
225	CIWN, MA.
226	MA; CIWN, PA.
227	CIWN, PA; CIWN, MA; MA.
228	MA; GF.
237	PA.
244	CPR.
245	BCA.
246	EB.
247	PA.
248	BCA; EB.
248-249	EB.
250-251	GF.
252	EB.
253	GF; EB.
254-255	City Archives, Vancouver.
256	CPR.
257	SHSW.

PICTURE STORIES:
The Editors wish to thank especially Henry C. Campbell, Chief Librarian, and his expert staff in the Toronto Public Library, and Helena Ignatieff and her colleagues at the Royal Ontario Museum, for assistance with the illustrations in this book.

The text for pictures and albums was written by Walt McDayter.

On the Making of this Book

The type chosen for the text is Times New Roman, a
design supervised by Stanley Morison and first issued
by the Monotype Corporation of England in 1932.
The face resembles Dutch and German fonts of the
late 17th and early 18th centuries.

Type was set in Canada by McCorquodale & Blades Printers Limited and Cooper & Beatty Limited.

The book was printed by Taylowe Limited. The text
paper is Evensyde Cartridge. The coloured paper is
Victory Tinted. The coated paper is Beaublade '21'.
It was bound by Hazell Watson & Viney Limited.

PRINTED AND BOUND IN ENGLAND